AF006389

Interventions is produced on the land of the Wurundjeri people of the Kulin Nation. We acknowledge the Traditional Owners of country throughout Australia and recognise their continuing connection to land, waters and culture. We pay our respects to their Elders past, present and emerging. Their land was stolen, never ceded.

It always was and always will be Aboriginal land.

INTERVENTIONS

First published 2022 by Interventions Inc

Interventions is a not-for-profit, independent, radical book publisher. For further information:
   www.interventions.org.au
   info@interventions.org.au
   PO Box 24132
   Melbourne VIC 3001 Australia

Cover design and layout by Belle Gibson
Interior design and layout by Viktoria Ivanova
Cover design from image of Andrew Blunden used with kind permission of Andrew Blunden

Author: Bobbie Oliver

Title: Hell No! We Won't Go!: Resistance to Conscription in Postwar Australia
ISBN: 978-0-6452534-1-2: Paperback
ISBN: 978-0-6452534-2-9: ebook

© Bobbie Oliver 2022

The moral rights of the author have been asserted.
All rights reserved. Except as permitted under the Australian Copyright Act 1968 (for example, a fair dealing for the purposes of study, research, criticism or review), no part of this book may be reproduced, stored in a retrieval system, communicated or transmitted in any form or by any means without prior written permission.

All inquiries should be made to the author.

 A catalogue record for this work is available from the National Library of Australia

# HELL NO!
# WE WON'T GO!

Resistance to conscription
in post-war Australia

Bobbie Oliver

INTERVENTIONS
MELBOURNE

# HELL NO!
# WE WON'T GO!

Resistance to conscription
in postwar Australia

In Memory of my friends
Vivienne Grace Abraham (1920-2003)
and
Kenneth Deakin Rivett (1923-2004)
without whose support and encouragement
this book would never have been written.

# Contents

| | |
|---|---|
| Introduction | 1 |
| **National Service in the Fifties** | |
| 1  'History shows no certain evidence that preparation for war ensures peace' | 11 |
| 2  'I do not feel satisfied that he holds a conscientious belief' | 29 |
| **The Sixties and Vietnam** | |
| 3  'War begins in the minds of men' | 45 |
| 4  'Why me?' | 59 |
| 5  'What kind of democracy is this?' | 73 |
| 6  'Under this government, it takes courage to be a conscientious objector' | 91 |
| 7  'Not to oppose conscription, but to wreck it' | 113 |
| 8  'Making a monkey out of the cops' | 145 |
| 9  'A stinking, rotten hole' | 173 |
| **Responses to being a Dissident** | |
| 10  'It made me a left-wing activist for life' | 193 |
| Appendix 1: Sample of 258 objectors and non-compliers, 1951–59 | 211 |
| Appendix 2: Sample of 530 objectors and non-compliers, 1965–72 | 241 |
| *Endnotes* | 267 |
| *Image Credits* | 277 |
| *Index* | 279 |

# Introduction

'So Australia is to have Conscription' read a front-page headline in the August 1950 issue of the pacifist newspaper, *The Peacemaker*. It was responding to announcements in the Australian press that the Menzies government would introduce a system of peacetime compulsory military training by July 1951. Australian pacifist groups were united against the move. They had foreshadowed it with a resolution passed at the Australian Pacifist Movement's annual conference, reaffirming 'unqualified opposition to compulsory military training' and urging pacifists to 'do their utmost to bring the case against [it] before the public, the press, parliament, and particularly the individual who will be conscripted'.

'The individual who will be conscripted' is the focus of this study of the National Service schemes of 1951–59 and 1965–72. Much has been written about National Service, the context of the Cold War and Australia's military activity in the countries to the near north over those decades, and some dissidents have published personal memoirs. There has not yet been a comprehensive history of the objectors and non-compliers. While I do not claim that this book is a comprehensive history – it does not and cannot include the experience of everyone who made a stand against military conscription – I have gathered many of their stories and attempted to answer the following questions: Who were they? What motivated them to take an unpopular stance

*The Peacemaker* front page August 1950, announcing the re-introduction of conscription.

– even to the extent of spending two years in prison? What experiences and sufferings did they undergo? Were they persecuted, then or afterwards? Did taking a stand against militarism and war make a difference to society or change their lives, then and later?

*Hell no! We won't go!* follows on from my earlier history, *Peacemongers*, which examined conscientious objection to military conscription from the implementation of the first compulsory military training scheme in 1909 to the end of World War II – a period spanning most of the first half of the 20th century. This book continues the story over the two decades in which the second and third National Service schemes operated. There was a gap of four years between the ending of the 1950s scheme and the introduction of a new conscription scheme that would soon require military trainees to fight in an undeclared war in Vietnam – finally breaking the time-honoured tradition of Australia sending only volunteers or professional soldiers offshore to fight wars. There were, of course, exceptions to this in 1942 and 1943, when militia soldiers fought in New Guinea – most famously, the 39th Battalion's defence of Port Moresby in August 1942. But, since the Australian public's second rejection of conscription for overseas service in 1917, frontline troops fighting outside Australian territory were either citizen soldiers or regular soldiers – until 1966.

I define a conscientious objector (CO) as someone who has a philosophical and/or ethical objection to undergoing military training and service, usually based on an abhorrence of killing one's fellow human beings. Some objectors felt able to perform non-combatant duties – support work for the military, such as clerical, kitchen, stores, medical and other duties – which, they assumed, did not involve training to kill, carrying arms or going into battle. This assumption was proved incorrect during the Vietnam War era, when all National Servicemen were trained to carry and use weapons. Other objectors believed that performing non-combatant duties was as immoral as being a combatant, because all such roles contributed to the war effort. During the Vietnam War, the term 'draft resister' became used more commonly than 'conscientious objector'. Some draft resisters applied for exemption; others refused to comply with the system, believing that applying for exemption as COs would be giving legitimacy to the *National Service Act* and also to Australia's involvement in the war. Rather than being COs, they were 'non-compliers' – sometimes called 'conscientious non-compliers'. I use 'dissident' or 'dissenter' when referring to more than one type of resister.

Much of the material in this book is based on collections of papers amassed by Vivienne Grace Abraham (1920–2003). Abraham graduated with an LLB from Melbourne University but did not complete Articles and so was not admitted to the bar. She could not practise as a lawyer, although she was employed by a Sydney law firm, F. W. Jenkins and Co. From the 1940s until the 1980s, she worked as a volunteer for many peace organisations, including the Australian Peace Pledge Union, the Federal Pacifist Council and the Women's International League for Peace and Freedom. She edited the pacifist newspaper *The Peacemaker* from 1953 to 1955 and from 1963 until the paper ceased publication in 1971. A collection of Abraham's papers is held by the National Library of Australia (NLA), Canberra, under the accession number MS9152 (referenced as Vivienne Abraham Papers, MS9152). I held the other collection while I wrote this book (referenced as Abraham Papers). These were lodged with the NLA after the manuscript was completed. Consequently, these papers (consisting of court transcripts, correspondence, notes, pamphlets and ephemera) had no accession number at the time of writing. *The Peacemaker* was another major source. Complete sets are held in the NLA, Canberra, and the Melbourne University Archives. Other material was drawn from government departmental files, security files in the National Archives of Australia, Canberra and Perth, contemporary newspapers and pamphlets.

I used interviews and surveys to collect information about the experiences of individual dissidents and those close to them. In its final form, the survey consisted of 26 questions, divided into four parts. The first section sought details about the dissident's background and whether he belonged to any support groups; the second asked about his stand against conscription; the third contained questions for those who were imprisoned; and the last asked about the impact of his experience on his later life. In 2000–01, when I began this research and sent the first surveys out, I received three replies from men who were called up in the 1950s and 10 from the Vietnam War era, including one from a mother of four sons, two of whom were conscripted. After resuming the research, I sent out a revised survey in 2020 and received seven responses, two of which resulted in interviews (one by phone and one face to face). The findings from these surveys are included in the chapters that discuss individual reactions to conscription and are used in drawing conclusions about the impact of resistance to the National Service schemes, individually and nationally.

Using accounts in *The Peacemaker* and newspapers from around Australia and the survey responses, I created two lists of dissidents. The first consists of 258 objectors who applied for full or partial exemption from military service in 1951–59 (see Appendix 1). The second list comprises 530 dissenters (objectors and non-compliers) to the 1965–72 scheme (Appendix 2). The only qualifications for inclusion in these samples were a name and sufficient information to determine that the person was a CO or non-complier: the type of exemption sought (total exemption or exemption from combat duties only) or evidence of non-compliance with the Act, and the outcome of the dissident's actions. I experienced some difficulties in collecting this information. In the first sample, finding adequate information about objectors from the second half of the 1950s was difficult because *The Peacemaker* published fewer court cases in the latter half of the 1950s (see Chapter 2), and the Trove (NLA) digital data base for many newspapers does not yet extend beyond 1954. Major newspapers, such as the *Canberra Times*, are less likely to have reported events in smaller, local courts. In the second period, the same difficulties applied with regard to major newspapers in Trove. Additionally, *The Peacemaker* ceased publication in December 1971, a year before the end of conscription. These samples are far too small to enable me to draw any conclusions, and it is important to note the likely biases: major newspapers are less likely to have reported events in smaller, local courts; and *The Peacemaker* may have been more likely to mention religious or politically based objections.

Nonetheless, the lists serve two purposes in this book. They record the names and actions of more dissidents than the text can possibly discuss, and they provide some useful information to add to other findings.

The book consists of three parts. Chapters 1 and 2 discuss the National Service scheme that operated from 1951 until 1959. They detail objections to conscription and the battle to widen the valid reasons for conscientious objection, and then include a right of appeal, in the *National Service Act* of 1951-59 (NSA). The Act provided exemptions for ministers of religion, students of defined theological colleges and COs to all military service. While the NSA made more adequate provision for COs than the *National Security Act* 1939 during World War II, the punishments were often harsher.

The first part of the book is mainly chronological. The second part, dealing with resistance to the second National Service scheme (1965-72) and Australia's involvement in the Vietnam War, is thematic. I have adopted this format because, from the second half of the 1960s, the various aspects of resistance and responses by police and military happened concurrently. For example, during the later 1960s, young men were being arrested and sent into military training, and subjected to military discipline such as solitary confinement in Holsworthy or other correctional establishments; or were entering military training and discovering a strong objection, or even revulsion, to it and applying for exemption. The government changed its policy in 1968, following protests about the treatment of Simon Townsend and other internees in military prisons. Henceforth, non-compliers who refused a court order to enlist were not regarded as enlisted and so not placed under military discipline. Instead, they were sent to serve their sentences in civil prisons. Imprisonment in civilian jails occurred throughout the late 1960s and the early 1970s, and the underground movement ran concurrently from the late 1960s. Secondly, many of the resisters' stories extended across several years and could not be accommodated in a designated time period of, for example, 1965-66 or 1967-68. The exception to this approach is Chapter 3, which provides the historical context for the Menzies administration's reintroduction of compulsory military service in 1964 and for early campaigns (1965-66) against the scheme. Subsequent chapters discuss the rise and increasing militancy of opposition to conscription and to Australia's part in the war; the experiences of individual objectors and non-compliers, including those in military detention or civil prisons; and the underground movement. In part three, the final chapter summarises findings from my research and draws some conclusions about the social and political impact of resistance to military conscription then and now. It discusses the attitudes of objectors and non-compliers, reflecting after five or six decades on their experiences as young men. While most of this material is drawn from the responses of Vietnam era dissidents, it includes a few from the earlier National Service scheme.

This project has been a very long time in the making, and I owe thanks to many people who assisted in its completion. My late friends, Vivienne Abraham and Kenneth Rivett, assisted with research for *Peacemongers* and encouraged me to write its sequel. Without Vivienne Abraham's generosity in entrusting her collection of files on war resisters to my care some 25 years ago, I would have been unable to complete this research. The Australian Army History Research Grants scheme and Curtin University provided funds that enabled my excellent research assistants, Carolyn Newman, Linley Batterham and Nick Oliver, to collect and catalogue material. *Hell no! We won't go* was completed while I was an Honorary Research Fellow in Humanities at The University of Western Australia.

It was always my aim to foreground the war resisters and to give a voice to their motivations, experiences and ideas, both then and in later reflection. Despite the wealth of contemporary material in the Abraham collection, this research wouldn't have been complete without former resisters who responded to my requests for information by filling in surveys, being interviewed and passing on their own material, including memoirs. In particular, the surveys and interviews enabled me to ask how resistance had affected those who made a stand and whether it had changed their lives since then. Special thanks are due to Ken Beale, David Bisset, Rowan Cahill, Peter Cook, Joan and Lloyd Davies, Douglas Dawson, Elsie Gare, Michael Hamel-Green, Keith Headland, Glen Huxley, Ken Mansell, Ian Marshall, Michael Matteson, Paul McKeich, Stephen Meredith, Frances Newell, Mike Payne, Jenni Perkins, Tony Pointon, Geoff Sandy, Bill Thomas, Adrian Walker, Peter Webb and John Wilson for their contribution to my research. Any errors of fact, omissions or misinterpretation of actions and events described here are, of course, mine. I also thank the institutions and individuals who granted permission to publish photographs. All are acknowledged in the Image Credits on pages 279-280, but I am particularly grateful to Leo Davis, Rowan Cahill, Ken Mansell, Michael Hamel-Green and Fran Newell for providing private photographs and to Andrew Blunden for permission to use his image on the cover.

Lastly, I thank Janey Stone, Lisa Milner, Belle Gibson, Viktoria Ivanova and Eris Harrison at Interventions Publications for making the published book a reality. It has been a pleasure to work with them.

# National Service in the Fifties

National Service
in the fifties

## CHAPTER 1
# 'History shows no certain evidence that preparation for war ensures peace'

The Menzies-led Liberal Party–Country Party Coalition government introduced compulsory military training in 1951 because, it later stated, global war was an imminent threat.[1] Three factors facilitated public acceptance of what might otherwise have been an unpopular policy: the Communists' victory in mainland China in 1949; the war in Korea that began in June 1950; and the initial absence of security pacts with a powerful neighbour – ANZUS and SEATO were ratified in 1951 and 1954, respectively.[2] The government claimed that, to meet its defence commitments, Australia's defence forces had to be increased from the existing total of 57,000 men. By the end of National Service in 1959, the scheme had reportedly produced 'a pool of 200,000 men with basic national service training and with some years of advanced training in the Citizens' Military Forces (CMF).'[3]

The *National Service Act* (NSA) became law on 17 March 1951. It was sub-titled 'An Act to provide for National Service in the Defence Force and for other purposes.' The reference to unspecified 'other purposes' drew early complaints against the Act, which required 17-year-old males, resident in Australia, to register within 14 days of a stated date and to continue to advise the Minister for Labour and National Service of their whereabouts until they had either completed their service or reached the age of 26. Penalties included a £50 fine for not registering or for not notifying the department of a change of address. National Service comprised 176 days of training, which had to be completed within five years of enlistment. Sometimes, the service was broken into two parts, with an interval between them. After his service was completed, the trainee remained a member of the CMF until he turned 26, although he was not obliged to undertake further training. The Act stated that a National Serviceman was enlisted as soon as he presented himself with his call-up notice. Opponents complained that complying with the instructions on a call-up notice appeared to make a person 'a member of the military forces and liable to military law'. Besides being fined, those failing to comply with the call-up notice could face imprisonment (possibly in a military detention centre) for a period equal to the period of service. If parents or guardians prevented youths from registering or obeying their call up, they were also liable for a £50 fine. Perhaps the Act's most disturbing aspect was the requirement for employers to dismiss employees who refused to register. Failure to comply meant a £100 fine.[4]

Oddly, most of the public accepted the Act's authoritarian mandates with little or no complaint. Yet, this easy acceptance didn't extend to other aspects of society. The extent of public hypocrisy was revealed in 1954, after the New South Wales (NSW) State Government had adopted legislation enforcing compulsory unionism in workplaces. There was an outcry because a man was sacked after he refused to join a union. On the one hand, it was acceptable to sack a youth who objected to being trained to kill his fellow human beings. On the other, it was 'a blow for decency' when the Arbitration Court forced the two engineering unions who had black banned the worker to raise the ban. The court's decision seemed to hinge on the man's right to earn a living; however, no such consideration entered into whether a youth who objected to military conscription had the same right. Further, the media – generally unsympathetic to young men who declined to enlist on the basis of religious principles – adopted a quite different attitude to workers who cited religious beliefs as a reason for not joining their trade union. One reader, clearly aware of the hypocrisy, asked whether conscientious objectors to unionism were prepared to take the benefits achieved by unions, such as holiday and long service leave and sick pay, or would they 'give it to a worthy charity because their genuine conscience worries them so much?'[5] Conversely, compulsory military service offered few benefits to the individual but a great deal of inconvenience, especially to those in training, such as apprentices or university students.

The NSA's opponents were anxious to ensure that there were adequate provisions for exemption. When the Bill was being debated in March 1950, the parliamentary Defence Committee proposed that exemption on the grounds of conscientious objection should be confined to four classes of personnel: conscientious objectors to all forms of military service (provided that they could prove their objection to police or a magistrate as required); theological students; ministers of religion; and members of religious orders.[6] These four classes were retained in the Bill. At the Second Reading of the Bill in the Senate on 5 December 1950, the Attorney-General, Senator Spicer, claimed that 'the government had given careful consideration to the position of conscientious objectors' and adhered to the principle established in the National Security (Conscientious Objectors) Regulations of 1943. This provided a total exemption for a person whose beliefs did not permit him to engage in any form of naval, military or air force service.[7] The beliefs didn't have to be religious. As during World War II, however, an objector who applied for exemption had to appear in the Magistrates Court and prove the sincerity of his beliefs. Some magistrates refused to accept that any objector had sincerely held beliefs,[8] although the Act provided exemption for men who held sincere pacifist beliefs. Some magistrates often ridiculed beliefs on the basis that they were irrational, rather than establishing whether they were sincerely held.

Granting non-combatant status also created difficulties. By the mid-1950s, there was considerable debate about what actually constituted non-combatant duties and how the training of a non-combatant National Serviceman differed from the regular training. The Minister for the Army, Josiah Francis, stated that, where a National Serviceman who had been granted non-combatant status by a court was called up for military service, the department would instruct the army not to train him in handling weapons or ammunition.[9] In reality, as the Army Department's Secretary admitted to his counterpart in Defence, non-combatant trainees were 'an embarrassment to the Army'. It was difficult to define non-combatant duties because, in a time of war, personnel of any army unit, including medical personnel, might be required to bear arms. Consequently, the army considered that there was little value in training such a person at all. It would be better for the court to grant complete exemption to anyone with a recognised objection to undertaking combatant duties.[10]

But the army tried to convey the message that non-combatants could be useful soldiers. Major-General L. G. H. Dyke, of Western Command, said in November 1956 that COs were 'playing important non-combatant roles in the Army' and that they 'had a good reputation for being hard workers'. He stated that COs had 'never been a problem in 17 National Training Battalion at Swanbourne [Western Australia]'. While admitting that the situation would be 'disastrous to Australia's defences' if all National Service trainees wanted to be exempted from combatant duties, the Major-General asserted that the army had a responsibility to place those with a partial or full exemption 'to the best advantage'. COs to combatant training were assigned to a medical platoon or clerical and orderly room duties. Major-General Dyke said that, out of each National Service intake of 670 men, the maximum number of COs had been nine, but it was usually between two and four.[11]

The new Act swiftly drew opposition. From the start, the pacifist newspaper, *The Peacemaker* – founded in 1939 by the Anglican priest Frank Coaldrake in response to the government's reintroduction of compulsory military service at the beginning of World War II – was a powerful mouthpiece in the opposition to National Service. *The Peacemaker* published international material; Australian objectors could read about the activities and ideas of war resisters in other countries. This made objectors aware that they were part of a worldwide community. Those whose age and gender determined mandatory registration for National Service could read how others in New Zealand, Britain, Europe and the USA responded to similar compulsory military service schemes. In June 1954, under a headline, 'Conscience had not made cowards of these', *The Peacemaker* pointed out: 'War resisters are being prosecuted in most countries today'. There followed accounts of prosecutions and penalties for war resisters in Belgium, France, Italy, Switzerland, Norway, Southern Rhodesia, the US and New Zealand. Sentences ranged from fines to several years in prison. The US Government still regarded more than 4,500 objectors who had been incarcerated during World War II as 'felons' long after their release from prison. France did not recognise any form of objection to military service; one prisoner, Edmond Schaguene, had been in prison for five years and had recently been sentenced to a further two years. Another French war resister, José de Guet, was granted asylum in Sweden.[12]

Most of the pacifist groups in Australia in the 1950s had been active during World War II and had maintained their vigilance during the early Cold War period. They were well placed to mount a campaign against the proposed military conscription scheme. In each issue from September 1950, *The Peacemaker* listed the contact addresses of six peace organisations: the Federal Pacifist Council (FPC) and the Christian Pacifist Movement (both in Victoria); the Australian Peace Pledge Union (Victoria, NSW, South Australia); the Women's International League of Peace and Freedom (WILPF) in Victoria; the Fellowship of Reconciliation (in NSW and Queensland); and the Tasmanian Pacifist Fellowship. There was also the Australian Peace Council, which other pacifist groups regarded as being a non-pacifist body connected to the Communist Party of Australia (CPA). Other groups, such as the Democratic Rights Council of NSW, while not specifically pacifist, objected to conscription as an abuse of personal civil liberties. *The Peacemaker*'s most valuable role, however, was to spell out in detail the provisions of the NSA; how to apply for exemption on the grounds of conscience; and the penalties for those who failed to comply.

Other groups quickly added their voices, criticising the Act. In April 1951, the Democratic Rights Council of NSW wrote an open letter to Prime Minister Menzies, signed by the organisation's President, the Reverend E. E. V. Collocott, an Anglican priest who had been an active campaigner against conscription during World War II. The Council objected to the title 'National Service' and to the unspecified nature of the 'service'. They asserted that Menzies' emphasis on producing more war goods and placing the national economy on a 'semi-war' footing, and his government's demands for 'more effective ways of dealing with strikers', gave the legislation a sinister aspect. The Democratic Rights Council claimed that the legislation was an underhand way of introducing conscription. Some of Menzies' statements suggested that a conscripted army would (or at least could) be used offensively – 'you have said that "an Australian Army raised for service in Australia would in all probability be raised for no service at all"' – yet, the government had made no 'determined and sustained efforts to settle international differences [peacefully]'. The Council urged the government to use methods advocated by the United

Front page of *The Peacemaker*, May 1951, detailing the *National Service Act* and an individual's obligation to undertake military service.

Nations for settling international disputes. Even if a plebiscite was passed on the issue, the Council argued:

> It is immoral for electors to obligate youths under 21, who are devoid of electoral rights, to train and prepare for war and death before they have had the opportunity to train and prepare for life and the pursuit of happiness.[13]

The WILPF wrote to Menzies in September 1951, deploring the extent to which governments were placing their faith in, and reliance on, armed force. Their letter contained a resolution passed by the WILPF International Executive Committee, stating:

everyone shall have the right on [the] grounds of conscience to refuse military service whether in time of peace or war, as well as of all work connected with the production, transport and distribution of armaments.

The resolution added that all objectors should be 'entitled to special international protection'. The Prime Minister's Department sent WILPF a non-committal acknowledgment.[14]

Another early critic was the Melbourne-based League for Freedom, a successor to the No Conscription Campaign, which had been founded by Maurice Blackburn in World War II.[15] In the March 1951 issue of its monthly circular publication, *The Anti-Militarist News*, the League for Freedom announced: 'We deeply regret...that "boy conscription" in Australia has now become an accomplished fact'. 'Boy conscription' was a reference to the original conscription scheme, which operated from 1909 to 1929, enlisting boys from the age of 14 years in compulsory military service. The League recorded its disappointment that the Australian Labor Party (ALP) had supported the reintroduction of conscription because a majority of one at the ALP Federal Conference had voted in favour of it. 'And thus', the League stated, 'the arbitrary vote, the whim of one man, determined the destiny of thousands of voteless Australian youths.' The ALP held a majority in the Senate and could have blocked the Bill. The League opined that the response – or lack of it – from the churches was even more disappointing. Its appeal to the churches to oppose conscription had elicited only three responses, drawing the League's withering condemnation:

> If one were to judge from the general lack of response by Christian ministers one would have to conclude that 99% of them do not really believe in the principles of their Founder as enunciated in the Sermon on the Mount – we say 'really believe' for, of course, real belief is shown in actions and conduct, not in mere lip service.[16]

Although the mainstream Christian churches did not oppose compulsory military training, individuals within their ranks did, and they were often active in the executives of the pacifist groups. The Reverend Collocott was one example. The Christadelphians, the Seventh Day Adventists, the Religious Society of Friends (known as Quakers) and the Jehovah's Witnesses preached either absolute non-compliance or limited compliance with the Regulations. In October 1951, the Mason family of Jehovah's Witnesses from North Bundaberg in Queensland wrote to Menzies expressing their desire as 'law-abiding citizens' to cooperate 'in anything apart from killing or learning how to kill'. The Department of Labour and National Service advised the Prime Minister's Department that, if any reply was warranted, it should state that a person claiming exemption from National Service on the ground of conscientious belief was 'required to establish his claim before a Court of Petty Sessions'. Like the original World War II National Security Act upon which it was modelled, the NSA initially contained no provision for an appeal against a magistrate's decision.[17] This right was instituted as an amendment agreed by Menzies' Cabinet early in 1953, and only after a vigorous campaign by the Australian branch of the World Council of Churches and others.[18]

In May 1951, *The Peacemaker* became the first newspaper to publish its support for young men who wanted to register as objectors and to offer instructions for registering. The paper merely stated that those who were liable for service and who wanted to talk it over might contact the secretary of their local pacifist group, listed on page 2. The groups, however, were located only in some capital cities – none in Western Australia (WA), the Australian Capital Territory (ACT) or the Northern Territory (NT). Young men seeking exemption had to register for National Service and then apply for exemption as a CO as soon as they received their certificate of registration. Forms were available from District Employment Offices and returned to them when completed. These offices forwarded the forms to the appropriate magistrate, who was empowered to direct that the applicant be exempted, either from combatant duties or from all training.[19] This instruction implied that the judgement would grant either non-combatant status or complete exemption. In many cases, however, the application was dismissed; and, initially, applicants had no right of appeal against the magistrate's decision, as many soon discovered. The proportion of successful to unsuccessful applications in this early period is discussed later in the chapter.

The Quakers were some of the first objectors to fall foul of the new Act. A young Perth man, Ronald Waddy, had his application for total exemption dismissed and received orders to be drafted in a non-combatant unit, the Ambulance Corps. Waddy, however, questioned the lack of a right of appeal in a higher court and took his case to his Federal Member, Paul Hasluck, the Minister for Territories. The question of a right of appeal had been considered and dismissed by a sub-committee of Cabinet, meeting in November 1951. Waddy was duly issued with a call-up notice but failed to report for service. The Minister for Labour and National Service, Harold Holt, could 'see no alternative but to proceed against him'. Waddy was arrested and imprisoned in a military detention centre.[20]

The League for Freedom (which, by November 1951, had changed its name to the League for Freedom and World Friendship) published details of the first Victorian cases, heard in the Melbourne Court of Petty Sessions on 16 to 18 October, 1951. In its *Anti-Militarist News* circular for November 1951, the League lamented the lack of a right of appeal and reported that Minister Holt had refused to defer calling up objectors whose applications for total exemption had been wholly or partially refused. Of the 20 cases heard over the three days, most were granted full exemption, and one was granted exemption from combatant service only. The two cases dismissed were an Anglican who objected on political grounds, and an applicant who stated that he had no religion but objected on 'Christian' grounds.

Christadelphians objected to any form of military service or work that would aid the military. One applicant said that a 'non-combatant corps' was part of 'the fighting machine and part of a worldly organisation', and he could take no part in it. Because the sect was firmly against any form of violence, and members were usually able to demonstrate consistency of belief, at least some secured total exemption. The Jehovah's Witnesses held more complex views. Many served as part-time ministers; they could apply for exemption as Christian ministers. The sect was not pacifist, stating that, if God called members to war, they would serve. In the witness box, many expressed contradictory views that seemed to irritate magistrates. For example, one said that he would serve in the Red Cross if it did not involve taking an oath. When asked what was wrong with taking an oath, he answered: 'It is part of the teaching of the Jehovah's Witnesses that we must not serve two masters.' He gave the same reason for refusing to serve in the Army Medical Corps; yet, he admitted to 'recognising an allegiance' to Australia and to Victoria. He also said that he would be prepared to sell fruit and vegetables to the army because 'the money would be my living.' That particular applicant was exempted only from combatant duties.[21]

In South Australia (SA) in mid-1952, the Quakers, the Women's Peace Crusade and the CPA all protested against the verdict in the case of Quaker Brian Keith Mason. He had been sent to Holsworthy Military Barracks, a correctional establishment outside Sydney, to serve a period of imprisonment. They claimed that Mason's case revealed 'a violation of what is accepted as British justice', because he had not been granted a right of appeal against the magistrate's decision. He had not sworn military allegiance, yet was 'taken against his will to a destination some thousand miles from his home.' Mason's widowed mother was totally financially dependent upon her son. The Quakers urged the Acting Prime Minister, Arthur Fadden, to investigate Mason's case and take steps to amend the Act to allow for a right of appeal and to protect civilians against 'arbitrary military law'.[22] Mason and another objector, Queenslander Keith John Bundesen, were each prosecuted by the department for failing to obey a call-up notice. They were regarded as enlisted in the CMF as soon as they were committed to military custody. They were sent to training camps in their respective states, where each refused to perform any training. Both were sent to Holsworthy to be detained until they had served 176 days.[23]

The Gospel Publicity League of Epping (NSW) expressed alarm that exemption was not granted as a matter of course to any sincere objector. The League cited the case of Norman David Topley, a Jehovah's Witness, who was refused exemption by Stipendiary Magistrate (SM) Solling. Solling's bias was clearly evident in his remark: 'You people obey the laws as much as it suits you. Explain that away.'[24] Similarly, the Christadelphians accused Judge Curlewis, presiding over an appeal in the District Court on 7 August 1953, of using language that conveyed to the public and the press that, in his opinion, Christadelphian beliefs were 'selfish in the extreme, cruel, cowardly, blind to the facts of life and seditious.' This was picked up by the media in a headline: 'Youths "Cowardly, Selfish": Judge'.[25]

These seemingly arbitrary judgements attracted the attention of the Australian Council for the World Council of Churches, who wrote to Menzies in August 1952 to protest against the lack of 'sufficient provision for appeal against the decision of the court.' Council representatives had spoken with Menzies about this matter in 1951. They again urged him to give it careful thought and to take it up with the relevant ministers.[26] When Christadelphians Colin Hill and Keith Bundesen from Rockhampton (Queensland) both had their applications for exemption dismissed in July 1952, and Bundesen was subsequently detained at Holsworthy, the Australian Christadelphian Central Standing Committee added its voice to the protest. Committee Secretary A. E. Davies had earlier informed Menzies that, during the century of its existence, his sect had been:

> conscientiously opposed to the bearing of arms, or taking part in warfare as combatants or non-combatants, on the ground that the Bible which [the Christadelphians] revere as the word of God commands them to refrain from killing or doing violence of any kind to their fellow men.

Davies added that, while grateful to the government for including exemption provisions in the Act, the Committee urged the adoption of an amendment granting the right of appeal.[27] Despite further evidence that the Christadelphians collected of Solling SM's bias against objectors, and considerable public debate, Menzies' Cabinet initially decided not to amend the Act.[28]

The Church of Christ took a different approach, simply asking for exemption for all of its members rather than campaigning for justice for all objectors.[29] Further pressure from the peace churches eventually brought an amendment. On 27 June 1953, Rockhampton's *Morning Bulletin* reported that Bundesen's application for complete exemption from military service was granted in June 1953 after he had served 132 days of a 180-day sentence in military detention. But Hill's appeal was dismissed, and he would serve a full sentence at Holsworthy, prior to being released in October 1954.

While these cases suggest that some magistrates had an ingrained bias against certain religious sects, especially the Jehovah's Witnesses, the Anti-Conscription Council of Victoria came to a different conclusion when it reported on outcomes of applications for exemption in late 1951, beginning with the original 22 cases heard on 16–18 October in Melbourne. Of those applying for total exemption, six Christadelphians, two Jehovah's Witnesses, one Christian Israelite, one Pentecostal, one Church of Christ member and one Anglican were successful. Another five were granted exemption from combatant service only; two applications were dismissed; one had left the state; and one didn't appear. The Anti-Conscription Council commented that these results and the outcomes of other court cases in October and December 1951 indicated that magistrates were *more* likely to grant exemptions to members of religious sects. In contrast, of the applicants who were refused, none was a regular church goer, and one's objection to military service was 'mainly of a non-religious nature'. The Anti-Conscription Council concluded, therefore:

> It is apparent that the non-religious objector is at a distinct disadvantage compared with an objector on doctrinal or religious grounds. It is at least conceivable that the objector who has had a conventional upbringing and has not been subjected to a religious teaching which is directly opposed to the traditional education in the spirit of patriotism and the obligations of men to the nation and the state, and still remains unconvinced, has thought more deeply on the ethics of military service than the boy who has unquestioningly accepted the beliefs of his parents and the teachings of a sect.[30]

This conclusion was based on cases in the Melbourne City Court. Vivienne Abraham's notes regarding cases heard in the same court in 1952 tend to confirm the assertion that sect members and trainees for the Christian ministry were more likely to obtain total or partial exemption than applicants who did not demonstrate that their objection to military service was on 'religious' grounds.

Abraham was the strongest and most dedicated supporter of conscientious objectors to compulsory military training. From the first application hearings, she regularly attended court cases in Melbourne and elsewhere in Victoria. In August 1953, she wrote to K. J. Kenafick, Secretary of the Pacifist Movement of Victoria, asking whether he could obtain copies of any Regulations gazetted since the *National Services Act (1953)*, which she required urgently for an appeal that was being heard at Wangaratta. Later that month, Abraham spoke at a Pacifist Movement meeting on 'Conscientious objectors: their problems and difficulties, ways of contacting them, methods by which they may be helped, and the need to assist financially in fighting their cases'. Despite Abraham's commitment, the Pacifist Movement appears to have had little connection with COs. At an April 1957 conference, groups discussed whether the Movement could 'do more than at present with its present membership, considering both numbers and the degree of commitment of individuals?'; whether it was 'desirable and practicable' to form sub-groups, including a CO Group; and, perhaps the most basic question of all: 'are we clear in our own minds on what we stand for?'[31]

In contrast, as already noted, the FPC adopted a more proactive stance through its newspaper *The Peacemaker*. The content on COs increased after Abraham took over editorship of the paper. *The Peacemaker*'s June 1951 issue published a long article by Roger Page, titled 'Conscientious Objection to Conscription', which argued that no CO should 'attempt a course of action unless he is convinced of its rightness for himself and confident of [having] the required spiritual strength'. This was important, Page asserted, because, if an objector failed, he failed 'not only himself but the whole movement'. Anticipating the argument that conscripted men had a duty to society, Page posited that the objector's duty to society was through his duty to the CO movement. In place of a duty to fight, the objector must substitute 'a duty to maintain a firm and sound witness to his belief'. He added: 'one defaulting, dishonest or backsliding conscientious objector can destroy the efficacy and witness of a whole group'. These were harsh words; given the pressure put upon objectors to submit to enlistment, one wonders whether they discouraged some young men from taking a stand for their conscience.

Brian Mason's case was the first CO court case to appear in *The Peacemaker*. Mason, a 19-year-old gardener and Quaker from SA, applied to be registered as an objector. The magistrate who heard his case in November 1951 determined that his beliefs did not prevent his performing non-combatant service. Mason was ordered to enlist but refused. In May 1952, he was fined £10 for failing to comply with the call-up notice, committed into military custody and sent to Holsworthy, where he may have been detained for the full 176 days of his training period. In its July 1952 issue, *The Peacemaker* urged readers to join with Brian's church leaders in appealing to Members of Parliament and other influential people to obtain justice. The church's pleas appear to have made no impact upon the government.

By mid-1952, COs faced increased criticism from certain sections of the public. One of the more extreme examples was a resolution that the Mount Tyson sub-branch of the Returned Services League (RSL) forwarded to the RSL's annual Queensland conference, expressing concern that so many COs were being granted either full or partial exemption from military training. The branch advocated the kinds of human rights violations that its members had supposedly been fighting against in World War II:

> if [objectors] are unwilling to assume their responsibilities with regard to the defence of their own country, they be defranchised [sic] and debarred from owning land.

Whether this resolution was carried at the conference is unknown, but it is probable that it was. In August 1952, the Queensland RSL President, R. D. Huish, called for all medical exemptions to be certified by military doctors, adding: 'there should be no exemption on occupational or conscience grounds.' Mr Leslie, a Federal Country Party member from WA, shared this view. The Queensland branch of the RSL sustained its attack on COs, using its 1954 conference to push again for closure of 'loop holes' in the NSA that 'allowed youths to shirk their responsibilities'. One of the delegates referred to objectors as 'gutless wonders'.[32]

Some citizens spoke out in the objectors' defence. B. J. Wooldridge wrote to *The Cairns Post* on 18 June 1954:

> Why should they be gaoled because their conscience will not allow them to go in the army? Surely their labour is more value to the country than that? After all, a true conscientious objector cannot go in the army, irrespective of the consequences, so unless something is done soon the gaols will be full. The objectors have proved this over and over again by their stand against those in authority.

Some magistrates, too, respected objectors' beliefs. On 28 August 1952, nine objectors appeared before Meagher SM in Sydney; seven were ordered to

*The Peacemaker*'s report on Brian Keith Mason's internment at Holsworthy Correctional establishment, July 1952.

undertake non-combatant duties, and two (a Christadelphian and a Quaker) were granted total exemption. William Ridden, a Quaker whose report of the trial appeared in the October issue of *The Peacemaker*, stated that Meagher gave a 'fair and impartial hearing', and that the National Service representative 'showed no animosity' towards the objectors. 'From their point of view non-combatants would be as useful to the army as combatants'.

A useful summary of applications for exemption by Sydney youths appeared on 28 November 1952, when *The Sydney Morning Herald* reported that 100 applications for total or partial exemption from military service had been lodged in the Sydney metropolitan area since the NSA came into operation in 1951. The paper reported that a majority had succeeded in being awarded non-combatant duties, and some had been granted total exemption, but that others would have to train for service in combatant units. 'Many' applications from country areas would be heard as soon as magistrates were available.

Most of the applicants who had appeared so far were Jehovah's Witnesses, Seventh Day Adventists, Quakers, Brethren or Christadelphians. There were also a few Anglicans, Methodists and Presbyterians and one Roman Catholic seeking exemptions. Possibly in response to the accusation that some magistrates were biased and were not adhering to their mandate of ascertaining merely whether beliefs were sincerely held, *The Sydney Morning Herald* concluded that its review of the applications heard so far indicated that 'objectors have been given every opportunity to prove their belief, with corroboration, if necessary, and have received sympathetic treatment by the Court'.

What emerges from newspaper reports in the early years of the National Service scheme is that magistrates quickly ascertained that Seventh Day Adventists would never serve in a combatant capacity but usually had no objection to enlisting for non-combatant duties. Consequently, their applications for non-combatant status were usually granted. Jehovah's Witnesses objected to any type of military service except that ordained by God. Their applications for total exemption often failed. An example of this differing treatment of religious sect members occurred in the Mount Gambier (SA) Magistrate's Court on 14 January 1953, where Williams SM heard applications from five youths for registration as COs. The four Seventh Day Adventists applied for non-combatant status because their Minister had told them that 'they would be violating the Communion of God by performing combatant duties in the services'. When asked the usual question about whether they would defend their mother if she was attacked by an assailant, they said that they would 'trust God for protection and strength, without using weapons'. Their church minister told the court that the Seventh Day Adventists' objection to taking life was based on the Commandment 'Thou shalt not kill':

> Our boys don't bear arms because we don't believe in killing, but they give honour to Caesar and are loyal to the Government where it does not conflict with their consciences. That allows them to do medical work and drive ambulances. The denomination's stand is the same throughout the world.

Each was granted non-combatant status. Raymond Norman, the fifth youth to appear in the Mount Gambier court that day, said that Jehovah's

Witnesses left it to the individual's conscience as to whether to bear arms. He believed that it was wrong to bear arms or comply with National Service. When Williams SM asked, 'Why is it wrong?', Norman replied, 'This world is controlled by Satan's organisation. Because of the selfish desires of the nations, they are not worth fighting for.' Jehovah's Witnesses would fight only when God commanded them to. Norman aspired to become a minister in the Jehovah's Witness church, which, he believed, was the only way to get everlasting life 'for at least a thousand years, when the Devil would be let loose again' – and those who followed him would be destroyed again. 'I want my chance to see that day.' When Williams asked whether his main reason for wishing to avoid military service was because it might prevent his becoming a minister, Norman replied that it was. His application was refused.[33] At a similar case in Perth one month later, four Seventh Day Adventists were granted non-combatant status, and the one Jehovah's Witness had his application for total exemption refused.[34]

Christadelphian objectors usually testified that their church did not permit them to engage with political or military matters, including voting in elections. They believed that, if they enlisted in the armed services, they would not have a place in the kingdom of God.[35] In some cases, this meant that military service would result in expulsion from the church. This defence often yielded total exemption from National Service. These cases indicate that, taking into account different beliefs, differing capacities to express those beliefs and the attitudes of individual magistrates, the experiences of young men seeking total exemption from military service varied considerably from one court to another across the country.

In the next chapter, I discuss the remainder of the National Service period and draw some conclusions, based upon my research into 258 individual cases of objectors.

## CHAPTER 2
## 'I do not feel satisfied that he holds a conscientious belief'

*The Peacemaker's* June 1953 issue reported that public protest over Brian Mason's detention had led Parliament to pass an amendment to the NSA in April, granting objectors the right of appeal. The amendment came into effect on 13 May. Because this was one year after Mason had been committed to Holsworthy, it had no impact upon his sentence; but it made a difference for others. Between May and August 1953, *The Peacemaker* reported that 50 youths had lodged applications of appeal against magistrates' refusals to grant them exemption. There were 28 appeals in NSW, eight in Victoria, 14 in Queensland, and two in each of SA, WA and Tasmania. These included appeals from judgements made before 13 May. Of the 329 men who had applied for total exemption on the grounds of conscience since National Service commenced in 1951, 170 had been successful, 64 applications had been dismissed, and 95 were ordered to register as non-combatants. Additionally, 238 men had applied for exemption from combatant duties; only 19 of these had been refused. *The Peacemaker* commented that the 170 men given total exemption represented 'only 0.14 percent of the total number registered for National Service'.[1]

From June 1953, *The Peacemaker* devoted much more space in its columns to Australian COs. This was, undoubtedly, partly because there were more cases to report upon once objectors had gained the right of appeal, but it also indicates the influence of the paper's new editor, Vivienne Abraham. In September, *The Peacemaker* reported on the outcomes of the first five appeal cases. Justice Ross in Adelaide and Justice Gibson in Burnie, Tasmania, respectively, granted total exemptions to Charles King (a Christadelphian) and John George Constantine (a Jehovah's Witness). In each case, the judge recognised that, irrespective of whether the men's views were rational, they were sincerely held; it would be against the applicant's conscience to enlist even in a non-combatant capacity. The applicants in Brisbane, Sydney and Melbourne were less fortunate, all having their appeals rejected. In Sydney, Judge Redshaw told Peter Berry that his views were 'servile and cowardly':

> You, of course, are looking at this from the Christian and what you believe to be the moral point of view. But with the selfish[ness] and egotism of youth you will not recognise any principles that conflict with your own.

The same could be said for the judge, whose task was not to convince the applicant of the error of his ways, but to ascertain whether his views were sincerely held.[2]

In November 1953, *The Peacemaker* reported evidence from across the country that some judges took this injunction seriously and judged accordingly. The Chief Justice of WA, Sir John Dwyer, upholding an appeal by Jehovah's Witness Donald Grondal in Perth on 11 September, defined a conscientious belief as:

> an inward conviction of what is morally right or morally wrong...a conviction that is genuinely reached and held by some process of thinking about the subject... It represents a conclusion that is uninfluenced by any consideration of advantage or disadvantage, either to oneself or others, and perhaps is combined with a willingness to act according to the particular conviction reached, although it may involve personal discomfort or suffering or material loss. If those characteristics are present, I think it is quite irrelevant to consider whether the conviction is reasonable or correct.[3]

Training to kill. Despite the army's promise, even non-combatants were given training in weapons handling. National Servicemen training at Woodside, SA, 1954.

*The Peacemaker*'s December 1953 and January 1954 issues reported on recent cases. In the Adelaide Supreme Court, Mr Justice Mayo espoused a similar definition of conscientious belief in granting Ian Reece Henig exemption from combatant duties. Nigel Leonard Noack in Townsville, Victor Paul Clements and Donald Stanley Morrisby in Hobart and Geoffrey John Beel and Graeme Phillips in Melbourne all successfully appealed for full exemption. The last two cases were heard by Mr Justice Read, who reiterated that the issue was not whether applicants held rational views but only whether their objection was sincerely held. Similarly, in Perth in October 1953, Resident Magistrate (RM) Taylor appeared willing to grant objectors what they asked for. Two Jehovah's Witnesses, Rodney Troy and Ian Youngman, were granted full exemption from National Service after Troy explained that Witnesses regarded the Medical Corps as 'one of the five columns of war', and it was unacceptable for them to serve in that capacity. Four Seventh Day Adventists – Robin Volrath,

Donald Till, Warren Bailey and Neville Borodale – explained that 'their faith did not conflict with their serving in a non-combatant capacity', and Mr Taylor accordingly ordered them to be registered for non-combatant duties.

How did a magistrate or a judge determine whether beliefs were sincerely held? My research on 258 cases reported by the media over the decade of the National Service Training Scheme indicates that the decision often hinged on two things: the extent to which the applicant demonstrated his knowledge of the Bible, and the amount of self-sacrifice evident in his personal life that was deemed to be consistent with his religious beliefs. Walter Henry Gray, a Seventh Day Adventist, appeared in the Innisfail (Queensland) Court in July 1954. Unlike most Adventists, who normally requested non-combatant service, Gray asked for full exemption. In his defence, he was able to quote not merely the commandment 'Thou shalt not kill' – which almost every applicant on religious grounds could cite – but the chapter in the book of Exodus where the Ten Commandments are found. He also cited many other verses in the Old and New Testaments, including *Acts* 5:29, where the Apostle Peter said: 'We ought to obey God rather than men'. Gray lived an abstemious life, eschewing meat, cigarettes and alcohol and not even attending the cinema. He was granted total exemption from military service.[4]

In many cases, where the applicant's knowledge of the Bible was poor, or the magistrate could find some inconsistency in his lifestyle or choice of employment, the magistrate either dismissed the application completely or ordered the applicant to undertake non-combatant service. This posed a particular dilemma for those Christadelphians who claimed that they would be expelled from their church if they undertook military service of any form. Two Queensland cases exemplify differences in Christadelphian teaching. Robert Archer O'Toole, appearing before the Rockhampton Magistrate's Court on 20 February 1953, said that his church would expel him if he joined the army.[5] On the other hand, Donald James Ross, from Urangan, who appeared in court in November 1954, stated that he would not be excommunicated by his church if he undertook National Service.[6]

Perhaps the most surprising cases of that time were reported in *The Peacemaker*'s March 1955 issue. Kenneth William Wrigley had already undertaken part of his National Service in WA. Because he was a student, Wrigley's training with the Royal Australian Air Force (RAAF) was divided into two periods of 88 days each. He stated that he was a Methodist when he undertook his first period of training, but that he became a Jehovah's Witness before beginning the second period. His application was based on his change of religion from Methodist to Jehovah's Witness. Wrigley said that the Jehovah's Witnesses believed that 'the Scriptures forbade anything to do with warfare'. He was granted full exemption from further training. His case wasn't unique in Perth. A similar application had come to court in January 1955, with the same result. Smith SM granted an application by Edward Davies for exemption from the remainder of his National Service training on the grounds that 'during his time in camp, he had become a member of a religious sect that opposed any kind of military service'.

As time passed, however, the magistrates appeared harder to convince. Perhaps this was because, as the number of objectors increased, both court and military authorities became concerned about applicants jumping on the bandwagon, and the RSL sustained pressure on courts to clamp down on 'shirkers'. Of five applications heard in December 1954 and January 1955, three in NSW were ordered to perform non-combatant duties; a Tasmanian application was completely rejected; and only the Perth applicant (Davies), who had completed half his training, was successful in achieving full exemption.[7] By June 1955, *The Peacemaker* was reporting cases where magistrates consistently turned down applications for either full exemption or exemption from combatant duties, on the basis of lack of evidence. Hearing the application of Leslie Prestidge in Sydney, McCauley SM remarked:

> While I am prepared to give the greatest latitude in dealing with applicants for non-combatant service, I must have some evidence of conscientious objection to the combatant service. If one has a conscientious belief, it is a very sincere belief, one might say a passion. There must be evidence of a definite condition of mind.

*The Peacemaker* continued to report on the actions of war resisters around the world in opposing conscription, including how a coalition of peace activists and church groups blocked a Bill before the United States Congress that would institute a permanent system of universal military training.[8] At a time when the post-World War II world was beginning to grasp the awful reality of

## "THE PEACEMAKER"
### An Australian Venture in Reconstruction

Vol. 16, No. 5.     MAY, 1954.     Registered at the G.P.O., Melb., for transmission by post as a periodical.    6d. per copy.

## COBALT BOMB ONLY FOR MADMEN

### Professor Oliphant Urges World Authority Whatever The Cost In National Sovereignty

On April 14, the Melbourne "Age" reported the following from Sydney:

"Only madmen or devils would contemplate the use of cobalt bombs, or other weapons designed to spread long-lived radioactivity over the earth."

"Only a devil would deliberately spread sterility and impotence among mankind, his own side included, or atoms up genetic monstrosities for the future," he said.

"I believe that men and women all over the world will demand of their leaders that, at whatever cost in national sovereignty and individual power, an international authority, backed by adequate policing strength, must be established to impose peace upon the world.

"This is no loss of freedom. It is the task of the newspapers, and of all organs of publicity, to spread knowledge of the threat which faces humanity and to help build a properly thought-out plan for preserving peace.

"Patience is needed, but so is speed. The hands of the clock point

Professor Marcus Oliphant, director of the Research School of Physical Sciences at the National University, Canberra, said this last night urging an international authority to impose peace upon the world.

new day will dawn, and war become a lost and incomprehensible sin of the past."

Professor Oliphant said that mankind faced the most important decision of all time. Push-button warfare with atomic weapons — impersonal, immoral and inhuman — could destroy civilisation.

Alternatively, atomic energy could provide unlimited power for use in industry and the home.

"Man, despite the teachings of all great religious leaders and moralists, has not given up warfare," he said.

"Perhaps, now that he is faced with the certainty that war means the complete devastation of the territories of both sides in any world conflict, he will find some alternative method of settling international quarrels.

will be found, perhaps by establishing a form of limited world government, with an adequate police force at its disposal. This implies the renunciation of all weapons of war in the hands of individual nations.

"To my mind it is useless to say that such proposals are idealistic and impracticable. I believe that restricted world government will come, because all men will wish to save their own lives, the lives and futures of their children and civilisation itself.

### BANS WORTHLESS

"There is much talk in some quarters of a move to ban atomic weapons.

"I do not believe that the most solemn agreement to ban the use of atomic weapons in war would be worth the paper on which it was written.

fought at first with conventional weapons, the side which faced defeat, or which felt that continued war would ruin it, would abandon all scruples and use every weapon at its command which it thought could stave off defeat.

"The last war taught us, surely, that even Christian morality is laid aside in all-out warfare. Gas was not used in the last war because it is not a good weapon. Atomic weapons are the supreme weapons of aggression and retaliation.

"Bacteriological and gas warfare are not likely to be used. Compared with atomic weapons, they are of little or no importance and adequate defences can readily be established.

"Therefore, an international ban on their use is likely to be effective, since neither side would wish to use

*The Peacemaker's* May 1954 front page, reporting Professor Mark Oliphant's stance against the use of nuclear weapons.

weapons that could annihilate humankind, many sections of society debated the moral and practical outcomes of producing nuclear weapons. The role of pacifists also continued to be discussed throughout the nine years that this National Service scheme operated, and *The Peacemaker* recorded much of this debate. Participants included one of Australia's foremost nuclear scientists, Professor Mark Oliphant, who declared: 'only madmen or devils would contemplate the use of cobalt bombs or other weapons designed to spread long-lived radioactivity over the earth'. As a member of the Manhattan Project, he had seen at close hand the devastation caused by the nuclear weapons that he had helped to develop. The sentiments that Oliphant and fellow scientists expressed were not confined to the Australian scientific community. In London, early in 1954, scientists debated the morality of atomic warfare.

Both sides were opposed to the use of the hydrogen bomb. Even those who argued that the bomb was 'a preserver of the peace' thought it 'too large and indiscriminate a weapon for use on military targets'.[9] Pacifists in Australia and overseas also debated an idea from the USA of a 'third camp' of non-aligned countries, committed to non-violent methods of negotiation, which would stand between the major power blocs. Contributors to the third camp discussions included Rev A. J. Muste of the USA; Dr Kenneth Rivett, an Australian academic who had been a CO during World War II; and Dr J. F. (Jim) Cairns, later a Minister in the Whitlam Labor Government.[10]

By May 1954, the Holsworthy Military Correctional Establishment held nine objectors: three detainees each from NSW, Queensland and SA. Seven were members of the Christian Assemblies; one was Christadelphian; one a Jehovah's Witness. Each served 140 days. John Fallding, who visited on behalf of the FPC on 23 May, reported that the detainees were being well treated.[11] The following week, Vivienne Abraham and two other members of the pacifist movement visited and spoke with the nine detainees. They found that, following the court's rejection of their application for full exemption from National Service, some detainees had presented themselves voluntarily and at their own expense to the military establishment where they were required to attend for call up. There, they had advised the authorities that they would not take the oath nor wear uniform. Others had ignored their call-up notices. In each case, the result was the same. Each had been summonsed to court, fined £10 and sent to Holsworthy. One had been told that he faced a court-martial, but this had not yet happened.

At Holsworthy, the objectors reported that they were well treated – permitted to wear their own clothes, send and receive mail and have visitors for half an hour on Sundays. They worked in the nursery by choice, not compulsion, and were kept segregated from other inmates. Facilities were available for reading or studying. Those who had presented themselves voluntarily to the military authorities were required to serve the 176 days that they would have spent in training; others were unsure how long they would serve. In contrast to the successful outcomes in 1953 after the legislation was amended to permit appeals, the objectors who ended up in Holsworthy said that they had not heard of any appeals against non-combatant duties being ordered. Abraham wrote:

CONSCIENTIOUS OBJECTORS TO MILITARY TRAINING
(From commencement of the National Service Act to 21st June, 1955.)

|  | N.S.W. | V. | Q. | S.A. | W.A. | TAS. | TOTAL |
|---|---|---|---|---|---|---|---|
| A. Applications for Total Exemption | 257 | 191 | 215 | 87 | 60 | 19 | 829 |
| 1. Totally Exempted | 41 | 109 | 120 | 57 | 37 | 6 | 370 |
| 2. Regist. Non-Combatants | 125 | 40 | 33 | 23 | 6 | 5 | 231 |
| 3. Applications Refused | 49 | 37 | 26 | 6 | 5 | 7 | 130 |
| 4. Applications Pending | 42 | 5 | 37 | 1 | 12 | 1 | 98 |
| A. Applications for Exemption from Combatant Duties Only | 224 | 127 | 102 | 48 | 88 | 36 | 625 |
| 1. Regist. Non-Combatants | 190 | 120 | 78 | 42 | 71 | 28 | 529 |
| 2. Applications Refused | 13 | 6 | 12 | 4 | 3 | 5 | 43 |
| 3. Applications Pending | 21 | 1 | 12 | 2 | 14 | 3 | 53 |
| C. TOTAL APPLICATIONS | 481 | 318 | 317 | 135 | 148 | 55 | 1454 |

SOURCE: Information supplied to Federal Pacifist Council by Minister for Labour and National Service.

Conscientious Objector figures 1951-55, published in *The Peacemaker*, December 1955.

certainly, a feeling was evident among these conscientious objectors as well as others I have spoken to, that there was little point in appealing, as it was not possible to convince a court of their conviction.

She stressed the need for anyone appearing before a court to be well prepared in advance, to know his rights regarding legal representation and the calling of witnesses, and to be 'clear in his own mind what he believes and how far and in what circumstances he would continue to believe and act accordingly'. She also raised the question of whether it was harder to secure a successful appeal in NSW or Queensland, the states where the majority of the Holsworthy detainees were tried.[12]

Abraham's suspicion about bias in NSW courts appears to have been justified by figures that the FPC obtained from the Minister for Labour and National Service: numbers of COs from the commencement of the scheme to 21 June 1955, and the outcomes of their applications for exemption. The figures show that 829 young men had applied for total exemption during this period. Of the 257 who applied in NSW, only 41 (16 percent) were granted total exemption, whereas in both Victoria (191 applicants) and Queensland (215 applicants), 57 per cent were granted total exemption. In SA and WA, the percentage of total exemptions granted was even higher (66 percent of

'I do not feel satisfied that he holds a conscientious belief'

An example of *The Peacemaker*'s reporting on international events, June 1955.

87 applications and 61 per cent of 60 applications, respectively).[13] The figures for Queensland courts do not clearly reflect Abraham's suspicion; however, 27 percent of those seeking total exemption either had their application rejected or were ordered to enlist as non-combatants. As the Holsworthy detainees indicated to Abraham, many simply refused to comply, which is why they ended up in a military correctional centre.

Nationally, to June 1955, courts had granted 45 percent of applications for total exemption, ordered 28 percent of applicants to perform non-combatant service and rejected 16 percent of applications. By contrast, 85 percent of young men requesting exemption from combatant duties only were successful. In all states except WA and Tasmania, the number seeking total exemption exceeded those seeking exemption from combatant duties only. This was most pronounced in Queensland, where 215 applied for total exemption and only 102 applied for exemption from combatant duties.

From July 1955, *The Peacemaker* had a new editor, W. J. Latona. In October 1957, D. V. Collocot succeeded him. Henceforth, COs featured much less in the paper; it was largely devoted to opinion pieces, happenings overseas, the continuing international debate on the use of nuclear weapons, and some indifferent poetry. Between July 1955 and June 1959, mention of COs was limited to the reports of a few court cases and an occasional article (such as 'Notes on Conscientious Objection', a two-page spread in the August–September 1956 issue). This omission is particularly odd, given the changes to the National Service scheme that occurred during this time. In 1957, the scheme was reduced in scope, with the period of service halved; the RAAF ceased to recruit trainees; and the method of selection changed from one where all young men aged 18 years and over were potentially eligible to the 'birthday ballot' system that, as later chapters show, became notorious during the Vietnam War. The RAAF's last intake completed its training in June 1957.[14]

The Minister for Defence, Athol Townley, announced that the government would suspend all National Service training from 1 January 1960. A new three-year defence plan, involving the reorganisation of the three services, would not include National Service. Trainees serving currently were expected to fulfil their obligations and complete their training by 30 June 1960. The *Canberra Times* reported the Minister as offering a rationale for these changes: 'while a global war was not impossible, it was considered unlikely, but limited wars could break out in various unstable areas.' The primary aim of Australia's defence forces, therefore, was to continue to improve Australia's capacity to 'react promptly and effectively with her allies to meet possible limited war situations.'[15] Official figures indicated that, by the end of 1959, over 500,000 trainees had been registered; 227,000 of them had been trained for military service; and 3,679 had applied for exemption.[16] Comparing these figures with the table published in *The Peacemaker* (discussed above) shows that nearly two-thirds of those seeking exemption did so between June 1955 and the end of the scheme.

My survey of 258 objectors from the 1951–59 scheme (Appendix 1) represents about 7 percent of the official figure of 3,679 men who applied for full or partial exemption.

Unexpectedly, most of cases in my sample were not from the most populous states. Although 77 of the objectors were in NSW, 82 (the majority) were in Queensland; only 18 in Victoria; 21 in SA; 43 in WA; 10 in Tasmania; and three in the ACT. The locations of the remaining four were unknown. The sample is too small for statistical analysis, but it is consistent with Abraham's suspicion that NSW magistrates showed an anti-objector bias. Of the 48 NSW applicants in the sample who applied for total exemption, only 14 (29 percent) were granted, compared with the Queensland courts' granting of 38 (50 percent) of the 76 known total exemption applications. In all states, some exemptions were granted only after an appeal, but the majority were granted in the lower courts.

In contrast, of 56 applicants for exemption from combat duties, only four were dismissed; some, however, were won by appeal. One example is the case of Carl Edwin Shipard, a Seventh Day Adventist from Kalangadoo, SA. When Shipard appeared in court at Mount Gambier on 14 July 1958, Special Magistrate L. K. Gordon dismissed his application for exemption from combat duties because:

> Having seen the applicant in the witness box, and bearing in mind his evidence as a whole, whilst he may hold a vague opinion regarding the taking of human life, which has become indoctrinated into him by teachings to which he has given little thought, I do not feel satisfied that he holds a conscientious belief.

Fortunately for Shipard, Justice Reed, before whom he appealed on 22 September, took a fairer approach. He accepted that Shipard believed the Adventist teachings (which he didn't regard as 'indoctrinated into him'); that he had held these beliefs for a number of years; and that it was generally accepted that, while Adventists were prepared to serve in the military, they were never known to bear arms. He upheld Shipard's appeal.[17]

Ten of the sample were non-compliers: they did not apply for exemption and/or refused to enlist when their application was dismissed. They were arrested and sent to Holsworthy or another military correctional establishment.

The sample shows a preponderance of members of sects rather than mainstream Christian denominations. A clear majority were Jehovah's

Witnesses (70) and Seventh Day Adventists (54). The latter, however, usually applied for – and were granted – non-combatant military training. There were 34 Christadelphians. A further 28 applicants for full exemption described themselves as being 'non-denominational', and 27 were members of the Assemblies of God, Brethren, Christian Israelites and similar sects. Only seven of the sample were Quakers, a denomination traditionally opposed to all forms of military service. Only two applicants described themselves as having 'no religion'. The results of the applications in the sample suggest that some magistrates may have been biased against 'sects', particularly the Christadelphians. Certainly, the Christadelphians believed this in the early years of the scheme; the church's Standing Committee in NSW corresponded with Prime Minister Menzies on several occasions, expressing the belief that magistrates were biased against their youths.[18] Thirty-five percent of Christadelphians in my sample, 42 percent of Jehovah's Witnesses and 58 percent of non-denominational Christians were granted total exemption, which is consistent with their viewpoint.

The sample suggests some interesting features of the CO cohort. As already noted, most of the cohort are from the first half of the National Service scheme (1951–55). Unsurprisingly, members of the Jehovah's Witnesses sect comprised the majority of applicants for total exemption in the sample, followed by Seventh Day Adventists, Christadelphians and then Christians who did not belong to a particular denomination. These last were mostly members of small local groups, some numbering less than 100 adherents. Surprisingly, few Quakers (traditionally known as a 'peace church') in the sample applied for total exemption from military service; but the number of Quakers in the sample was small.

Minister Townley's 1959 announcement that the National Service scheme was being suspended was a step forward in converting Australia's military from a citizen army, raised in times of emergency, to a highly trained, professional force in which conscripts would have no place. Unfortunately, there would be one more reversion to the strategies of yesteryear, and it would prove to be more socially and politically divisive than anything since the conscription referenda of 1916 and 1917.

The following chapters discuss Australia's fourth and last National Service scheme. The Menzies government and its successors introduced this scheme in 1964 and administered it between January 1965 and December 1972, when it was disbanded by the incoming Labor administration of Gough Whitlam. Of similar duration to the 1950s scheme, the 1965-72 scheme was the catalyst for massive social and political division. In contrast to the 1950s, resistance took many forms, with the ultimate aim of smashing the system rather than complying with it and seeking individual exemption.

# The Sixties and Vietnam

## CHAPTER 3
# 'War begins in the minds of men'

After a four-year interval, the Menzies administration reintroduced National Service in November 1964, effective from January 1965. This chapter explains the context in which the government decided to reintroduce military conscription, differences from the earlier scheme, opposition groups and public opinion. Because the government announced the recommencement of military conscription shortly before it committed Australian troops to the war in Vietnam, the National Service scheme that operated from 1965 until 1972 has always been associated with the Vietnam conflict. According to the government, however, the scheme was restarted in response to the political situation much nearer to Australia, in Indonesia and Malaysia. During the early 1960s, Australia anxiously watched the Indonesian government's increasingly belligerent stance towards the emerging nation of Malaysia, including territorial disputes over the northern part of the island of Borneo. The new military conscription scheme, which – like the last few years of National Service in the 1950s – was selective rather than universal, was introduced hurriedly and agreed to in principle before the legislation was drafted.[1]

Several peace organisations immediately wrote to Menzies, deploring his government's reintroduction of military conscription. These letters were published in *The Peacemaker*'s November–December 1964 issue. The Religious Society of Friends (Quakers) 'greatly regretted' that the government considered it necessary to compel young men to undertake military training and to allocate £404 million for armaments. The Quakers argued that combat training 'instils habits of violence and inculcates wrong values'. Military training was 'an unethical substitute for real diplomacy, tolerance and negotiation', because it constituted preparation for war. The WILPF quoted a statement by the United Nations Educational, Scientific and Cultural Organization (UNESCO): 'war begins in the minds of men' and argued that 'mature citizens' had a responsibility to guide 'impressionable [young] minds...into channels of service to, and concern for, their fellow-men of all races and nations'. The Peace Pledge Union's Annual General Meeting passed a resolution recording a strong protest against the government's action. The Fellowship of Reconciliation used even more emphatic language, declaring compulsory military service to be a sin because they rejected 'war and preparation for war and reliance on armed force as incompatible with the teaching and example of Jesus Christ.'

Even those who didn't actively oppose compulsory National Service were unenthusiastic about it. In March 1965, *The West Australian* reported that one-fifth of the 20,000 20-year-old youths who were in the first National Service ballot would not be called up because they were married or planned to marry – which begs the question of how many married chiefly to avoid National Service. Another significant portion, the paper stated, would not pass fitness tests. In the Federal Parliament, Labor MP Clyde Cameron asked why the government balloted 20,000 young men when only 4,200 were required, and why was the ballot secret? William ('Billy') McMahon was the Minister for Labour and National Service and had introduced the Bill into parliament. He didn't answer Cameron's question but declared that the government wasn't prepared to give assistance to anyone planning to evade registration. 'We have found as a result of long experience that it is better not to publish the birth dates,' he said.[2] This policy was changed in 1970, when the dates drawn were published.

McMahon's statement heralded the hardening of attitudes that would characterise the second National Service scheme, including much more severe penalties for anyone who refused to accept a magistrate's ruling. A week later, *The West Australian* reported that psychologists would be used to detect attempts by eligible 20-year-olds to fail their education tests deliberately to avoid National Service training. Despite this, by the end of March, a number of applications for exemption had been lodged on the grounds of conscientious objection, while others had requested deferment. The Act contained a provision for university students to defer their training until completion of their degree. Those seeking deferment on grounds of hardship or exemption as COs would have their applications heard by a magistrate.[3] Fines were levied under Sections 48, 49 and 51 of the Act for, respectively, failing to register, failing to attend a medical examination and failing to obey a call-up notice. A later amendment imposed a seven-day jail sentence for refusing to enter into a recognisance to obey a future call-up notice. There were also penalties for leaving Australia without permission. A 1971 amendment placed a liability on travel companies to check whether young men who booked overseas travel were eligible to register and be balloted.[4]

The National Service scheme introduced in 1964 was significantly different from the earlier scheme of the 1950s, although both came under the same *National Service Act 1953* (NSA), with its various amendments. In early May 1965, the government announced that National Servicemen would be liable for service 'anywhere in the world during a war or defence emergency under the provisions of legislation brought down in Federal Parliament.' National Servicemen might also have to serve more than the conscription period of two years. The government announced the changes to the legislation just one week after deciding to expand Australia's military role in Vietnam by sending 800 combat troops instead of increasing the number of army trainers already working there. The amendment replaced the *Defence (Citizen Military Forces) Act 1943*, which limited CMF areas of overseas service to the South West Pacific. Henceforth, all members of the military forces, conscripted or voluntary, could be called upon to serve either in Australia or beyond Australia's territorial limits.[5]

The amended NSA required trainees to serve a period of 24 months' continuous service – more than twice as long as the previous scheme – followed by three years in the Army Reserve. Another difference was that, for the first time, conscripted trainees were considered a part of the Regular Army. Attempts to force conscripts to serve overseas had been defeated in two plebiscites in World War I; in 1964, the policy was made law by parliament, with the public having no say in the matter. And, although the recruitment age had been lifted from 17 to 20 years, it still compelled young men to serve and defend a nation where they were legally too young to vote. Imprisonment for non-compliance involved a proportionately lengthy jail term of up to two years. The first conscripted soldiers arrived in Vietnam in April 1966.[6]

The US Government had neither invited nor expected Australia to contribute active service personnel to the war effort. Although the USA first approached the Australian Government in December 1964 about the possibility of 'a substantial Australian military commitment in Vietnam,' President Johnson asked only for a further 200 military advisers to supplement the 83 Australians already engaged in training soldiers of the South Vietnamese Army. Not until after the first contingent of US Marines arrived in Vietnam in March 1965 did the President and his advisers express the wish to see 'more flags' from Allied nations before they would make a larger military commitment. Yet, in April 1965, the US Government again asked both Australia and New Zealand for 'instructors' and merely 'hinted at a possible request for a battalion.' The Australian Cabinet rejected the request for instructors and advised that it would send a battalion if the South Vietnamese Government publicly requested Australian troops.[7] Some Australians were suspicious of the government's motives when they learned that the South Vietnamese Government had complied reluctantly; further, Menzies had announced the troop commitment in parliament late one afternoon, in the absence of both the Leader and Deputy Leader of the Labor Opposition. Journalist Gerald Stone, writing soon afterwards, accused the government of mercenary motives. When Menzies made the announcement in parliament, Harold Holt, the Federal Treasurer, was in Washington holding talks with the US government to avoid threatened cuts to US investment in Australia. This provoked the charge – emphatically denied by the Government – that it was a case of 'diggers for dollars.'[8]

Between January 1965 and December 1972, over 804,000 20-year-old men registered for the National Service scheme. Of these, 63,735 were conscripted by the infamous twice-yearly 'birthday ballot', conducted in much the same way as modern-day lottery draws: celebrities drew numbered balls (representing birth dates) randomly from a barrel.[9] Within a month, those whose birth dates had been selected were advised whether they were required to enlist. Nineteen thousand conscripted Australian soldiers served in Vietnam. They comprised 44 percent of the 42,700 serving soldiers and almost 50 percent (200) of the 414 Australian Army personnel killed in action during Australia's involvement in the conflict.[10]

The National Service scheme was terminated after the ALP won government in December 1972. By then, most of Australia's troops had been withdrawn from Vietnam. Military conscription has never been reintroduced.

Despite the numerically small commitment of troops and relatively few fatalities, compared with the World Wars, Vietnam became Australia's longest and most divisive overseas war of the 20th century. Major controversies, coupled with graphic television footage of actions in Vietnam – the first televised war – changed the Australian public's perception of the 'rights' and 'wrongs' of the conflict. There were anti-war protests on Australian streets months before Menzies' successor, Harold Holt, announced in March 1966 that his government would more than treble its troop commitment to 4,500; 500 of these would be conscripts. A significant minority among the population opposed Australia's troop commitment from the outset, objecting to this particular war. Despite the efforts of government and some conservative groups to marginalise protesters as a cowardly, disloyal 'lunatic fringe', the dissidents represented a much wider section of the public than those who faced the prospect of being conscripted. They included returned services personnel from previous wars.

There were some similarities to those who had objected to conscription under the National Service scheme of the 1950s – and many differences too. Chapters 1 and 2 revealed that most of the early dissenters were adherents to a Christian denomination and believed that it was wrong to take life. In the first few years of the new scheme, however, most dissidents who were liable to be conscripted registered and applied for exemption as COs. Their reasons for objection were much broader in scope. Prior to 1968, few were conscientious non-compliers (CNCs): refusing to register, attend a medical examination, obey a call-up notice or apply for exemption as COs. When summonsed, CNCs usually failed to appear in court. They refused to pay fines, and many went underground to avoid prison sentences of up to two years. As the Vietnam War continued into the 1970s, CNCs or draft resisters – those who actively worked to smash the scheme – comprised a much greater proportion of dissidents than COs. Many would protest specifically against conscription,

Despite their quiet and orderly protests and respectable, well-dressed image, some Save Our Sons members fell foul of the law. This SOS demonstration in Melbourne opposed the imprisonment of the so-called Fairlea Five. In 1971, Joan Coxsedge, Jean McLean, Chris Cathie, Jo Maclaine-Cross and Irene Miller were jailed for 11 days in Fairlea Prison. They were charged with wilful trespass for distributing leaflets on conscientious objection to men registering for National Service.

51

*The Peacemaker*'s reportage of the first CO court hearings in 1965, after the resumption of compulsory National Service.

rather than objecting to taking human life. The most aggressive stance was taken by the Draft Resistance Movement (DRM), a later development of the anti-war protest movement. The DRM formed 'not...to oppose conscription but to wreck it', openly intending to 'resist the draft by *all* available means' – including staging demonstrations and providing information about how to fail medical examinations.[11]

In Australia, opposition had begun tentatively and often sporadically. The labour movement was mobilising opposition to the NSA by May 1965. Delegates at an ALP Conference in Townsville reportedly clashed during a debate on the party's attitude to Australia sending troops to Vietnam. A motion, carried by 89 votes to 45, condemned the sending of troops and supported the Federal Parliamentary Labor Party calling for a negotiated settlement. In WA, the Trades and Labor Council (TLCWA) carried a resolution opposing the federal government's decision and agreed to call a public meeting in Perth, coinciding with meetings in other states to oppose sending troops.[12] On 26 May, the Communist paper, *Tribune*, reported on a protest in Canberra, during which 300 people stood on the lawns outside the Prime Minister's office in a two-hour silent vigil and prayer. The group comprised church members and leaders, including Canon Frank Coaldrake, founder of *The Peacemaker*; trade union representatives from the Building Workers' Industrial Union, the Waterside Workers' Federation, the Amalgamated Engineering Union, the Teachers' Federation and the Sheet Metal Workers' Union; and representatives from peace groups in the ACT and every state except WA and Tasmania.

Joyce Golgerth convened the first meeting of Save Our Sons (SOS) in Sydney on 13 May 1965. From a founding group of nine enthusiastic supporters, SOS grew in four months to almost 100 supporters in the Sydney metropolitan district alone. A Brisbane branch of SOS formed on 30 June, when 56 women stood for one hour in Anzac Square on the day that Queensland conscripts left for camp. Similarly, the first protest staged by SOS in Adelaide occurred at the airport where South Australian conscripts embarked for Puckapunyal training camp in Victoria. A branch formed in Newcastle (NSW) on 5 August. Jean McLean founded a group in Melbourne, also with 56 supporters, on 18 August. The SOS's stated aims were:

> to oppose conscription of youth into the armed forces for service overseas, especially in the present conflict in Vietnam, [and] to seek the amendment or repeal of the *National Service Act* with regard to objectionable clauses providing for long periods of compulsory service, engagement in military action abroad and severe penalties for infringements.

SOS declared itself non-party political and non-sectarian. Despite this, the Australian Intelligence Security Organisation (ASIO) spent much time attempting to prove that SOS was a communist organisation, because it participated in anti-war demonstrations and shared members with such groups as the Union of Australian Women and the CPA. Early activities included a Week of Protest from 12 to 19 September 1965, organised by the Vietnam Action Committee.

SOS's most distinctive form of protest was to stand silently outside recruitment offices, such as the Marrickville Army Training Depot in western Sydney, holding placards denouncing conscription. The second intake of conscripts was scheduled for late September 1965; SOS intimated that it would again 'demonstrate forcibly' against conscription. At a demonstration staged during the first 1966 intake of conscripts, the ASIO Field Officer reported that SOS conducted itself:

> in an extremely orderly fashion. These women merely stood quietly and handed out leaflets and it was interesting to note that of all the people who accepted these leaflets, the vast majority were women.

The leaflets bore emotive titles such as: 'Must these 600 go into the Valley of Death?' and 'Calling all parents'. They presented valid arguments against involvement in the war, including that Australia was breaking the Geneva Agreements by sending troops to Vietnam. The leaflet 'Calling all Parents' asked: 'Should our sons be forced into an army that is breaking the Geneva Agreements by being in Vietnam?' It quoted the Geneva Agreement of 20 July 1954:

> With effect from the date of entry into force of the present agreement, the introduction into Vietnam of any troop reinforcements and additional military personnel is prohibited.

The leaflet also quoted the American representative, Walter Bedell Smith, holding the USA to the agreement when he signed on their behalf.[13]

Unfortunately, the SOS's image of respectability and peaceful protest was blemished by an event that occurred the following year. The Perth branch of SOS formed on 29 March 1966. Unlike most other SOS branches, Perth admitted men to its membership, including the secretary, Raymond Collie. SOS organised its first protest only four days after forming. About 50 protesters marched to the Perth Esplanade, carrying placards. Their protest attracted media coverage, which reported that it was 'well received' by the public. But it was a different matter when an incident occurred during another protest.

As Prime Minister Harold Holt's plane landed on the tarmac at Perth Airport on 21 April 1966, it was greeted by a small group of placard-waving protesters from the Perth branch of SOS, standing on a balcony about five metres above the entry into the airport lounge. Holt emerged from the plane, walked down the steps and approached the airport, accompanied by his retinue. As he neared the entry below the group, he looked up at the protesters and smiled his broad, toothy grin. This was too much for Joan Davies, one of the SOS members. She removed a shoe and threw it at Holt. The shoe missed him but struck another member of his party on the head. Joan was arrested and charged with creating a disturbance. She was fined $20. *The West Australian's* front-page headline read: 'Woman hurls shoe as PM arrives'. A report of the court case the following day was headed: 'PM's smile angered Perth shoe thrower'. Interviewed after her court appearance, Joan Davies said: 'I don't think war is a laughing matter'. Neither did the SOS, but the group quickly distanced itself from her actions. Branch Secretary Raymond Collie immediately rang the press, dissociating SOS from any violent action, and said that the shoe incident had not been planned. Joan remained unrepentant and proud of her action more than three decades later.[14]

The first conscripted soldier to be killed in action was South Australian Errol Noack, on 24 May 1966, barely a month after conscripts began arriving in Vietnam. His death made headlines and sparked anti-war and anti-conscription demonstrations around Australia. The futility of his death was emphasised by the fact that Noack was probably killed by 'friendly fire' from another Australian company.[15] This incident may have sparked doubts for some who had supported Australian military action in Vietnam.

In the World Wars, mainstream churches had usually supported the war effort unequivocally; in the 1960s, the churches' response to Australia's involvement in the Vietnam War was much more complex and varied. As early as March 1966, the Commission on Peace of the Methodist Church of Victoria and Tasmania opposed the government's decision to send conscripts to Vietnam. In May, the Victorian Congregational [Church] Union similarly opposed both the 'use of chance', in selecting National Servicemen, and the principle of sending conscripts to fight overseas unless they volunteered for active service.[16] Two Catholic newspapers in Victoria, the *Catholic Worker* and the Melbourne diocesan publication *The Advocate*, spoke out against conscription, leaving some readers 'astounded' and 'disgusted'. The *Catholic Worker* labelled ardent pro-conscriptionists as supporters of the Democratic Labour Party. They possibly had in mind the Bishop of Bendigo, who claimed that the war in Vietnam was a 'holy war against Communism'; therefore, he believed, conscription was justified.[17]

An Anglican bishop, J. S. Moyes, attracted national attention by preaching on the theological implications of Australia's involvement in the Vietnam War. He argued that the war could never be termed 'just' because it was a war of aggression, it was instigated by the CIA rather than the US Government, and its purpose was not to right wrongs and rescue the poor from the hands of evildoers.[18] While this may have been the lead that some Anglicans sought from Australian bishops, the bishops themselves were certainly not united. The Archbishop of Perth, George Appleton, regretted the government's decision to send troops to Vietnam, a move that he felt had 'lessened Australia's ability to influence neighbouring Asian nations and enlist their help in efforts to bring about a peaceful settlement'. The Dean of Brisbane, W. P. Baddeley, regarded Australia's entry into the war as 'a grave mistake' and mentioned the lack of a declaration of war. But three Sydney bishops, in the absence of their archbishop, published a letter calling for parishioners to exercise 'sober thinking and calm judgement'. They believed that the government should be trusted to make the right decisions, even when these affected the lives of thousands of young Australians, because it was privy to information that was not available to the public. Therefore 'Christian men' should do their 'duty' to government and God by registering to be conscripted.[19]

Later, in October 1967, two mainstream Protestant denominations indicated that there was growing concern among their memberships about conscription. At their annual conference, the NSW Methodists resolved to urge the federal government to permit COs to undertake civil aid work as an alternative to military service and recommended that a panel of representatives should talk with objectors 'to decide if they had a case'. The Victorian Presbyterian Church's State Assembly came out much more strongly, unanimously expressing its 'abhorrence of the Vietnam war'. Although not calling for the withdrawal of Australian troops, nor specifically condemning Australian involvement in the war, the Assembly condemned the 'inhumane treatment of prisoners' and the use of napalm. The Sydney Anglican Synod, however, rejected a proposal calling on the federal government to provide increased civilian aid to South Vietnam.[20]

The divided opinions among and within groups such as the Christian churches were also reflected in newspaper editorials, among parliamentarians and in public opinion expressed through 'letters to the editor'. But perhaps a more accurate barometer of public opinion may be obtained from the results of Gallup polls during the period. In September 1965, shortly after 1 Royal Australian Regiment (1 RAR) was established at Bien Hoa base in South Vietnam, 56 percent of Australians polled believed that the government had made the right decision in committing armed forces to the conflict, while 28 percent favoured withdrawal and 10 percent were undecided. By May 1967, 62 percent supported military involvement; then the percentages for and against began to be reversed. In August 1969, 55 percent of Australians polled favoured withdrawal.[21] Even when a majority favoured the Australian Government taking military action in Vietnam, there was less enthusiasm about the use of conscripted soldiers in the war. A nationwide Gallup Poll, published in January 1966, showed that 52 percent of Australians believed that, if their battalion was sent to Vietnam, National Servicemen should remain in Australia, with only 37 percent stating that they should go to Vietnam and a further 11 percent undecided. Even on gender and political lines, there was no clear majority in favour of sending National Servicemen to the war, with men and Liberal–Country Party voters being 'evenly divided' and women and ALP voters recording a two-to-one majority against.[22]

No doubt, those early days of protest were heady days for some. University campuses became sites of protest, both for and against involvement in the conflict. On 17 May 1965, anti-war students from the Young Labor Club and pro-war students from the Democratic Labour Party (DLP) Club at The University of WA (UWA) clashed at a meeting outside Council House in Perth, addressed by the ALP's Senator-elect John Wheeldon. Wheeldon said: 'We are here to protest against the killing and maiming and crippling of young Australians in a war which has been condemned by General de Gaulle.' The State Secretary of the DLP, John Martyr, was among the counter-demonstrators.[23] Anti-war protesters would have drawn encouragement from reportage in the CPA's newspaper, *Tribune*, that the New Zealand Government had been forced to temporarily abandon plans to commit troops to Vietnam, as a result of public protests. Unfortunately, the delay was indeed temporary, with the first New Zealand troops arriving in Vietnam in July 1965.[24]

For many young men who 'won the lottery' in those early days, when public support for the government ran high, the experience of refusing to enlist was isolating and alienating. The next chapter relates the stories of some of those in the early ballots who decided to disobey the law: by ignoring the requirement to register; by registering but refusing to enlist; or by defying a court ruling to undertake military service, either combatant or non-combatant, after their application for total exemption from military service had been dismissed. It also discusses the situation of young men who were not supported by conscientious objectors' groups, either because they did not know of their existence or because they were physically isolated in rural Australia.

## CHAPTER 4
# 'Why me?'

Rowan Cahill sat on a bus travelling to Sydney University. He had just learned that his marble had been drawn in the second ballot in 1965. Many years later, he reflected on the experience and his subsequent actions:

> I leaned back in the hard, public transport seat and looked at my fellow passengers absorbed in their own preoccupations. I wanted to yell, 'Fuck you! Why me?' but didn't and turned instead to look out the grime-streaked windows... [Back on campus] I looked at the throngs heading homewards; students laughing, cuddling, hand in hand, discussing the latest lecture, the next assignment, the next party. Between them and me I felt no link, no bond. Feeling like an outsider looking in on life, I sought refuge in the Cellar, the campus basement coffee shop. It was empty. With a black coffee, and the juke box belting out the Rolling Stones' *Little Red Rooster*, I found an arrogant chorus for my anger and loneliness.

Cahill's first reaction was to register, followed by a successful application to defer call up until the completion of his studies. Later, he changed his mind, burnt his draft card and then, overwhelmed by his action, applied for another. His 'letter of regret' to the Minister for Labour and National Service was ignored until February 1969, after he had applied for exemption from all military duties. Then it was produced and used in court as evidence of his inconsistent beliefs. Rodgers SM heard the case and exempted Cahill from combatant duties only. His subsequent appeal was upheld in August 1969.[1]

Isolation was a common experience for young men who were 'balloted in' during the early months of conscription. In Melbourne, Michael Hamel-Green was another early draftee. He recalled his feelings in March 1965, when the letter arrived informing him that his birth date had been drawn from the barrel:

> As I stared at the letter, Gail's [his mother's] arm around me, it was like a harpoon barb lodged in my flesh. All my personal hopes, ideas of writing and overseas travel, pursuing life at university, collapsed as I visualised what the army wanted to do to and with me. I could foresee it would leave me either deeply compromised with myself or suffocating in a prison cell. My future stolen. The only brief reprieve was that university students could defer the actual call-up till the end of their studies, in my case for two more years. So time to think (which others who had gone straight from school to work did not enjoy).

Having arrived with his family as 'ten-pound Pom', Hamel-Green had the option of using his British passport to travel to Britain, complete his university degree and escape the draft, but this presented the emotional difficulty of leaving loved ones behind in Australia. To accept his fate and join the army 'would mean complicity with genocide – a repudiation of all the values for which I was seeking to live'. Refusal to join the army would mean 'two years in jail, with all the humiliations, brutality, monotony and indignity of prison life.'[2]

These feelings, recorded by two articulate men who both went on to have successful academic careers, were experienced in similar ways by a generation of young men confronted with the same choices. Most did not have the tempting option of escaping to another country, but they all had to choose between abandoning their beliefs and proceeding to register for National Service – with the spectre of active service in Vietnam looming over them – or risking a two-year jail term if an unsympathetic magistrate dismissed the grounds of their objection, and they refused to enlist.

Ken Mansell, a poet and songwriter from Melbourne's eastern suburbs who described himself as 'lower middle class', found inspiration in folk music to pour out his anguish at the prospect of being conscripted and forced to fight in a war that he opposed. Like many others, he was enraged by 'the injustice of having one's life chances subject to a lottery (especially when one could not yet vote)'. People around him were not supportive. He recalled: 'there seemed to be no one, least of all my parents or the church, I could turn to for advice or sympathy'. His colleagues at Kraft Foods in Port Melbourne, where he was employed as a purchasing clerk, 'sniggered "it would make a man of me"' to be conscripted. Even his mother joked, 'you'll be off to war, son' after the government introduced conscription and then announced that it would send active service personnel to Vietnam. Despite his opposition to the war, Mansell did register – as most young men did in 1965. He suffered months of anguish before a letter arrived from the Department of Labour and National Service, stating that his call-up was 'indefinitely deferred'. For many, this let-off would have provided a handy escape. Mansell, however, became deeply involved in the anti-war movement as Australia's military involvement in Vietnam escalated; he even undertook acts of civil disobedience. He reflected: 'if the Liberal Party had wanted to avoid producing a phalanx of life-time anti-war activists, they sure went the wrong way about it.'[3]

Taking a stand and demonstrating against conscription and the war was not easy. In the hope that Labor might win the 1966 election, Hamel-Green joined the Youth Campaign Against Conscription (YCAC) and picketed the Swanston Street National Service Office when the lottery was being drawn for each intake. The protesters' banners proclaimed: 'No Conscripts for Vietnam' and 'End the War Now'. In those early days in 1965, the press largely ignored demonstrators. Hamel-Green recalled that passers-by were hostile:

> One woman spat in my face. Some shouted out, 'traitors, communists and cowards.' Our hope was to win support for the Labor Opposition in the lead up to the election, but everything seemed against us.[4]

Unfortunately, the November 1966 election, when Labor sustained a crushing defeat, would prove them only too correct.

*The Peacemaker* recorded the first objector court hearings on 3 and 10 June 1965 in Melbourne. In the first, all three applicants were granted total

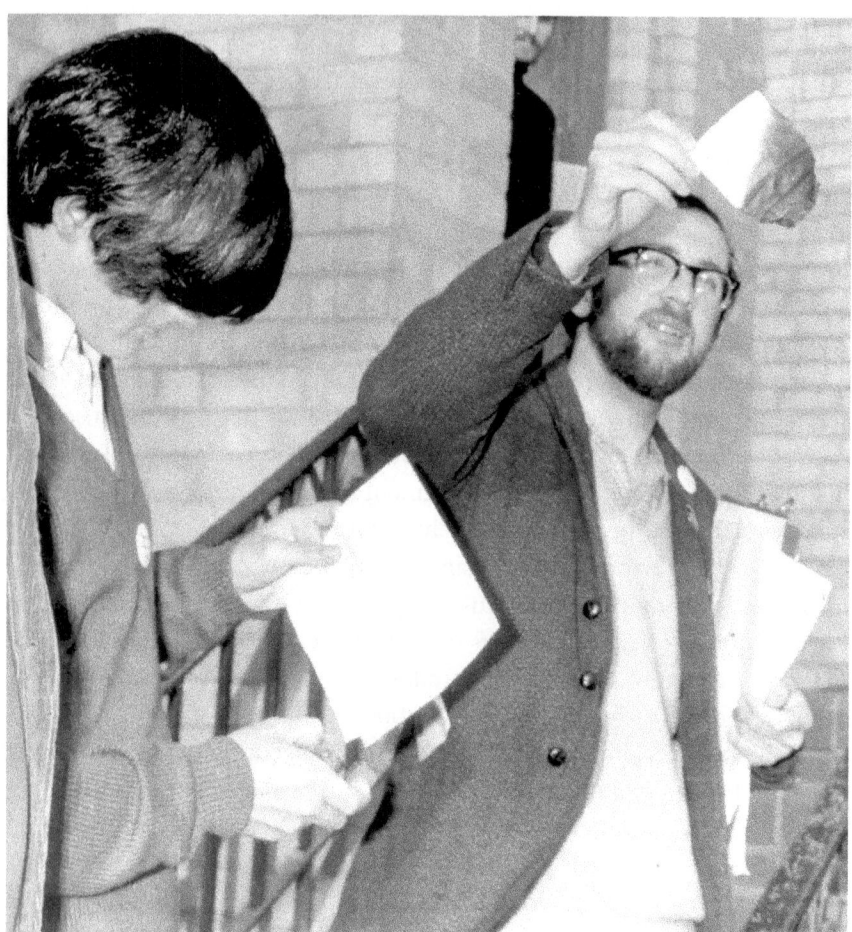

Michael Hamel-Green (right) and David Day (left) burning their National Service Medical and Registration Notices.

exemption: two on religious grounds. In the second, five applicants applied for exemption from combatant status only, but then two asked to change their applications to total exemption. E. L. Ross SM asked these to withdraw their applications and reapply. The other three were granted exemption from combatant duties. *The Peacemaker* reported: 'the hearings took place in a small court room with very little formality'. The paper also published the questions that each of the objectors had been asked, including:

Do you belong to any religious faith or sect?

Do all the members of that particular faith hold the same views as you?

Do your parents hold a similar belief to yours?

When did you first discuss this with your parents?

Do you think you gain any benefits from the society in which you live?

Do you not think you have a duty to defend that society?

Imagine the country were being invaded. Would you assist the army to repel the enemy?

If the invader were attacking your family (your bishop or your monarch) would you kill to save lives?

If the country were invaded and you knew that they [presumably meaning the invaders] would exterminate your particular faith, would you fight the invasion?

If a constable were being attacked and called on you for help, would you go to his assistance?

If you were in a situation where you were to be killed, would you kill the invader to save your life?

Prosecutors asked variations of these questions *ad nauseum* in courts trying young objectors over the next seven years. Sometimes, the questions centred on mothers and girlfriends, as in the exemption hearings from the 1950-59 National Service scheme: 'If your mother/girlfriend was being attacked, would you go to help her?' The aim of this question was, apparently, to demonstrate that a youth who objected to going to war was a coward who would not defend women, but one who was prepared to use physical violence in defence was inconsistent in declaring that he had a conscientious objection to war. Similarly, the questions about defending one's religious faith were designed to show that anyone who would not use violence to defend his faith didn't hold it in high regard. Conversely, anyone who would use violence in any situation was being hypocritical by refusing to join the armed services. The questions were shaped with the aim of trapping the objector into an indefensible position, rather than ascertaining whether his views were sincerely held. While articulate young men could and did acquit themselves creditably under such transparently biased questioning, those who came less well prepared were sometimes reduced to silence or tears.

As early as mid-1965, it was evident that youths appearing in courts around the country could expect very varied results. From the beginning, court judgements could be as much of a lottery as birth dates, as some WA cases show. In the Albany Court, a 20-year-old farmer, John Christopher Lamont, a Jehovah's Witness, was given an exemption; another farmer, Kevin Darrell Hilgert of Mount Barker, was given a one-year deferment. Two other applications for deferment heard on the same day were dismissed. In Bunbury, three youths were granted deferment on the basis of hardship, but two other applications were refused. Danilo Covich, a net maker of Beaconsfield, received a year's deferment to train someone to work in his business while he undertook military training, but another application for a deferment was refused. At Bridgetown Court, Leigh Alexander Hales, Geoffrey Peter Muir and Peter G. Millington were all granted deferments. Similarly, three Geraldton youths – farmers Adrian Johnson and Michael Vincent McMahon Clune and pastry cook Norman Anthony Edwards – had their training deferred on the grounds of hardship, but Roderick O'Donnell, a Jehovah's Witness, had his training 'permanently deferred.'[5]

Sometimes, newspaper headlines indicated media prejudice against those applying for exemptions. 'Young Red ordered into NS training' ran a headline in *The West Australian* of 27 July 1965, relating to the case of Robin Peter Kitching in Sydney. Kitching's case was interesting. He had been a member of the Eureka Youth League's (EYL) Peace Committee in WA, moved to Sydney and joined the EYL in NSW. He applied for exemption in March 1965, on the grounds that, as a member of the peace movement, he had 'a moral and humanitarian obligation to struggle for peaceful co-existence between nations.' He 'believed in settling world problems by peaceful negotiation' and was 'strongly opposed to military power being used.' In the Sydney Court of Petty Sessions, Phillip Street, in July 1965, Kitching was grilled on his relationship with, and understanding of, the tenets of the EYL and also on his connection with the CPA, despite his claims that his beliefs were not politically based. The magistrate ordered him to perform non-combatant duties. Kitching's appeal was heard before Judge Monahan at the Sydney District Court on 14

September. At the opening of proceedings, Mr Smail, counsel for the Minister for Labour and National Service, was obliged to state that reports appearing recently in *The Australian* newspaper, purporting to be from the Minister for the Army, were unauthorised. 'What the Army thinks about the eligibility of a Communist Party member for National Service has nothing to do with the matter'. After another lengthy examination into his beliefs, Kitching managed to convince the judge of his sincerity, and he was granted total exemption from military service.[6]

In the Melbourne City Court in September 1965, objector Jeffrey Ross Foley told Humphries SM, that 'all those who live by the sword, die by the sword'. He was granted total exemption from National Service, as was German-born Martin Ernst, who had arrived with his family in 1949. However, on the same day, the magistrate dismissed Stanislas Van de Wiel's application and ordered Brian Gray to perform non-combatant service.[7]

Even at this early stage of Australia's military commitment to Vietnam, the objectors had supporters among the public. On 23 June 1965, Perth's evening paper, the *Daily News*, published a letter from J. G. Boardman of Scarborough, who found it 'incredible' that another correspondent, 'Opinionist Jan Ressing', could equate the Vietnam War with Christianity, when there were 'un-denied reports of atrocities by the South Vietnamese troops and Americans: phosphorus bombs and napalm'. He asked, 'Would Ressing consider that Christ... would volunteer to pilot a napalm bombing aircraft?' Another letter writer, Jeff Payne of Mt. Lawley, objected to a Gallup Poll asking 15 year olds their opinions on conscription and to the 'groundless' reasons for introducing conscription, such as that 'it is good for young men'. He asked, 'Is it good to have young Australian men shot and maimed in civil wars such as Vietnam?'

Yet another correspondent, N. Mitchell from Austinmer, NSW, wrote to *The Australian* in support of Robin Kitching. Afraid that the paper might not publish his letter, he sent a copy to Kitching. He wrote:

> It has long been the practice of the old men of the world's tribes to send out the young men to kill each other. No advance for the human race out of barbarity towards civilization has resulted from this sacrifice of the young to the hatred and hopelessness of the old... The stand of such a young man as Robin Peter Kitching, who refuses

to be trained to kill, promises an immeasurably greater hope for the future of the human race than do all the actions and statements of men who, by perpetuating their elderly blood-lust, are likely to destroy the world in a nuclear holocaust.[8]

This searing criticism of society was made more effective by Mitchell's admission that he was not a young person, so it was not the voice of an 'angry young man' but a sadder, wiser, old one. On the bottom of the typed copy that he forwarded to Kitching, as if feeling that he had not been supportive enough, Mitchell wrote in red ink, 'Don't feel that you are on your own!'

Benedict Bun Gee Chu, who faced Rodgers SM in the Phillip Street Court on 19 August 1965, was in a unique position. A Catholic from Kingsgrove in NSW, he had been born in Canton and had formerly been a Chinese subject. Two days after being naturalised in November 1964, he was informed that he might be liable to conscription to 'fight against people of my own race in SE Asia'. He stated that it would be completely against his 'will, principle(s) and conscience to commit such a revolting act'. Although he applied for total exemption, Rodgers granted him exemption only from combatant duties. Chu's appeal was heard by Judge Head on 1 June 1966. In addition to his objection to being asked to fight against people of his own race, Chu asked for consideration to look after his ageing parents and younger siblings. The judge admitted the uniqueness of a case where an appellant's convictions had formed 'substantially as a result of family influence', compared with a person whose beliefs were based on membership of, or adherence to, the tenets of a religious group. He also accepted the evidence that Chu was deeply affected by warfare – resulting from his family's experience of war in the Japanese occupation of China and Hong Kong in the 1930s and 1940s, during which one of their children had died. Chu's appeal was upheld.[9]

Stanislas Van de Wiel was another immigrant whose family had lived through wartime occupation. Van de Wiel, who had migrated from the Netherlands as a child in 1959, appeared before Humphries SM in the Melbourne City Court on 16 June 1965. Van de Wiel stated that he had no religion but was opposed to violence leading to injury or death. He said that his father was opposed to military service and had 'wanted to come to a country where there was no likelihood of war or military service'. Counsel for the

Phillip Street Court of Petty Sessions in Sydney, where many objectors were tried.

Department of Labour and National Service, Mr Fowler, quizzed Van de Wiel about an incident five years earlier when he had blinded his brother in the eye. Fowler also asked whether he held 'this belief' because 'you feel it will protect you from any harm?' When pressed about his motives for objecting to being called up, Van de Wiel responded that 'more civilians usually get killed in a war than military personnel.' Fowler then switched to questions about whether Van de Wiel believed 'in paying for what you get?' In other words, the benefits provided to Australian citizens should be defended by being prepared to serve in the military. Further questions ranged from how he would have responded if attacked by the Japanese, to why he drove a car, because there was always a chance of killing someone on the road. This distasteful and aggressive method of questioning of a man whose parents had lived through the Nazi occupation of the Netherlands was clearly not aimed at establishing the sincerity of his beliefs. His application was rejected. Van de Wiel was later exempted on medical grounds.[10]

In its September–October 1965 issue, *The Peacemaker* published the results of all the applications for complete exemption that the editor was aware of: NSW (13); Victoria (25); Queensland (6); SA (6); WA (1); and Tasmania (3) – totalling 54. In NSW, Kitching was the only objector to gain full exemption, and this was on appeal. Ten were ordered to perform non-combatant duties, and two had their applications dismissed. Of the 25 Victorian applications, 15 were granted complete exemption, five were ordered to perform non-combatant duties, and five were dismissed. All but one of the Queensland and SA objectors were granted complete exemption. Two in Tasmania were ordered to perform non-combatant duties, and a third application was dismissed. The one Western Australian was granted complete exemption. These records were certainly incomplete, unless *The Peacemaker* was not counting applicants for a deferment. But even this small sample suggests that the pattern of harshest judgements in NSW, apparent in the previous National Service scheme, seemed to be repeating itself.

By the end of the first year of National Service, over 50 objectors had lodged applications for total exemption from military service; a lesser number had requested exemption from combatant service only. Public opposition to conscription increased after the government announced that National Servicemen would be liable for war service in Vietnam. The objectors' most strident critic, the RSL, swung into action again. At its 39th Congress in the ACT in August 1965, it resolved that the COs' Advisory Committee was 'dangerous' and asked the government to keep it 'under constant surveillance' and 'act immediately to scotch its activities.'[11] Surprisingly, men who had personal experience of the horrors of warfare seemed the keenest to force their sons and other young men into the armed forces, in the full knowledge that they were likely to be sent on active service.

Some cases began attracting much media attention, with detailed accounts being published, sometimes in several different newspapers; other cases received no publicity. Max Beddow's case is one that would have remained almost unknown but for Vivienne Abraham's documents. Beddow was a farmer from Liston, NSW.[12] In 1965, he became a vegetarian because he did not want his eating habits to cause cruelty to animals. Although he registered for National Service in July 1966 and passed a medical examination, Beddow was reluctant to enlist. However, he thought that, having 'obeyed the other laws of the country,' he should comply. He felt that it would be wrong to take part in military service, so he applied to be exempted from all forms of military training. His case was dismissed at Tenterfield Magistrates Court in September 1967. For financial reasons, and also because he thought that he had little chance of proving the sincerity of his beliefs, Beddow decided not to appeal. His application to defer his National Service because his father needed him to help run the farm was also refused. He didn't receive his call-up until July 1968.

In court in December 1968, with no legal representation and none of his family present, he pleaded guilty to having disobeyed a call-up notice and was fined. The magistrate told him that if he obeyed his call up, he could then apply again for exemption as a CO. Beddow refused to 'have any part of the army.' He was sentenced immediately to two years' imprisonment and sent to Glen Innes Prison Farm. He became very depressed at the prospect of two years in prison, especially when informed that he might be transferred from the Prison Farm to Grafton Prison, a much harsher environment for hardened re-offenders. The prison governor told him that he might be released if he agreed to do his National Service.

Although he had never contacted any pacifist group, Beddow received a visit from Vivienne Abraham and two other members of the NSW Peace Pledge Union, Ian and Louise McIntyre, soon after his arrival at Glen Innes Prison Farm. Beddow told them that he was against the Vietnam War and all war, killing and violence. He believed that he couldn't serve as a combatant, and he wanted to do some humanitarian work. Although he had known that, by refusing to pay his fine and ignoring his call-up notice, he risked a two-year sentence, Beddow was ill prepared for prison. After he accepted the call up, he was allowed to go home for Christmas, prior to formal enlistment, and was then sent with other recruits to train at Kapooka, near Wagga. Despite his preference for non-combatant duties, the army authorities informed him that he must do the same basic combat training as every other recruit. Was this just bloody-mindedness on the part of the authorities, or were they making their own interpretation of Minister for the Army Malcolm Fraser's statement: 'conscientious objectors would be excused all duties and training connected with weapons except training necessary to learn how to make weapons safe?'[13] Beddow was forced to undertake bayonet drill with dummies simulating the enemy. The recruits were told to twist their feet about on the dummies as they withdrew their bayonets. This did not comply with Fraser's statement that he would learn only how to make a weapon safe. Beddow was told that it was 'likely' that he would be placed in Ordinance, Catering or Service – all non-combatant units – after training, but he was so sickened by the bayoneting of dummies that he decided not to return to Kapooka after his first leave. He made this decision without seeking advice from Abraham or his legal counsel, Mr Dew.

Abraham met Beddow in Canberra when he was absent without leave (AWL), and took him to several COs' meetings, including an Orientation Week presentation at the Australian National University (ANU) entitled 'Register or Resist'. She persuaded him to rejoin his unit and make the application for exemption through his commanding officer. Beddow was sentenced to seven days' detention for going AWL and was then given leave without pay to prepare his case, which was heard in the Liverpool Street Court of Petty Sessions in Sydney on 31 March and 1 April 1969. Mr Carruthers, Counsel for the Crown, cross-examined Beddow about his answers in his first court case at Tenterfield. Carruthers contested Beddow's claim that, before he went to Kapooka, he was unaware of the existence of the Army Medical Corps. He argued that Beddow knew the Australian Army Ambulance Service was a military unit because he had refused to serve in it. Beddow was also questioned about a violent incident at a dance several years previously, where he claimed that he had not defended himself when set upon by two other men; he said that they had soon desisted, possibly because he would not fight. Carruthers asked what Beddow would do if a female 'under his protection' was threatened with violence. He answered that he would try to 'talk them out of it or get her out of the road or to hold them off.' Carruthers tried to prove that Beddow was influenced by Abraham's letters and actions, questioning him on whether he had 'attended meetings of the pacifist defence.' Throughout the hearing, Beddow appeared to be calm and in control of the situation. He gave brief answers, insisting that he had not discussed his application for conscientious objection with anyone except Mr Dew, his legal counsel. His application for exemption from military service was successful. On 12 April 1969, he received a telegram informing him that he need not return to his battalion after his leave without pay ended. His ordeal, from the dismissal of his initial application at

'Why me?' 71

No. 1589    Incorporating The Guardian (Victoria) and Qld Guardian    WEDNESDAY, DECEMBER 18, 1968    10 Cents

## "Political prisoners of Govt."
# CHRISTMAS CALL TO FREE ZARB, BEDDOW

PART OF THE poster parade through city streets preceding last Friday's Sydney Town Hall meeting protesting against the Government's use of the National Service Act to gaol conscientious objectors John Zarb and Max Beddow. See story, Page 1.

*Tribune* page 1 headline and photograph on page 12, showing demonstrators with placards demanding the release of John Zarb and Max Beddow. Whilst Zarb's case was well-publicised, this is the only known public reference to Max Beddow.

Tenterfield in September 1967 until his release from the army in April 1969, had lasted 19 months.[14]

From this point, with the numbers of both draft resisters and opponents of the war increasing, the lot of a CO remained difficult but became less lonely – although this was not true for all. John Wilson, a pacifist from Biloela, Queensland, was called up in 1971. Wilson had withdrawn from medical studies with depression and was working on his father's cattle property. He had no support structures, later recollecting that he felt 'particularly isolated'. His parents told him that it was his decision whether he obeyed the call up or not. He did not know that he could seek legal advice or representation when he appeared in court. At the Gladstone Police Court on 12 May 1972, Wilson was sentenced to two weeks in prison, which he served in the Gladstone police lock-up. Recollecting these events some 30 years later, he was vague about the charges, but it is likely that they concerned failing to register or attend a medical examination and refusing to agree to obey a future call up. Upon his release, he went to the media to tell his story. Rearrested, he spent another night in the Biloela lock-up and was then transferred to a padded cell in the Rockhampton lock-up. The police seem to have feared that he would self-harm. Wilson believed that his second arrest and imprisonment resulted from his interview with the ABC, but it was probably the result of non-payment of fines. Wilson served two weeks at Etna Creek Prison, where 'there were no other conscientious objectors... I have never met any others then or since'.[15] He was not listed among the non-compliers in 1971 issues of *The Peacemaker*, so it does indeed appear that no one in pacifist circles was aware of him. His story shows that, even in 1972, after involvement in the anti-war movement reached its peak with the massive Moratorium demonstrations (one of which Wilson attended in Sydney in 1970), some dissidents remained isolated and unsupported outside the movement. For some, dissent could be very lonely indeed.

The next chapter charts the rise of opposition, firstly to sending conscripts to the war in Vietnam and, later, to any Australian involvement in the war.

## CHAPTER 5
# 'What kind of a "democracy" is this?'

'Holt punched, car attacked at night rally' ran *The Sydney Morning Herald*'s front-page headline on 24 November 1966. During an electioneering rally the previous evening at the Rockdale (NSW) Town Hall, Prime Minister Holt had been forced to defend the government's handling of what became known as 'the Bill White case'. The demonstration outside turned violent when a rowdy and divided crowd both 'hooted' and 'cheered' Holt. Eight of White's supporters, all members of the Sydney COs' Group, declared that they would go to jail rather than enlist if their applications for complete exemption failed. They included Simon Townsend, whose application for exemption had been dismissed and who had lost his appeal. He refused to attend his medical. Townsend finally had his application for complete exemption from military service granted by N. J. Hunt SM in the Court of Petty Sessions on 14 June 1968, but only after enduring horrific punishment at the hands of the military (see Chapter 6).[1]

William Phillip Orrick ('Bill') White was a school teacher who lost his position in the NSW Education Department because of his stance against conscription. In November 1965, White had applied to be registered as a CO, giving as his reason his inability 'with a clear conscience, [to] kill a person, or be part of any organisation that is able or willing to kill or make war'. He represented himself at his application for total exemption in the Phillip Street

Protesters at a demonstration against Prime Minister Harold Holt at Rockdale Town Hall, 23 November 1966.

Court of Petty Sessions on 20 December 1965. The prosecution pursued banal issues, such as: whether (as a teacher) he would ever 'chastise' a child; whether he would ever use the cane on a child; and whether he believed that penalties should be exacted on law-breakers – none of which involved killing. White was also asked whether, in paying taxes, he was belonging to 'an organisation?' Although he had stated that he would never 'take part in any form of activity that would take a life', the prosecution pointed out that White held a driver's licence and asked him whether he knew what the annual road toll in NSW was. When White said that he didn't think this line of questioning had anything to do with war, he was told by the bench that the purpose was to 'try to understand your beliefs.' White's application was dismissed, and he was ordered to perform non-combatant duties. He appealed.

White's appeal was dismissed in the Sydney District Court on 22 March 1966. In June, he received a notice to report to the Eastern Command Personnel Depot on 18 July. When he failed to comply with his call-up notice, his employer, the NSW Education Department, dismissed him, complying with the NSA, which stipulated that an employer would be liable for a $200 fine for continuing to employ a person who was refusing to enlist. Despite this, a Mr Douglas McPherson offered White a job tutoring his son, aware that he was also risking a fine. His action spurred a wave of support from children and parents at White's former school. A group of parents, teachers and other supporters formed the Bill White Defence Committee and appealed for assistance with White's mounting legal fees. They also challenged the legislation that resulted in White's dismissal by the Education Department. McPherson spoke with officials of the Department of Labour and National Service, seeking an amendment to the Act that would remove the clause requiring employers to sack employees who were refusing to undertake military service. Despite promises, the Act was not amended.

White was summonsed to court on 3 August and charged with refusing to comply with the NSA, but the court was adjourned when about 50 women and children staged a protest outside the courthouse. White's life was in limbo until a further appeal was heard in November. This time, he was appealing against the ruling that an objector could make only one application to be registered. There was nothing in the Act that specified this. While awaiting the hearing in November, he applied for unemployment relief, was rejected,

'What kind of a "democracy" is this?' 77

Bill White, being presented with a petition containing signatures of trainee teachers, in support of his stand against conscription, Sydney Town Hall, 1966.

and was then granted a 'special payment' of the same amount. His application to reapply for registration as a CO was dismissed on 9 November. On 17 November, Rodgers SM committed White to military custody.[2]

Tense days passed while White awaited arrest at his parents' home. He had received 500 letters of support and only three (anonymous) letters criticising him, with supporters ranging from school children to a Gallipoli veteran. On 22 November, *The Sydney Morning Herald* suggested, mockingly, that the Australian Army was observing 'Procrastination Week', because of their tardiness. Some believed that the arrest wouldn't take place until after the federal election on 26 November. A band of up to 30 supporters kept a round-the-clock vigil outside White's home, to avoid the possibility of his arrest in the middle of the night with no cameras present. They nailed placards to the front fence, one of which said: 'Brave enough to say "No"' – a reference to the charge that objectors were cowardly. Despite the support, White admitted to feeling the strain, which also impacted on his fiancée, Clare Seale. White's forcible arrest on 22 November, with photographs appearing in the press of the teacher being dragged between two hefty police officers, provoked outraged letters. One, from 15-year-old John Briot in *The Sydney Morning Herald* of 25 November, asked: 'What kind of a "democracy" is this where actions of conscience are so treated?'

Media interest in White did not diminish after his arrest. The Sydney press reported daily on his internment at Victoria Barracks in Paddington – when he received visitors (including his mother and fiancée) and the punishments he endured. On 29 November, the army court-martialled White, for refusing to wear a uniform or obey orders, and sent him to Holsworthy. While he was there, the press could do no more than speculate on his conditions of incarceration. Possibly because of his high profile, White seems to have been treated well – or, at least, much better than some later internees at Holsworthy.[3]

White was released from the army on 23 December 1966, after his second application for complete exemption from military service succeeded. The second application was made possible by a legal precedent set by the case of a Queensland Christadelphian. Noel Collett had enlisted as a non-combatant but had made a fresh application for exemption as a CO after he had undergone several days' training at Kapooka. Collett's application argued that, after study, he better understood the beliefs of the Christadelphians and realised that he could not undertake any form of military service. His application was successful.[4] Thereafter, objectors were able to lodge a second application if their first application and a subsequent appeal had been dismissed.

To his credit, Rodgers SM, who had dismissed White's first application, believed that it was not in White's interests for him to hear the new application. He referred the application to Sydney's Central Court, where it succeeded. Despite the verdict, White wasn't immediately reinstated in the Education Department. Apparently, a majority of the public agreed with the department's reluctance. A Gallup Poll of 1,700 people in February 1967 found that only 23 percent believed that White should have been granted exemption. Of the 72 percent who believed that he should have been made to complete his military service, however, only15 percent thought that he should have served as a combatant.[5] This poll may indicate that White's principled stand had begun to influence public opinion.

Two National Servicemen, both of whom objected to serving in the Vietnam War, stood in the 1966 federal election. John Thurwall stood in the Brisbane seat of Ryan. Despite polling only 756 votes, he believed that he'd achieved his main objective: to 'enlighten people on the permanent lies about Vietnam'. Brian Dennis King stood against the Minister for Labour and National Service, Leslie Bury, in the NSW seat of Wentworth. Rogers SM had dismissed King's application for full exemption on 2 May, and his appeal in October was also unsuccessful. King then lodged an application to the Supreme Court of Appeal on the grounds that he had been denied natural justice. This also was dismissed. In January 1967, King was convicted of not obeying a call-up notice to complete his two years of National Service (interrupted by his appeals and his election campaign). After being taken into custody at the Eastern Command Personnel Depot, he went AWL. In February, he was arrested and court-martialled. Like Thurwall, King's main objection was to serving in the Vietnam War. A third objector candidate, Thomas Joseph Yates, a school teacher, polled 2,000 votes in the Victorian electorate of McMillan. His application for complete exemption was rejected in the Morwell (VIC) court in January 1967, and he was ordered to perform non-combatant duties. He appealed.[6] The outcome of the appeal, heard on 14 March, is unknown.

On the day before the federal election, 25 November 1966, *The Sydney Morning Herald's* political correspondent had forecast correctly that conscription would be an issue in the election, but that Arthur Calwell's unpopularity would cancel out 'the great public unhappiness over the William White case'. *The Sydney Morning Herald* asserted that Holt's threat to amend the *Electoral Act* to outlaw rowdy demonstrations was unnecessarily heavy handed, because: 'Rowdiness is not new in Australian politics.' The newspaper remarked philosophically that, to some extent, the fault lay with the 'political parties in Australia, which have failed these young people by not appealing to their idealism', but also claimed that the instigators of the demonstration at Rockdale were Communists, who had 'exploited

Bill White being dragged from his house.

the anti-conscription and anti-Vietnam demonstrators during the present campaign.' The *Bulletin* was more outspoken in support of White; its correspondent stated that White was:

> not a coward. He is determined not to give up his stand; that killing is wrong, that war is wrong, and that he cannot take part in any organisation whose purpose is to kill.[7]

The Rockdale demonstration indicated the rise of more militant forms of opposition to conscription and to Australia's role in the war; these would increase during 1967. Already, in 1966, the YCAC had begun staging demonstrations at which conscripts burnt their registration certificates (or 'draft cards' as they became known, using the American terminology). Barry Robinson, Wayne Haylen and Greg Barker, who burnt their cards at a demonstration in Sydney on 2 February 1966, were some of the first to perform this symbolic act.[8]

On 8 June, during the first welcome home parade of troops who had served in Vietnam, Nadine Jensen staged a lone protest by splattering herself with red paint and dashing out in front of the soldiers of 1 RAR and other troops during the salute to the Governor-General, Lord Casey, outside the Sydney Town Hall. A crowd estimated at 300,000 to 500,000 lined Sydney's streets to cheer the soldiers; yet, Jensen's protest has stayed in the public memory as evidence that soldiers returning from Vietnam were not welcomed and applauded. In court the following day, Jensen was fined $6 and placed on a good behaviour bond. Typical of contemporary attitudes towards women, Riley SM wondered whether she should be remanded for psychiatric assessment, apparently believing that no sane woman would commit such an act.[9] *The Peacemaker*'s July–August issue published Jensen's statement to the court, which showed that she had carefully considered her action before undertaking it. This was no spur of the moment whim of a deranged mind, as the magistrate seemed to suggest. Jensen said:

> My action was directed not so much against the instruments of higher authority [the soldiers], but against the authority itself. That is why I chose the location that I did [the Sydney Town Hall] for my action.

Even here, perhaps, I was wrong, wrong because it should have been directed against apathy and complacency of many, many of the Australians who allow themselves to be drawn into a conflict where the moral issues at stake are far from clarified.

My countrymen are noted for their physical bravery. This, I feel, is true. However, I wish that they would show a corresponding intellectual and moral heroism, by at least questioning our reasons for being in Vietnam. Under such an examination I feel there is not sufficient justification for our involvement.

According to *The Peacemaker*, Jensen paid a similar price to Bill White: she was sacked from two jobs as a result of her actions, although that does not appear to have been reported in the mainstream press.

Shortly after Jensen's action, YCAC, SOS and the Vietnam Action Committee jointly organised a large protest in Forrest Place, Perth on 11 June 1966. It attracted about 500 people. The rally turned violent when police moved in to take the name and address of a young man addressing the crowd. Some of the crowd abused the police, calling them 'fascist pigs'. An opposition group, comprising Young DLP and DLP University Society members, urged the police to shoot the demonstrators. Police arrested four university students for burning their draft cards and charged them with disorderly conduct. These events were labelled 'The Battle of Forrest Place'; eventually, all the offenders were acquitted.[10]

Although the YCAC regarded itself as being fairly radical, some of its members went out on a limb with protests that the organisation disowned. Two such protests, in Perth in April and June 1966, involved planting a 15-foot (4.6 metre) cross near the war memorial in King's Park and setting fire to it. On the second occasion, the cross carried a placard: 'Ours not to reason why, ours but to do or die in Vietnam.' The protest leader, UWA Arts student Rupert Gerritsen, was arrested and fined $10 and $20 restitution to the King's Park Board for damaged cables. Gerritsen refused to reveal the names of his fellow protesters. YCAC did not sanction the burning of either draft cards or crosses.[11] In 1971, Gerritsen would be involved in a much more serious crime; but that story is for Chapter 7.

Protests during the visit of US President Lyndon B. Johnson in 1966. Protestors lying in front of the United States President's car during Lyndon Johnson's visit to Sydney in 1966.

Protests during the visit of US President Lyndon B. Johnson in 1966. A protestor being arrested during the US President's visit to the NSW Art Gallery, Sydney, 1966.

Meanwhile, the court cases proceeded, continuing to demonstrate the serendipity of magistrates' judgements. Christopher Campbell, a British immigrant, became aware of his liability under the NSA only after arriving in Sydney in April 1966. Campbell maintained that he always intended to return home after two years. He had belonged to the Campaign for Nuclear Disarmament in Britain, and he concluded that 'absolute' anti-war was the only tenable position for him to hold. Consequently, he did not apply to register as a CO. On 22 October, he was arrested at an anti-LBJ demonstration during the US President's visit to Australia, but the magistrate discharged him. Campbell failed to register under the NSA by 6 February 1967 – the deadline for his age group. Making his stance public, he wrote to the Minister for Labour and National Service, Leslie Bury, on 26 February, advising of his refusal to register. Bury replied, enclosing a registration form and telling him that applying to register as a CO would not compromise him. Campbell disagreed. He returned the form and wrote to *The Peacemaker*. He also sought help from Vivienne Abraham in his demand for the Act to be repealed. *The Peacemaker*, recognising his stance as something new, commented:

> Christopher Campbell is saying something different. He...does not believe that anyone should be obliged to cooperate with an Act of Parliament whose purpose is to force citizens to participate in what he, and many others, regard as immoral – war and preparation for war.[12]

Campbell argued that, although war 'has not been made unlawful', many individual acts committed in warfare (genocide, murder and war crimes) had been held to be unlawful, and individuals are punished for them: 'In other words, an individual is responsible even in wartime for actions he personally commits.' The FPC stated that Campbell was the first person 'to openly inform the Minister for Labour and National Service of his refusal to be conscripted for military service and to publish that correspondence.'[13] Many draftees would follow his example as aversion to the war grew and, with it, the desire to destroy the NSA.

For 13 months, Campbell waited to be prosecuted, living in daily expectation of a summons. He was able to continue his employment. Finally, he was served with summons to attend court on 26 February 1968, charged with failing to register for National Service. Campbell attended court, waiting there all day until his name was called at 2.45 pm. He stood up in the public gallery and called out that he did not intend to appear as a defendant, because he considered the NSA to be immoral and the court to have no jurisdiction under it. He made further statements, expecting to be charged with contempt of court, but instead the magistrate – the same Rodgers SM who had presided at so many dissidents' cases – adjourned the case until 4.10 pm and then to 12 March. Campbell had come to Australia as an assisted immigrant, on condition that he surrendered his passport to the Australian government for two years. As the second anniversary of his arrival in Australia approached, he decided to return to England. He applied for the return of his passport, expecting his request to be rejected. The passport was returned to him on 3 March; he found a berth on a ship and sailed immediately for England. On board the *Northern Star*, bound for Southampton, he wrote to Vivienne Abraham, indicating the strain he had suffered over the past few months and the value of her assistance with his case:

> I cannot thank you enough for making it all possible, nor for that matter can I express my gratitude for the last year. At times my mental state was pretty low. I'd have probably gone under if it hadn't been for...the fact of having someone I could talk to... I slept for 15 hours as soon as we were away from the wharf. Not only was I exhausted. I can still detect symptoms of shock, actual physical symptoms, similar to something received in a car accident... I had wanted to get you some sort of gift that could fully express my gratitude; unfortunately, I left it far too late and anyway couldn't think of anything sufficiently demonstrative... I think you can probably appreciate what last week's decision meant for me.

The postscript to his case was that he was fined $20 in his absence for failing to register for National Service.[14]

Cases such as Campbell's, White's and Beddow's were all protracted. It wasn't merely a matter of either registering and applying for exemption, or stating their intention not to register and being summonsed to court.

Sometimes, many months passed before an application was resolved in court or the department responded to a failure to register. One of the lengthiest was that of Laurie Carmichael. Carmichael sent a statutory declaration to the Minister in January 1967, the date by which he was liable to register, stating that he had a conscientious objection to any form of military service. He did not appear in court until November 1968, almost two years later, when he was convicted of remaining unregistered and fined $40.[15] He was finally granted total exemption by Foley SM in Melbourne on 10 September 1971.[16] His case, from the time he was liable to register until his application for total exemption was finally granted, had taken more than four and a half years. This raises many questions about the inefficiency and the cost of enforcing the NSA, as well as the effects of protracted strain on resisters, so well described by Christopher Campbell.

There were other examples of the pressure placed on young men to register. Bernard Cannon was training as a school teacher in Armidale, NSW. He learned that, if he didn't register for National Service, he would lose his Education Department scholarship, and the people who had acted as guarantors for his bond would be financially liable. Despite his objection to the Act, he registered and planned to keep a low profile. The following year, he asked Abraham not to include his name in a list included in a 'Don't Register' pamphlet, presumably fearing the consequences of making a public stand.[17]

Several of the protesters mentioned in these chapters spent time in military detention. This practice was later discontinued in favour of sending dissidents to serve their sentences in civil prisons. The next chapter examines the experiences of those who, most unwillingly, wore the uniform of the Australian Army, or bravely refused to wear it, and who suffered barbaric punishments within the walls of its correctional establishments.

## CHAPTER 6
# 'Under this government, it takes courage to be a conscientious objector'

It was often much harder for objectors to gain exemption after they had enlisted, as Max Beddow's case showed. This chapter discusses the experiences of seven dissidents whose cases illustrate the comparisons and contrasts in the way men were treated when they had enlisted before applying for exemption. These seven are Robert Stead and Simon Townsend from NSW; Denis O'Donnell from Victoria; and Western Australians John Poole-Johnson, Desmond Phillipson, Ken Beale and Paul McKeich. I refer to other cases, too, although in less detail. Despite the differences, one experience was common to all: there came a point at which they felt utter revulsion for their army training and believed that they could not continue.

Robert Stead had not been a pacifist, or even an objector to conscription, before he was called up on 2 February 1966, entered training and was sent to Kapooka. Stead's family were writers and academics.[1] His aunt was the novelist Christina Stead. His step-grandmother, Thistle Stead,[2] held university degrees in science and education and was a writer and teacher. Stead was from a 'religious' background but had rejected Christianity while at high school and regarded himself as an atheist. He did not consider himself a pacifist, at least in the sense that he understood the term, because he didn't believe that killing was wrong in all circumstances (for example, it might be justified in self-defence); but he did believe that most of the evil in the world arose 'from

[the] interference of one person with another person.' He found it 'totally repugnant' to con a person into military service, whether voluntary or not.

Stead's story is possibly unique in that he enlisted, then applied for exemption, was unsuccessful in the Magistrates Court, appealed, and then cancelled the appeal, completed his training and spent the obligatory two years in the army. He did not perform active service. Throughout his period of service, Vivienne Abraham maintained a friendship and a regular correspondence with him. They met both at Kapooka, where he was stationed, and when he was on leave. The correspondence provides a window into the way Abraham related to some of her clients and her determination never to give up on someone, even after he had decided not to continue as an objector.

Like Beddow, Stead was revolted by exercises at Kapooka. Within three days, he informed his superior officer that he could not continue training. He applied for exemption as a CO from all forms of military service. The application appears to have been delayed and was not heard in court until 21 May. In dismissing the application on 20 June, Rodgers SM observed that Stead was 'a deep thinker, [an] intelligent, well-educated young man', but that he objected to 'having his personal rights interfered with' rather than military service itself. The army had employed Stead in clerical work while he awaited the outcome of his application for exemption, a compromise that both he and they accepted. Acknowledging that his position was 'not the fault' of his superior officers, Stead was prepared to cooperate with the authorities to some extent. This cooperative attitude didn't work in his favour as far as his application for exemption was concerned; rather, it seems to have convinced the magistrate that he wasn't a sincere objector.

Stead lodged an appeal, which was set down for hearing on 8 September 1966 at the District Court in Sydney. The army now changed its attitude, demanding that Stead recommence his military training (as ordered by Rodgers SM) while awaiting his appeal hearing. Stead refused to return voluntarily to Kapooka and was taken there on 14 July under escort. He wore civilian clothes to emphasise his refusal to cooperate further in any way with the military training, although he was willing to return to his former clerical work at Eastern Command's Watsons Bay depot.

In July 1966, in her role as Secretary of the FPC, Abraham attempted to raise a deputation to the Minister for the Army, Malcolm Fraser, consisting of representatives from the Society of Friends, Dr Kenneth Rivett of the University of NSW and the Reverend Frank Coaldrake. Writing to the Society of Friends with this request, Abraham stated:

> There seems to be no legal ground for challenging the provisions of the [NSA] under which persons are 'deemed' to be enlisted, whether they present themselves in response to a call-up notice or whether they are committed by court for refusing to so present themselves.

She cited Bill White's case, then in progress, which she hoped would clarify the matter when he appeared in court for refusing to obey his call-up notice. (It didn't, but the law was amended in May 1968, as detailed later in the chapter). Abraham added:

> It may be that the result of serving two years in army detention could be less damaging, from a legal point of view, than two years in a civil gaol with a civil conviction. But this does not to my mind alleviate the principle here; unfortunately, I do not see how to challenge it at present, much as I would like to do so.

Abraham hoped that it might be possible to convince the Minister that it was not normal practice to carry out the decision of a court while an appeal was pending. Additionally, she stated, conscientious objection to conscription for military service was 'as valid an objection on the grounds of conscience as objection to military service itself', although objection to conscription was not covered in the NSA. She observed that 'whether to suggest there should be conscientious objection to a particular war [permitted] is more controversial', as she did not know of anyone arguing this before an Australian court during the present conscription period. This would change in later years. Mr Bury, the Minister for Labour and National Service, received the deputation on 26 January 1967 but made very little comment.[3]

After returning to Kapooka and recommencing his training, Stead experienced the same revulsion that he had felt in February. Abraham and his solicitor, David Cooper, visited him in July. Stead then changed his mind about proceeding with his appeal; on 17 July, he wrote to Abraham advising that he was 'officially cancelling' it. In his letters, his only stated reasons for making this decision were that he was not a pacifist, and that he had actually lied in court when he said that he could not go back into training.

Their correspondence continued over the next 18 months. Stead often used Abraham as both a sounding board for ideas and a confidante. On 5 August, he wrote of the disturbing ways in which soldiers were conditioned to conceptualise 'the enemy':

> According to most 'instructors' here, the enemy invariably has one, two or all of a yellow face, a yellow belly and slit eyes. According to one corporal ...the enemy 'gibbers' and is somewhat 'lazy'. And according to same authority, the enemy has for at least one of 'his' names, Charlie Nip.
>
> The fact is that the enemy today is not just Japanese (almost out of fashion), not just Chinese (too unthinkable), not just C.T. (Communist terrorist, forgotten), not just Indonesian (temporarily hors de vue [out of sight]). The enemy is (South East) Asian.
>
> If Australia has always been a little xenophobic, in a quaint, parochial fashion, there seems now to be developing in the Antipodes a definite, unmistakable case of Asiaphobia.

Ironically, when Stead completed his training in September, he was judged to be one of the best soldiers in the platoon. Throughout his training, he did not hide his views; he spent much of his time arguing with other soldiers about the war, pacifism, Christianity and various other topics – at some personal cost, because his outspokenness didn't make him popular. He sent Abraham some reflections, although he didn't think they were suitable for publication in *The Peacemaker*. After completing his training, Stead was transferred to the Psychology Unit at Kapooka, where, as he wrote on 31 January1967, he was about to endure 'the tedious routine of another NS intake.' Later in the same letter, he commented bitterly:

1967 could not possibly be more rewarding or valuable in my life. It promises only to be 12 months of soul-destroying monotony, enlivened only by increasing conflict with Bateman [his superior officer], not serious as yet.

The monotony did not ease. Stead literally counted the days until his release, writing on 1 April: 'at the close of this weekend [370 days] shall remain to be endured. And each day is a true test of endurance.' He was also 'tiring a little of wisecracks re COs.' Perhaps only the military could fail to see the irony of employing a man who constantly opposed its values in a position in the Psychology Unit.

A month's leave in June 1967 merely exacerbated Stead's misery. On 5 July, three days after his return to the unit, he wrote of the:

> barrenness of the environment; the distasteful work; the inaccessibility of other activities;...incompatibility with the social habits of my 'colleagues'; a general lassitude as regards any activity, let alone those I choose to think of as 'my own'; too many people too close; lack of companionship; outright hostility with some, uncomfortable acceptability with others; bugles from 5.50am; unpalatable food; noisy nights; too much smoking; indifference with the present breeding indifference with [sic] the future; lack of accomplishment inhibiting accomplishment. Tired of just waiting.

Stead had enough self-knowledge to realise that release from the military would not end all his problems, merely the immediate ones related specifically to army life:

> In many ways these two years [are] just a short suspension of my poor, struggling existence, where many problems are shelved merely by the imposition of a state of being.

Perhaps so, but it is easy to imagine how a man who read Simone de Beauvoir, played and listened to music and wrote poetry (some of which appears in his letters) could be suffocated by the tedium of his work and life in

National Mobilisation to Holsworthy Prison to protest conscientious objector Denis O'Donnell's imprisonment, 19 May 1968.

the military. The letters show, too, that Stead kept abreast of the cases of other objectors, especially Bill White, whose case had run concurrently with his in 1966, and Simon Townsend. There are few copies of Abraham's letters in the file, but, from his comments, it seems that she asked Stead's opinion on these and other cases.

Stead's last letter on the file, dated 6 December 1967, contained news of his promotion to sergeant. He had 71 days still to serve, but the tone was quite different from previous letters, defiant and even optimistic. He seemed to feel that he had beaten the army. The copies of Abraham's last two letters to him, conversely, are somewhat judgemental in tone, asking him to take up the cause after his release, perhaps in assisting the campaign to have the NSA repealed or in other ways. In her penultimate letter, she pleaded with Stead to remember the idealism of his stand in court in 1966: 'I'm asking if whatever it was engendered that thinking and action is still present?' She added:

> Do you want to go out with a clear record or do you feel able to consider another stand – albeit on a more minor issue maybe?.... Or it may be that having demonstrated your ability to conform, it would seem childish to act up now.
>
> Maybe I'm still regretful of the lost opportunity. Maybe I want action for action's sake. I still think what happened to you iniquitous. And I've no doubt it happens to a lesser degree to others.... You said repeatedly...after deciding not to go on with your appeal that you were not a pacifist. Your transcript doesn't from memory indicate this.

Abraham's last letter, dated 22 January 1967, was written on the train between Melbourne and Sydney, a route that she travelled regularly while maintaining her work in both capitals. She wanted Stead to write something for *The Peacemaker*. Then, returning to her previous letter's theme of making some kind of a 'last stand gesture', she asked:

> Have they indoctrinated you to the extent that you'll take what they decide... Of course, it would spoil your record... Your conscience I leave to you.

The letter ends with an oddly personal note: 'Drunk with joy, that [I] can soon sleep without dreaming of you as I go past [Wagga on the train].' Stead's response to either of these letters is unknown, because there are no further communications in the file. Perhaps he just wanted to put it all behind him. Several of his letters had indicated his reluctance to embark on the 'absolutist' route of some other objectors, including Bill White and Chris Campbell.

We will never know why Abraham indulged in this lengthy correspondence with someone who, from mid-1966, indicated that he was not going to return to the CO path. Did she feel some inclination to go after the one lost sheep, although she had many others to tend? Perhaps she was attracted by Stead's highly developed intellect, evident not only in his ability to understand and absorb ideas from his reading, but also in his capacity to express original thought. Abraham spent most of those years in a state of frantic busyness, always travelling between her sister Shirley's home in Hawthorn East (Melbourne) and her own home in North Sydney, frequently exhausted. In her last letter to Robert Stead, she wrote that she had been advising 60 CO cases all around Australia. Some of these were connected with her law firm, F. W. Jenkins and Co. Others, including one in WA, clearly were not. Additionally, she was involved a wide range of other causes: taking editorial responsibility for *The Peacemaker*; Secretary of the FPC; and campaigning for a 'Yes' vote in the 1967 Referendum on rights for Aboriginal and Torres Strait Islander Australians.[4] Somehow, in the midst of all this activity, she found time to write copious letters to a man who was lost to the anti-war cause.

Why Stead changed his mind and decided to complete his army service is not entirely clear from his letters. It is possible that he was unnerved by the way the army treated dissidents. Both Denis O'Donnell (from Victoria) and Simon Townsend (NSW) experienced brutal treatment while in military detention. O'Donnell, like Stead and Beddow, had applied to become a CO after he had enlisted in the army in 1967. After both his application and his appeal were rejected, O'Donnell had gone AWL. He was arrested, court-martialled and imprisoned initially at the jungle training camp, Puckapunyal, where he was kept in solitary confinement in an unlighted cell and made to eat meals without any utensils. After 48 hours, he was transported to Melbourne in a cage on the back of a truck. O'Donnell's letters show the incredible stress he was under. 'I am nearly insane... I cannot take much more,' he wrote in a letter that was published in the National Union of Students newspaper, *National U*. He was disappointed that no pressure had been put on anyone 'to see me or have me released somehow.'[5]

Apart from solitary confinement and deprivation of sleep, light and food, O'Donnell experienced 'psychological brain scrambling exercises' used on objectors to break their spirit. He was denied bathing facilities for several days; when he was permitted to shower, he had to change back into his dirty clothes, because no others were provided. A leaflet issued jointly by Melbourne University's Labour and Pacifist Clubs around April 1968 stated that O'Donnell was being treated as though he were a dangerous criminal.

'Under this government, it takes courage to be a conscientious objector'   99

Simon Townsend (top left) headed a leaflet setting out the reasons why nine young men refused to enlist.

Water was brought to him by 'guards with fixed bayonets, and food is handed to him through a slot in the door.' The leaflet criticised the pacifist movement for standing by O'Donnell until he was arrested and then doing nothing:

> when he was imprisoned there were no large demonstrations; nor was there any mention in the press of his actual removal to Holsworthy. We supported him but only to the extent that was necessary to keep him out of gaol. Then we left him on his own. Most people would feel bitterly disappointed if they were in Dennis' place and received this sort of support.[6]

Townsend was also imprisoned, for 28 days at Holsworthy, for disobeying orders. During 48 hours in solitary confinement, he was detained in a 9-foot square (2.7 x 2.7 metre) cell and given only bread and water. He was woken by guards every half hour from 7 pm to 6 am and made to stand to attention and give his name. Townsend's treatment did, however, raise a

A selection of leaflets produced by the various anti-war and anti-conscription organisations in operation during the Vietnam War.

## CONSCIENTIOUS OBJECTORS ADVISORY COMMITTEE

"THE PEACEMAKER"

*Speakers:*
Hon. A. A. CALWELL
Mr. FRANK CREAN, M.H.R.
Mr. ALAN FRASER, M.H.R.
(N.S.W.)

## PRINCESS THEATRE
Spring Street, Melbourne

### SUNDAY, MAY 22
at 2.15 p.m.

Glen Tomasetti and other artists
"Singing Against War"

**ALP** Victoria

...ustralians being ...ed for Vietnam?

### S.O.S.
WHY CONSCRIPT VOTELESS YOUNG MEN FOR AN UNDECLARED WAR

YOUNG MEN LIABLE ... MILITARY SERVICE

EXTRACTS FROM THE NATIONAL SERVICE ACT 1965

## CONSCIENTIOUS OBJECTION
AND
NATIONAL SERVICE ACT, 1951-1965

WHY QUAKER ... TO ALL

debate in the Federal Parliament. In May 1968, several Labor MPs interrogated government ministers. Doug Everingham asked whether the Minister for the Army, Phillip Lynch, was aware that the Townsend's punishment was likely to cause 'serious psychological effects'. Lynch replied that 'no attempt has been made to break down any man' at Holsworthy. The treatment that Townsend suffered (such as semi-starvation, isolation, prolonged deprivation of sleep) was 'the normal code of military discipline'. The half-hourly checks had been instituted 'for the safety of prisoners' but they had been reviewed and discontinued. Clyde Cameron pressed the Minister further, pointing out that solitary confinement 'with or without a bread and water diet' had not been imposed in South Australian civilian prisons 'for many years', even against 'the worst murderers, garrotters or rapists'. Lynch asserted that Holsworthy, as 'a military correctional establishment', could not be compared with other prisons. Len Devine then asked Acting Prime Minister John McEwen whether he would instigate an open inquiry into 'all aspects of military detention and treatment at military establishments' and whether he would call for Lynch's resignation. McEwen said that he would not. According to him, Townsend's punishment for disobeying a 'legitimate Army instruction' was entirely in line with 'penalties that have been prevalent for a long time in the Army'.

Fred Daly was utterly appalled by this response:

> Now we have the Minister for the Army condoning what is, in effect, torture treatment being given to a man who conscientiously objects to serving in Vietnam. Every half hour this man is awakened in his cell. There is a knock on the door and he is told: 'Wake up, we want to see if you are alive.' They cannot allow him to sleep all night because they fear he might be dead in the morning. What a fantastic situation that is in this day and age! Can you imagine the character of the man who sentenced him to solitary confinement and to be awakened every half hour? Do people want me to believe that that sadistic individual was really fearing for the health and welfare of the man? Of course he was not. He knew that the man would be there in the morning, without his having to be awakened every half hour from 7 p.m. to 7 a.m. The fact is it

was sadistic treatment. The officer responsible for imposing this treatment – whatever his rank – ought to be court martialled on the charge of inhuman treatment, because I would never justify it, and no honourable member on the Government side could justify it... [U]nder this government, it requires a lot of courage to be a conscientious objector.[7]

Following more questioning by other ALP members, McEwen stated that the matter of objectors who refused to obey a call-up instruction being subjected to military discipline had also been reviewed; amendments to the legislation would mean that, henceforth, objectors whose applications had been dismissed and who refused to obey a military call up would be subject to civil, not military, law.[8] Consequently, as Chapter 9 outlines, objectors and non-compliers who refused to accept the decision of the court were liable to two years in a civil prison – later reduced to 18 months. But, of course, those men who had already enlisted prior to expressing dissent remained under military law until they were released from the army, as the following cases show.

Three of the Western Australians whose experiences are described here all enlisted in 1968. John Poole-Johnson, Desmond Phillipson and Ken Beale all entered National Service with personal doubts about the scheme and, like Beddow and Stead, experienced a strong revulsion when they began training at Puckapunyal. Later, writing in the UWA student newspaper *Pelican*, John Poole-Johnson described the effect one aspect of the training had on him:

> There was a target in the shape of a soldier dressed in real clothes, which was holding something like a gun pointing towards us.
> Then one shot was fired at the centre of the soldier-dummy target. Unknown to us, concealed in the clothing of the dummy, there was a 4-gallon metal drum filled with red fluid and jelly.

> The effect of the single bullet hitting the target was horrible. The whole of the lower part of the clothing was torn away by the bullet which penetrated the drum. The hole caused by the bullet entering the drum was only a small one but there was a huge gaping hole left

at the back of the drum by the bullet passing through. In addition, there was a large cascade of this red fluid and jelly, which was a terrible shock to me.

After this we were all taken up close to the targets. One of the NCOs pointed to the back of the drum and said, 'Imagine what that would do to a man's guts.'[9]

Like Stead, Poole-Johnson also objected to the overtly racist overtones in the training, including references to 'the little yellow men' and the fact that '1,700 million South East Asians' could easily overrun Australia if the National Servicemen were not prepared to fight. One of his fellow recruits, a primary school teacher who noticed his revulsion at the training methods, said to him: 'If I was up in Vietnam and you were there, too, I'd shoot you first before a Viet Cong.' Poole-Johnson deserted and returned to WA. The military police soon tracked him down and took him back to Karrakatta Barracks. Poole-Johnson applied for exemption as a CO. He remained in the army to undertake non-combatant duties while awaiting his court hearing. He knew the difficulty he faced in convincing the court that his objection was sincere, despite having held reservations when he enlisted. The army came to his aid, giving him another medical examination and pronouncing him unfit for further service. Overall, he had spent five weeks in the army.[10]

Desmond Phillipson's escape from army service was by a harder and longer road. He was inducted into the army at Karrakatta Barracks on 7 February 1968. Like Poole-Johnson, he was quickly sent to Puckapunyal, where he completed five weeks' training. In the third week of training, he experienced the same incident with the dummy that had had such a profound effect on Poole-Johnson. Phillipson's response was similar, although more cerebral than emotional. In the statement supporting his application to be exempted, he wrote:

> Whereas before I thought of killing in only the abstract sense, at this point it became a harsh reality – there was no evading the question of killing any more. [The dummy incident] had the effect of making me think about killing more deeply than I had before and [made] me realise that the object of all this training was to teach me to kill. I also

became aware of just how brutal warfare had become and that any position I might fill would be contributing to this killing.[11]

Phillipson was granted four days' leave at the end of his five weeks' training. He returned to WA and became engaged to be married. He discussed his beliefs with his fiancée and members of his family. On returning to camp, he informed his commanding officer that he wanted to lodge an application for exemption from military service. He also stated that, once he had lodged the application, he would perform no further military training, because it was against his conscience. Because he refused to carry out orders, he was imprisoned for a month. A further refusal resulted in a court-martial on 18 April and 40 days confined at Holsworthy. He served 28 days' detention before being given leave to prepare his application for exemption. After the court-martial, Phillipson refused to cooperate in any way, refusing even to eat, walk or talk. He later revealed that he was carried onto and off the plane that took him from Melbourne to Sydney, pulled out of the truck that conveyed him to Holsworthy and dumped on the ground. He was also pulled by the hair, and his arms were bruised. When he refused to shower, he had cold water poured over him; his clothes were thrown into the cell with him, but no towel to dry himself. When he refused to leave his cell, he was transferred to the cold, sunless side of B block, where he spent seven days. The officers and NCOs accused him of cowardice and fear of being shot in Vietnam.[12]

Abraham visited Phillipson at Holsworthy on 22 April and again on 1 May 1968, both times in the presence of the commandant, despite her wish to speak with Phillipson in private. She had received information from Dennis O'Donnell, who was in the next cell, that Phillipson had arrived at Holsworthy on 19 April 'with a bloody head'. O'Donnell repeated this accusation to Labor MP Jim Cairns; he said that Phillipson had been 'bashed up' and that he heard him crying, but that Phillipson insisted he wouldn't give in. Cairns took part in the debate in the House of Representatives, mentioned above, where he and others severely criticised the treatment of prisoners in military detention.

Phillipson was in solitary confinement when Abraham visited him. He had been denied writing materials and couldn't communicate with his family. Abraham obtained the commandant's permission to contact Phillipson's family on his behalf. Phillipson had fasted for five days and spent 24 hours in hospital. His attitude to military service had hardened to the extent that he believed that obeying any order, even something as apparently harmless as cutting grass, was equally as bad as obeying a command to perform combatant duties. However, when the commandant advised him that, if he continued to disobey orders, the army wouldn't grant him his wish to have his hearing transferred to Perth; he would continue to be court-martialled; and he would be taken to court in Sydney under military escort, Phillipson relented and agreed to obey orders. He asked Abraham to explain this when she wrote to his fiancée, requesting that she send Phillipson some civilian clothes. He was transferred to Kapooka, where Abraham and his legal counsel visited him on 26 May.

On 30 May, Phillipson was given leave without pay and put on a train to Melbourne. He succeeded in having his court hearing transferred to Perth, where his application was rejected by Bateman SM in the Court of Petty Sessions on 26 July 1968. His appeal was dismissed in the Supreme Court of WA on 24 September 1968. In December, Phillipson lodged a second application for total exemption from military service, but, prior to the hearing, the army gave him another medical examination and dismissed him, as they had done with Poole-Johnson.[13] Was it because they feared adverse publicity, or did they, like the law courts, see the value of a precedent?

A third WA recruit who enlisted in 1968 also changed his mind about serving during his training. Ken Beale already had concerns about participation in war, despite a proud family tradition of war service stretching from the Boer War through both World Wars. His father, who served with the 13th Australian General Hospital in Singapore in World War II, was imprisoned by the Japanese forces. His experiences as a prisoner in Thailand and Burma resulted in lifelong health problems. Apart from the impact of his father's experience, Beale read books about World War II and concluded that war was 'horrific'. He saw World War II as a transition, 'a black period that we are now out of.' He believed that there was no more need for war; warfare didn't solve the world's problems.[14]

Beale had no desire to join the army. After three years of anxious waiting, his number came up in a selection process that he regarded as being unfair. It was as much a lottery as buying a ticket in the hope of winning money. On TV, he saw Simon Townsend:

National Service recruits training at Puckapunyal, prior to serving in Vietnam. Despite the myth that trainees could choose whether they served in the war, Paul McKeich recalled, 'I was not given a choice, despite what the official records state.'

forced into the back of a police wagon and driven away to prison. For what? He had turned 20 and was a male. He was expected to leave his career, which he was very good at, and serve in the army.

Prior to enlisting, Beale sold his car at a loss. He knew that he would initially be confined to barracks at Swanbourne for the first few weeks, then flown to Melbourne and on to Puckpunyal, so he had no need of a vehicle; but being without a car disadvantaged him when he returned to civilian life. In his first 12 weeks of training, he had only one weekend off. Marching and rifle drills were designed to make the recruits respond to commands and become instinctively obedient. As he felt himself becoming like a machine, doubts began forming. Education programmes in the evening included films like *Zulu*, emphasising that the British troops were victorious over much larger numbers of Zulus because they were disciplined. Beale recalled an incident when the officer asked the class, what was the purpose of a soldier? Responding to the recruits' answers, he told them that protecting their country, the queen, etcetera were purposes, but the real purpose was 'to kill'. 'The purpose of a soldier is to kill,' he reiterated. One of the 'Nashos' asked, 'What if there's women and children' and was told: 'You should obey in all circumstances.' A hush fell over the room. It was a turning point for Beale. He felt that he could not fire upon women and children, even if refusing to do so meant disobeying an order. He decided then that he wanted no part of the army. He reflected on his training experience:

> It is that loss of freedom, the bullying and punitive consequences (comply or go to jail) that I objected to. At Puckapunyal we weren't treated with respect, we were spoken to as if we did not have any common sense or intelligence. When I wrote to my parents about the way we were treated my father was surprised.

After training at Puckapunyal, Beale's group went to an artillery camp on Sydney's North Shore to 'a 9 to 5 job'. While there, he met some COs who invited him to a support group that met at the Quakers' hall, where he met Vivienne Abraham. The group's aim was to prepare young men for making their own decision about whether or not to enlist and informing them of what to expect as a result of their decision. Beale became friends with one of the group members, who invited him to stay in a share house in inner Sydney while he lodged his application for exemption from military service. When Beale told his commanding officer what he was going to do, the officer said, 'You can't listen to your conscience.'

Awaiting the outcome of his application in the court, Beale didn't feel optimistic. On unpaid leave from the army, he was living in a squat in Glebe, sleeping on a flea-ridden mattress. When he fell ill with flu, a doctor who attended him asked what he was doing there. After hearing Beale's story, the sympathetic doctor arranged for him to see a military psychologist. He had to enter a military hospital, where he stayed for about a month before being judged unfit for further service. Beale received a non-disciplinary medical discharge and returned to WA.

New Zealand-born Paul McKeich was the fourth WA recruit to experience ethical difficulties with being trained to kill people. Like those before him, he sought total exemption after a period of time in the army. McKeich worked in the Department of Labour and National Service in Perth when his marble was drawn. Despite his closeness to the process, he had no idea that his birthday had been drawn until he received a telegram informing him that he must enlist. The birth dates that were drawn in the twice-yearly lottery were not published until September 1970. McKeich, who was granted a one-year deferment to complete a Bachelor of Arts at UWA, described himself as being 'not openly opposed' to Australia's involvement in the Vietnam War. Reflecting on his experience years later, he admitted that he was 'apathetic, open-minded and willing to enter into army training,' which he regarded as being 'a necessary evil'.

By the time he was called up in January 1971, McKeich had been married for eight months to Lorraine, a trainee nurse. He wrote: 'This would be our first time apart. The goodbyes...were gut wrenching'. To add to his emotional stress, the recruits were immediately taken from Karrakatta Barracks and put on the 'red-eye special' – as the midnight flight from Perth to Eastern States capitals is still known locally. From Melbourne, they were bussed straight to Puckapunyal army base for haircuts, medical and dental checks and training. Over the next three months, the recruits were trained to handle a range of weapons, including rifles, sub-machine and machine guns and grenades. Although he became a 'good soldier' and was awarded a Marksman Badge for shooting accuracy, McKeich's beliefs became increasingly at odds with his training:

> The more I realised I was being trained to become an efficient killer, the more it cut across my beliefs. This was just not me – I am not that type of person. And it was crazy for the government to force people into this role. It is clear in my first letters from Puckapunyal that I was not happy about using a rifle and bayonet against a so-called 'enemy', and I was questioning Australia's role in the Vietnam War.

Although he applied for a non-combatant position when his initial training was completed, McKeich was allocated to Infantry and sent to further training at Singleton, NSW. When he complained, the army staff told him that there could be no change to his allocation, but that he might not be sent to Vietnam. A week into training at Singleton, 'they announced that my infantry company was on its way to Vietnam. I was not offered a choice, despite what the official records state.'

McKeich's experience illustrates flaws in a system that claimed that, if a soldier 'volunteered' for a non-combat unit, he would not be sent to Vietnam. A soldier might well volunteer, but if his choice was ignored and he was placed in a combat unit, he was certainly likely to be sent on active service. McKeich's response was, firstly, to sabotage his military training by deliberately firing inaccurately on the rifle range, much to the annoyance of his commanding officer, and then to apply for status as a non-combatant. He then changed his application to total exemption as a CO. Initially, he was pleasantly surprised by the way the army dealt with him:

> The captain's attitude was more understanding and respectful and he gave me the paperwork to fill in. Going through the formal processes, I was surprised that I did not initially receive the ridicule I expected. Later at less formal moments I was called a 'coward' and a 'communist' by both army and non-army people, then and later.

Lorraine McKeich had been planning to move to NSW to be near her husband, when the army suddenly sent him back to WA. McKeich's court appearance was set for 16 August 1971. He was represented by Peter Dowding (later a Labor Premier of WA), who had defended a number of COs. McKeich was a member of the Maylands Baptist Church. His aversion to killing was based on Jesus' teachings that we should love our enemies and do good to those who hate you. But he saw 'flaws' in the pacifist stance:

> For instance, I believe the Second World War to be a 'just' war by its nature, probably the only 'just war' in modern history and one which I would have fought.

The leaders of McKeich's church refused to provide the character references he needed for his court appearance because they disagreed with his pacifist stance. But another Baptist minister, the Rev. Glen Brooks, came to his aid with a character reference and also supported him in court, along with McKeich family members. The Crown Prosecutor appeared anxious to disprove the sincerity of McKeich's beliefs. If the prosecutor succeeded, it would mean a prison sentence of almost two years. But the magistrate ruled in his favour, and he left court free from any further obligations to the army.

These stories indicate that the military could sometimes be merciful when it came to deciding that a man was unsuited to army training, but subjected those who refused to obey orders to extremely barbaric treatment. Undoubtedly, some dissidents were made examples of, possibly to dissuade other recruits from imitating them. Reports of the training illustrate a pretty bleak picture of military life. Recruits were expected to show blind obedience to their officers and not allow their conscience to dictate their actions. The 'enemy' was demonised, to instil hatred in the recruits and enable them to kill another human being without compunction or compassion.

While no one mentioned experiencing or witnessing sexual abuse, bullying by both trainers and fellow recruits was evident in Stead's, Poole-Johnson's, McKeich's and Beale's accounts. There is anecdotal evidence, too, that a number of trainees suicided or attempted suicide during their training. Glen Huxley, a National Serviceman who completed his training, could not substantiate these stories but knew of one fellow trainee who attempted suicide by taking a drug overdose and was discharged from the army days later. Huxley was not a dissident, but he wrote that the effects of the military training on his own attitudes were 'not all positive':

> I was disappointed to discover that many recruits and servicemen were interested in Vietnam service simply 'for the benefits.' [Did the training make me] more aggressive? Hard to say. Personally, I would say the end product of my two years in the army was a balance between aggression and the value of good communication skills.[15]

The more educated and reflective 'Nashos' revolted against the indoctrination and threats. Naturally, it begs the question of how much the training affected those who were less aware of its attitude-altering capacity. Peace activists have often argued against the psychological and cultural dangers of militarising society, on top of actual physical harm sustained in warfare. The impact upon the young men described in this chapter indicates that those dangers are very real.

The years 1967 and 1968, when the stories in this chapter occurred, can be seen as pivotal in opposition to the National Service scheme. Resistance changed from the personal (individuals seeking exemption from military service) to 'smashing the draft', so that no one would be conscripted. Beyond that, many also opposed any military involvement in the war. The next three chapters discuss the forms that this all-out resistance took.

## CHAPTER 7
# 'Not to oppose conscription, but to wreck it'

From the beginning of 1968, the anti-war protest movement became more widespread and militant and the police response more violent. Opposition to the entire NSA, rather than specific parts of it, also increased. Delegates of the Australian Student Christian Movement (ASCM), meeting at a convention in Sydney in January, carried resolutions condemning Australia's involvement in the Vietnam War and urging the Australian Government to withdraw all troops 'as speedily as possible and to mediate a just and humane peace.' The ASCM declared that the suffering in Vietnam was an offence against God and humanity. It also called for the repeal of the NSA.[1] The ASCM's actions were indicative of a rising tide of resistance to the war that swept across Australia in 1968.

Increasingly, non-compliers (referred to in *The Peacemaker* as 'conscientious non-complier' or 'CNC') who refused to register, to apply for exemption, to obey a call up or to attend court when charged outnumbered COs who complied with the system, registered and applied for exemption from military service. David Bissett, a non-complier from Melbourne, wrote:

> [We] felt that the conscientious objector provisions of the conscription laws were in fact a method by which the government coped with a small number of articulate, committed pacifists while

Protesters marching to a sit-in outside the Prime Minister's Lodge, Canberra, 19 May 1968.

'A pretty 'ruley' bunch. The quiet, orderly police arrests of protestors at the Prime Minister's Lodge sit-in, Canberra, May 1968, contrasts with the following images of Sydney arrests just two months later.

continuing to conscript the wanted numbers. Some non-compliers were also true pacifists, while others including myself were totally opposed to conscription per se and to the purpose for which it was then being applied, but would possibly have *volunteered* for service if convinced that it was just and necessary.[2]

As the war ground on, resistance to the Act grew. Rather than objecting to conscription and warfare on the grounds of private religious or pacifist beliefs, non-compliers called for the NSA to be repealed. They questioned the government's legal right to conscript and the morality of involvement in this specific war. Although Vivienne Abraham had hesitated, in mid-1966, to suggest that the Act should be amended to enable objection against a particular war, this objection became common in 1968 and 1969. Among the groups to protest specifically against conscription, the DRM took the most aggressive stance. They formed 'not...to oppose conscription but to wreck it.' The DRM intended to 'resist the draft by *all* available means', including staging demonstrations and providing information about how to fail medical examinations. The DRM reminded potential members that this action would cost money – 'legal costs, fines, etc., for those we will be supporting in resisting the draft.'[3]

By March 1968, the mainstream press was beginning to pay attention to COs' groups. In a satirical piece for *The Australian*, journalist Martin Collins wrote of his experience visiting the Sydney Conscientious Objectors Group, whose organisers included Vivienne Abraham. Abraham pointed to the 'unreasonable' decisions of some magistrates, who:

> ask the boys if they've consorted with peace groups or discussed their objection with interested parties, and try to use it as a weapon against them.

She said that the group's aim was not to tell people what to think but to help them clarify why they objected to being conscripted.[4]

The ASCM and the Conscientious Objectors' groups acted within the law, but illegal forms of resistance mounted as protest intensified. Student Democratic Action (SDA) groups formed at the universities of Sydney and Brisbane. University students staged a mass sit-in outside the Prime Minister's

Examples of police brutality at demonstrations. Police arrested *Tribune* photographer Noel Hazard after he took these photographs at a demonstration in Martin Place, Sydney in July 1968.

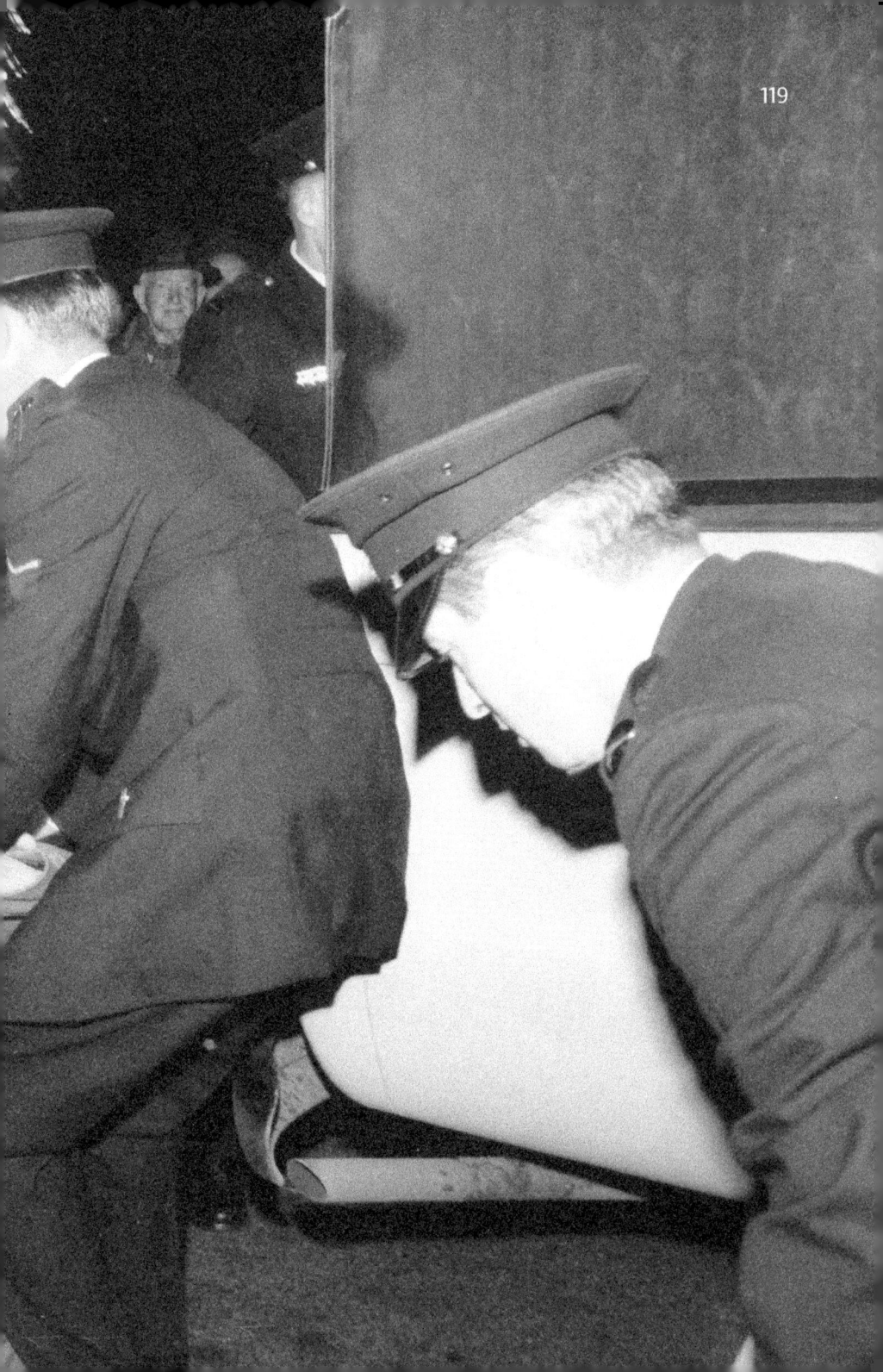

Lodge in Canberra on 19 May 1968. Although a majority came from Monash, over 30 organisations sent representatives from almost every state; around 400 people participated. The demonstration opposed conscription and demanded the repeal of the NSA and the release from prison of Denis O'Donnell and Simon Townsend. In what *National U* described as 'perhaps the first completely organised act of civil disobedience', half of the protesters courted arrest by sitting on the road leading to the Lodge.

The police, however, had been instructed to be 'gentle' with the protesters. Despite their determination to be arrested, the more radical sitters experienced the humiliation of seeing their fellow protesters queueing voluntarily to be taken in police cars and buses to the police station, where eight were released on bail and the remaining 61 of those arrested were locked up for the night. The police conduct was 'perfect at all times', according to *National U*. They provided the prisoners with blankets, hot meals and drinks. A police sergeant reportedly commented that the demonstrators 'proved their point to their own satisfaction and they were a pretty "ruley" bunch on the whole.' Ironically, he added: 'Most of them would make excellent soldiers.' In court the next morning, the magistrate was not so generous. 'I am not prepared to convert any of these people to heroes or martyrs,' Dodson SM declared. 'There are no vacancies on the list for martyrs.' Some of the students refused to pay their fines and, the following month, were facing the prospect of five days in jail.[5]

Police in other locations were less tolerant. News of increasing police brutality at demonstrations featured in both the alternative and the mainstream press. *Farrago*, the University of Melbourne's student newspaper, had published complaints of assault against anti-conscription demonstrators as early as March 1966. Two years later, *Tribune* published photographs of police – many of whom had removed their numbers from their uniforms to avoid identification – grabbing demonstrators around the neck, forcing them to the ground, handcuffing them and dragging them along the street. *The Australian* criticised police for removing their identity badges at a demonstration involving the Prime Minister, John Gorton; for 'needlessly marching Mr. Gorton straight into the demonstration'; and for not 'barricading off his car or [his exit from the building].'[6] *Tribune* of 10 July 1968 reported on violent incidents at a demonstration where students from Sydney University, the University of

New South Wales and Macquarie University invaded the Liberal Party's staff headquarters, chanting 'Gorton's got to go' and 'No conscription'. One placard read: 'Conscript the 7,000 Young Liberals' and another, 'Why should WE have the courage of THEIR convictions?' About 100 students barricaded themselves into rooms on the upper floors of the building. When police gained entry, they threw some protesters down the stairs. One student, Andrew Martin, who was dragged down the stairs on his back, was sent to hospital in an ambulance. Another student kicked a police officer in the face, purportedly by accident when he was being thrown down the stairs. After being detained and questioned for several hours, the student was released without charge.

Around Australia, a wide range of groups used the US national day, 4 July, as a focus for protests. In Melbourne, protesters tore down the American flag at the US Consulate and smashed windows with stones. The Vietnam Coordinating Committee held a rally at the Assembly Hall in Collins Street. Other protests occurred at the Australian American Association premises and at the City Watch House, in Russell Street, where some of the protesters were held after arrest. The protests at the Consulate and the Watch House were particularly violent. *Tribune* claimed that mounted police 'were ordered to gallop their horses indiscriminately into a crowd of people sitting down in the driveway of the Consulate grounds.' At the Watch House, several officers wielding truncheons set upon a demonstrator. Dozens were arrested. In contrast, demonstrations in Brisbane and Perth were peaceful.[7]

With the DRM's foundation in 1968, protests became much more organised. The DRM held a conference on 24 August 1969 and published a 'Declaration of Intent':

> Should the government at any stage in the future attempt to gaol any one of us for our conscientious defiance of the *National Service Act*, we will initiate nation-wide resistance on a massive and unprecedented scale – in universities, work places, and on the streets.[8]

Unfortunately, this belief in its own powers was optimistic. No general strike resulted from the imprisonment of any draft resister.

Anarchist Mike Payne recalled a protest in the office of the Department of Labour and National Service in Perth on 7 August 1970, where demonstrators experienced similar levels of police violence to those in Sydney and Melbourne in 1968. The 24 students involved included Payne, CPA activist John Rivo Gandini and Rod Moran, who was:

> pulled down three flights of stairs not, it looked, very gently, singing the 'Fixing to die Rag' – and dumped on the pavement where a little old lady kicked him because she had a relative serving in Vietnam.

In the East Perth lock-up, the arrested students annoyed police officers by 'larking about, singing, swinging on the bars and that sort of thing'. In retaliation, the police picked up Payne, stripped him and locked him in a damp and totally dark room, where 'there was absolutely no way to judge the passage of time.' This was in the middle of winter. After those arrested were bailed out, Payne told others of his experience. Brian Tennant, later famous as a civil rights campaigner, publicised it and worked for reforms to police treatment of detainees.[9]

Early in 1969, 23 non-compliers were facing the prospect of two-year jail sentences, and those who undertook various forms of protest also risked imprisonment. After John Zarb was jailed for two years in October 1968 for failing to obey a call-up notice, two protesters, Ken Mansell and Adrian Desailly, began painting 'Free Zarb' signs around various Melbourne suburbs. One night, just as they had painted 'Free Z' on a railway bridge in Northcote, police caught them. They were locked up overnight in 'a stinking Northcote police cell', followed by 'a free trip to the Bluestone Hotel in Coburg for cruel haircuts and a "roughing up"'. The following Saturday morning, activists converged on the bridge. Robert Tillett completed the three missing letters of the sign. He was arrested and sentenced to three months' jail – 'one month for every letter'. Students at Monash University donated $100 to help pay for his defence. Magistrate A. H. Pfeifer fined Desailly and Mansell $200 each for their part in painting the sign – and questioned their sanity. As payback, 'raiding parties set out from the Bakery [the headquarters of the Monash Labor Club] in the wee hours to paint the magistrate's footpath and fence in Murrumbeena'.[10]

Thirteen other protesters were charged with publishing material that 'incites young men not to register for National Service'. *The Peacemaker* argued that everyone who authorised or distributed the leaflet titled 'Why Register for National Service?' was 'equally guilty' of this offence. 'But is it a crime,' *The Peacemaker* asked, 'to hand out a leaflet, not to incite young men not to register, but to ask them to obey their moral convictions?' The leaflet merely set out 'the alternatives available to those liable to register, and the consequences of the choices open to them.'[11] In Burnie (Tasmania), *The Advocate* had already proclaimed the act of issuing pamphlets detailing acts of sabotage that a draftee could perform while in the army as 'close to treason'.[12]

In March 1969, several people appeared in the Melbourne City Court charged with incitement or encouragement to commit an offence against the NSA. They were students Michael Hamel-Green, Frances Newell and Robert Pendlebury; laboratory assistant Brian Currie; librarian Brenda Ford; and freelance journalist Philip West. The cases were dismissed on a technicality. Griffin SM determined that, although the pamphlets were intended to dissuade people from registering for National Service, which constituted 'incitement', handing out the pamphlet was not the same thing as publishing it. A decision on the case of Nicholas Beams, who appeared in the Hobart Court on the same charge, was reserved until 28 April. *The Peacemaker* reported that there were a further 40 charges pending in Tasmania. In an act of bravado, *The Peacemaker* published extracts from the pamphlet 'Why register for National Service?' and included a list of names of the people who had authorised, published and printed the leaflet. These included several whose charges had been dismissed in the Melbourne Court.[13]

In its May–June 1969 issue, *The Peacemaker* profiled the 23 CNCs, including several young men who would become some of the most well-known war resisters of their time: Geoffrey Mullen; the Mowbray triplets, David, Graham and Robert; Brian Ross; Stephen Townsend; and Michael Matteson. All had committed themselves by taking the initial step of advising the Minister that they would not register for National Service. Matteson and Townsend had both done this as early as January 1967, but, as we have seen in other cases, the department was often very slow to respond.

Geoff Mullen had registered for National Service in February 1967; in December, he decided not to comply with the Act. He was one of the first people to take this course of action. He twice refused to attend a medical examination, in February and again in August 1968. Having refused to pay the resulting fines, he served 16 days in jail for the first offence and 28 days

# Will Geoffrey Mullen return to gaol?

## ...or will the National Service Act be repealed?

Geoffrey Mullen has served one month in Long Bay Gaol for refusing to attend a medical examination. He was released today. He has refused to obey a call-up notice, and will be imprisoned for two years.

He believes that conscription is the first step towards a totalitarian state; it narrows — and for those conscripted — obliterates the difference between Australia and the Communist regimes that we oppose.

"While I am opposed to the Australian intervention in Vietnam, I feel that conscription and Vietnam are two separate issues; I would reject conscription even if it were not for the Vietnam war.

"I consider that non-cooperation with the Government is the only effective method of working for the repeal of the National Service Act."

As long as there is military conscription, Geoffrey Mullen and 17 other conscientious non-compliers will be imprisoned for two years, rather than comply with the National Service Act. Of the 17 in N.S.W. who have openly refused to comply, 12 have already been prosecuted.

Open Meeting Tomorrow Night
February 18th at 7.30 p.m.
119 Devonshire Street, Sydney
(over Elizabeth St., up from Central Stn.)

## TO MEET GEOFF MULLEN

AND OTHER CONSCIENTIOUS NON-COMPLIERS FROM WOLLONGONG AND SYDNEY

TO PLAN FURTHER ACTION TOWARDS SUPPORTING THESE MEN AND THEIR OBJECTIVE – THE ABOLITION OF MILITARY CONSCRIPTION

National Campaign Against Conscription aims to secure the repeal of the National Service Act
If you can assist this campaign in any way; if you want more information about it; if you want to challenge the government's right to conscript YOU, please contact us immediately:
Ian McIntyre, 63 Huntley's Point Rd, Huntley's Pt. Tel: 89-1312
Vivienne Abraham, Box 2598, G.P.O., Sydney, 2001. Tel: 929-6640

Printed by Comment Publishing Co., 22 Steam Mill Street, Sydney 2000

A poster produced by the National Campaign Against Conscription, calling for the *National Service Act* to be repealed.

for the second. Just after his release from Long Bay prison in February 1969, Mullen wrote to his member of parliament, Dan Curtin, inviting Curtin to join him and 'thousands of other Australians, young and old, in our opposition to the *National Service Act*'. He warned that, if members of the Labor Party and other parliamentarians chose to decline his invitation, and if the issues of conscription and involvement in the war were not decided in the House, 'they will be decided on the streets'.

Mullen disobeyed a call-up notice served on 2 December 1968. Incredibly, he did not appear in court until 1971, despite maintaining a public profile during that time. He stood as a candidate for the seat of Wentworth (NSW) in the 1969 federal election. During his campaign, he circulated a statement saying that, unless the government changed, he was likely to spend his 23rd and 24th birthdays in Long Bay prison. He demonstrated why this should concern not just him but everyone: 'a vote for the Liberals is an endorsement of their violent and dangerous policies.'[14]

On 22 March 1971, the Phillip Street Court was crowded to hear the magistrate sentence Mullen to two years in prison. One woman was ejected for shouting, 'Shame, shame! Hang your head in shame!' on hearing the judgement, and she was later fined $5. When asked by Anable SM if he had anything to say, Mullen responded:

> I thank you. I have often thought that I did not do enough to show that I cared about the Vietnam War. If you convict me today you will show that I do care and I thank you for that.

Anable asked whether he wanted to hear the exact wording of Section 26 of the NSA, regarding call up for service. Mullen replied:

> There is no need for that. I think that you might learn by now that I do not intend to comply with any call up notice or with the *National Service Act* in any way... This is a game. You know I will not obey any future call up notice.

Anable, nevertheless, persisted: 'Before you answer the question put to you...' Mullen interrupted:

Members of the Draft Resisters' Union meeting in Sydney, 1970. Back Row L to R: Michael Hamel-Green, Karl Armstrong, Tony Dalton, Geoff Mullen, Simon Townsend?, Peter Hornby. Front Row L to R: Mac Gudgeon, Lou Christofides, David Mowbray?, Errol Heldzingen, Robert Mowbray?

I have answered this twice. I have had five years to think about this. It has taken the Government that long to do something about it.

Finally, the magistrate advised Mullen:

The Court now formally asks you: If you will comply with the requirements of any notice that is subsequently served upon you under Section 26 of the *National Service Act*?

Mullen replied: 'As George Bernard Shaw said, "Not bloody likely"'. He was sentenced to two years in prison.

Mullen's supporters who could not enter the crowded court sat on benches outside the building. Tom Uren, the Federal Member for Reid (NSW) and Jack Page of the Draft Resisters' Union (DRU) – another militant group, formed in late 1970 – addressed them before court proceedings started. Page was later arrested for refusing to leave the vicinity of the court. Supporters staged a 48-hour vigil in the Melbourne CBD, followed by a march from Melbourne

University to the Commonwealth Government offices in Flinders Street. Police arrested nine demonstrators.

Michael Matteson's case was another example of how long it took the department to act, even after a non-complier had written to the Minister advising his intention. Matteson was born in Georgia, USA in January 1947 to an American father and an Irish Australian mother. He came to Sydney at the age of six after his father's death but retained his American citizenship after arriving in Australia. He had refused to register for the American draft at the age of 18 in 1965; in January 1967, when he turned 20 and became liable for National Service in Australia, he again refused to register.[15] A self-described anarchist, Matteson entered university to study social work. He defined anarchism as being:

> If you take the view that people should act according to conscience and accept that there is some conscience other than your own that might be right, it means you cannot force people to do anything, which leads you automatically into an anarchist position.

Peter Manning, a *Bulletin* journalist and former fellow student, described Matteson as highly intelligent and 'terribly reserved with loads of quiet assurance. He had a way of putting you on the spot in a conversation.' Manning recalled that other students worried about Matteson:

> He, like a lot of us, had been called up, but, unlike any of the people I knew, he would not seek endless deferments, enjoy university and hope that on the evil day a CO clause would provide an 'out'. He took the then unusual course of flat rejection. Refusal to register.[16]

In December 1967, almost a year after he had failed to register, Matteson wrote to the Minister, stating his reasons for his action:

> Were I to register and then plead as a conscientious objector, I would be pleading only my own case, saying...that the *National Service Act* is just, and soldiers go in this door, conscientious objectors the other. Yet I don't think the *National Service Act* is just, but because of my

special beliefs wrong for me. I think that it is wrong for everybody – that the government has the right to conscript no one. If I objected only for myself, I would be tacitly affirming that the law was 'just' (right) for others.[17]

Matteson wrote to the *Herald* with Geoff Mullen and Stephen Townsend. The letter expressed support for Bill White, who had been arrested and taken to Victoria Barracks (described in Chapter 4). A year later, on 9 December 1968, the law finally caught up with Matteson. He was convicted of remaining unregistered and fined $40 plus $17 court costs. A further five months passed before he was arrested for failure to pay his fine and sentenced to 29 days in Long Bay prison. Matteson did not regard himself as a pacifist or a CO. In both his 1967 letter to the Minister and in his statement before entering Long Bay prison for the first time in May 1969, he distinguished his beliefs from those of many other objectors and non-compliers:

> It is argued that conscription is necessary for the defence of freedom. But those who are conscripted are not free and in the final result of war, there is freedom only for the conqueror. Therefore, I support neither side in the Vietnam conflict. But Vietnam and conscription are two different issues...
>
> I do not suggest that conscription is undemocratic. There is nothing in the theory or practice of democracy that disallows the use of coercion when backed by a majority. If 90 per cent of Australians wanted conscription I would still oppose it as I would oppose a decision by 90 per cent of Germans to kill all Jews. If conscription is both legal and democratic, it is still nothing more than legal and democratic slavery.[18]

The Mowbray triplets, Graham, David and Robert, Methodists from Killara in Sydney, also hit the headlines in this period. In August 1967, each took the step of writing to the Minister, Leslie Bury, stating that he would not register for National Service. After that, their stories differ. David, who had already completed a Bachelor of Science degree, was summonsed on 9

The Mowbray triplets decided to make a stand despite not being in the ballot.

December 1968 for failing to attend a medical examination, but his trial was adjourned until 27 February 1969, pending an appeal. Graham was convicted on 20 December 1968 of remaining unregistered; he was fined $40. He failed to attend a medical examination on 19 February 1969. Robert, who also held a Bachelor of Science degree, had accepted a voluntary science teaching position in Papua (then still under Australian administration). The government refused to permit Robert to leave Australia. He was convicted on 1 October 1968 of remaining unregistered and fined $40 plus $12 court costs or 26 days' imprisonment. He failed to attend a medical examination on 8 November 1968.[19]

Apart from the newsworthy story of triplets being called up for National Service, there was added interest – the Mowbrays' birth date did not come up in the ballot. They knew this when they decided jointly to make a public stand against the draft, because a friend with the same birth date was not balloted in. By refusing to register as COs – in which they would probably have succeeded, all being Christians with pacifist beliefs – they challenged the law. Initially, rather than believing that the law should be scrapped, as most non-compliers did, they wanted it amended to enable objectors to do civil work in Vietnam. Refusal to register incurred a $100 fine and compulsory drafting into the army. Like Matteson, the Mowbrays made their stand to help all potential conscripts. The triplets acknowledged that they could 'easily have avoided all this fuss' and knew that they faced jail sentences, but they believed that they 'had to take a stand on this for the sake of every conscript.'[20]

The Mowbray brothers issued a joint statement in 1967. They wrote that peace could only be achieved by 'removing injustices, poverty, suspicions and fears.' To this end, young men and women should be encouraged to work in underdeveloped countries in civil aid projects and programmes aimed at removing injustice. They were each undertaking further university study to enable them to contribute in the fields of agriculture and social work, either in Australia or overseas. They asked the government to repeal the NSA. Their rationale was 'a strong Christian conviction in the power of love...as exemplified by Jesus Christ.' Further, they believed that: 'the Christian position is clear; Christianity rejects violence.'[21]

In separate statements, written in February 1969, each enlarged on his beliefs. These statements indicate their increasingly radical beliefs, undoubtedly influenced by events of 1968, when a revolutionary spirit swept much of the northern hemisphere.

David, then working as a part-time teacher while furthering his studies in social work, stated that all of the government's policies must be challenged:

> Whereas the revolutionary spirit is gripping creative and imaginative men [sic] throughout the world in their strivings for peace, social justice and human rights, our government continues to cling to old reactionary policies of self-interest, militarism and fear.

Graham wrote of turning the dream of peace on earth into a reality. He distinguished the difference between Christ's teaching on non-violence and the church's attitude to war and peace that 'became established as that of the world after rapprochement with the Emperor Constantine', adding: 'But the spirit of Christ is not changeable...the call is still to non-violence in all our dealings.'

Robert observed:

> The tragedy of today is that we all too often misunderstand the upheavals in developing countries. Too often we tend to identify

the cries for self-determination, social justice and opportunity with 'communist agitation'.

He believed that Vietnam was one such example. Robert demonstrated common ground with other non-compliers, even anarchists like Michael Matteson, in stating that he rejected the right of any government to conscript young men for military service: 'I believe this is an unjust law and therefore "no law at all".' In March 1969, Robert served seven days in the Metropolitan Remand Centre at Long Bay prison for 'refusing to obey a future medical examination'. *The Peacemaker*'s March–April issue reported that he was the first person in Australia to be imprisoned on this charge, which resulted from a 1968 amendment to the NSA. On his release, he was fined $54, or a further 27 days in jail, for failing to attend a previous medical examination.

Throughout 1969, resisters expressed a great urgency to change what they believed to be a morally corrupt system. On Good Friday, 15 Christians, including David Mowbray, staged a silent protest at Sydney's St. Andrew's Cathedral. They stayed seated at the back of the cathedral until Archbishop Loane was about to begin his address; then they advanced down the aisle to the steps below the pulpit, bearing placards proclaiming: 'Christians crucify Christ in Vietnam' and 'Silence is a Potent Political Weapon of Oppression'. Some of the church wardens tore up the posters and dragged one of the protesters, Paul Duncum, out of the church. The others remained on the steps. About halfway through Loane's address, two police officers arrived. The archbishop paused in his sermon and said: 'Gentlemen, there is no disturbance here. Could you please leave things as they are?' The astonished police officers withdrew. After the service, the protesters spoke with the archbishop, who refused to comment on 'controversial issues'. They were surprised by the level of support they received from some members of the congregation.

Graham Jensen, a theological student at Sydney University, sat down on the road opposite the Sydney Town Hall during the Anzac Day march. Jensen, who was already facing 25 days in jail for non-payment of a fine for refusing to register, was arrested and fined $15 for 'obstructing traffic and offensive behaviour'. In court, Jensen stated that his opposition to:

Sydney University students in Parramatta Road, March 1969.

that [Anzac] day when the glories of men fighting are stressed and Hiroshima forgotten. I am opposed to the Anzac Day that suggests to our school children the idea that by killing your neighbour you serve your country.[22]

Jensen was arrested on 30 July and taken to Long Bay prison to serve his sentence.[23]

In May 1969, Graham Mowbray served seven days in prison for refusing to enter a recognisance to attend a future medical examination, having already been fined for not attending on a previous request. Webb SM – who showed empathy with Mowbray's position but stated that he had no option but to sentence him – refused the prosecution's request for costs. Graham served the sentence in the police cells at Armidale, while studying for a university examination. He was the third Mowbray brother, and also the third person, to be convicted for refusing to agree that he would undergo a future medical examination.[24]

David Mowbray's imprisonment was delayed because he had appealed his conviction on 27 February 1969. The appeal did not come before the NSW Supreme Court until 11 February 1970, when it was rejected. As ordered, Mowbray was presenting himself at the Phillip Street Police Station on 26 February, when he was arrested. *The Peacemaker* described the following arrest in dramatic terms:

> Scene: Footpath outside the Phillip Street Police Station, Sydney.
> 
> Cast: David Mowbray, hand in hand with his girlfriend and accompanied by [family members]; a number of newsmen and two TV cameras; three plain clothes members of the NSW Police Force.
> 
> Enter Right: David and his family, crossing the road to enter the police station, are intercepted by the newsmen on the footpath outside the police station. David starts to answer questions as to why he is going to gaol for seven days for refusing to attend a medical examination, as his brothers Robert and Graham have done before him.

Enter Right: Three plain clothes police, who say excuse me to the newsmen, pull David's arms behind his back and drag him into the police station, refusing to answer any questions put to them by the newsmen and the Mowbray family as to why this treatment is necessary.

David Mowbray's father eventually succeeded in getting an interview with a senior police officer to complain of the unnecessary and unwarranted coercion used upon his son, who was 'quietly and peaceably complying with an agreed-upon arrangement to present himself to the police.' It was a public relations disaster for the police, because the two TV Channels, 2 and 10, filmed the whole event. Channel 10 showed it repeatedly.[25]

In a poem written in September 1970 to celebrate the Mowbray brothers' third anniversary of not registering for National Service, David Mowbray welcomed the prospect of 'revolution'. While still referring to himself as 'a Christian, a pacifist, an ecologist', he added that he was 'a revolutionary... within a mass movement' which, he hoped, would be 'non-violent, not violent, but this is up to you.'[26] Ultimately, it seems, the government took the easy road with the Mowbrays, granting them all complete exemption in separate cases in Sydney (Robert and David) and Armidale (Graham) in March 1971.[27]

Amendments to the National Service Regulations, gazetted on 27 August 1970, introduced a new Conscientious Objector Referral scheme. This enabled the government to force draft resisters into compliance with the Act. Under Section 32A, the Minister could direct a Registrar of National Service to 'refer the question of a person's objection on the grounds of conscience to taking part in military service to a competent court'. Non-compliers were summonsed to appear in court, to be examined as a CO, and could, even in their absence, be judged to have gained exemption.

WA Labor Senator John Wheeldon argued in parliament that, if a person did not wish to exercise his rights under the NSA for classification as a CO, and was prepared to take the consequences of that action, he should be entitled to refuse to comply. Wheeldon believed that the amendment affected the rights of the individual in several ways:

A man may be a conscientious objector within the meaning of the law of our country. He may refuse to make application under the Act. Yet for some reason or other he may find himself brought before the court and the court may find he is not a conscientious objector because in fact he has produced no evidence to establish that he is a conscientious objector, although in fact he has not claimed that he is a conscientious objector. This, in itself, is an infringement of this person's rights. The other – perhaps more substantially material – infringement of his rights would follow if this were to have the consequence that were he to change his mind, not about his conscientious objection but about his particular objection to the operation of the Act, and if he desired at some later date to make an application to be classified as a conscientious objector, the previous finding of the court that he was not a conscientious objector would prejudice any subsequent application he may make.[28]

Nevertheless, the motion to disallow the amendment was defeated, the government having a majority in both houses.

Writing in *The Peacemaker*'s May–June 1969 issue, non-complier Michael Hamel-Green challenged the government's actions as a 'façade of legitimacy'. He wrote that a person who saw a child being beaten to death wouldn't wait for approval from bystanders before rushing to the child's aid:

> [N]or should we, when half a million children have already been burned by napalm or killed outright, wait for the next election (and the next and the next) before we act. The time to resist is now – at every point that the Government requires our acquiescence or compliance. Conscientious objection and deferments are no longer morally sufficient. It has become obvious that the provisions for conscientious objection were merely a means of giving the *National Service Act* an appearance of legitimacy.

Figures released by the Minister show that, in the period between 1 January 1965 and 30 June 1969, out of 431,351 registrations: 133,686 young men had been balloted in; 44,229 had been rejected as medically or psychologically unfit for military service; and only 34,498 had been called up and enlisted in the army. Of 577 applications for total exemption so far determined, the courts granted 335 (58 percent); exempted a further 125 (22 percent) from combatant duties; and dismissed 117 (20 percent). Of 122 applications for exemption from combatant duties, the courts granted 108 (88 percent).[29] These figures did not include non-compliers, because the department did not publish figures of those who were eligible to register, only those who did register. What they do show, however, is that surprisingly few of those registering (about 25 percent) had been enlisted, and one-third of these had been rejected. The remainder were deferred either temporarily or indefinitely; had been exempted; or were awaiting either the outcome of applications for exemption, or call up. These statistics, placed in the context of the government's efforts in pursuing resisters who evidently were never going to submit to the system, and the rising tide of protest across Australia, clearly demonstrate just how inefficient the so-called democratic system of selection by means of the 'birthday ballot' was.

By the end of 1969, it was evident that many more young men were prepared to defy the system. In its November–December issue, *The Peacemaker* listed the names of 45 non-compliers who had either refused to register or, having registered, then refused to attend a medical examination, to obey a call-up notice, to attend court when charged with these offences or to pay fines. While this list was not comprehensive, it showed that non-compliance was increasing.

Non-compliers believed that those who registered and sought deferment of their National Service were not making a stand. This belief is demonstrated in letters that non-compliers sent to the Minister for Labour and National Service, copies of which were published in *The Peacemaker*. Letters from two Victorians to Billie Snedden, who was the Minister in January 1970, not only exemplify the position of some non-compliers, but also indicate that they knew and fully understood the cost of the decisions that they chose to make. Ian Turner advised Snedden that he had instructed his solicitor to withdraw his appeal against the decision of Ross SM to dismiss his application for total exemption as a CO. He had concluded that:

> A conscientious objection is not a strong enough gesture of condemnation of the foreign policy and general attitude of the

Australian government. Had my appeal been successful, the case would have been swept quietly under the carpet and I would probably have gone off and taken some secure job in industry (I hold a degree of Bachelor of Mechanical Engineering at Monash University), and thought little about the matter again.

Ian Pearce returned his registration card to the Minister, stating that he was 'a man, not a number' and that he objected to 'a totalitarian law made by a government not renowned for its liberality', which turned 20 year olds into soldiers. He believed that:

> What makes a man is his capacity to reason and choose – two qualities that the army takes away... To turn a man into a thing which kills when it is told and which bears no responsibility for its killing is a terrible wrong against Man.[30]

*The Peacemaker* continued to publish letters in a similar vein throughout 1970.[31]

While non-compliers regarded it as dodging the issue, deferment sometimes provided the space a young man needed to develop his thinking about the morality, not only of the war, but of the entire National Service scheme. Geoffrey Sandy's birthday had been in the first lottery on 10 March 1965. Sandy already had a long-standing 'personal distaste towards all things military' and felt outraged both by Australia's participation in the Vietnam War and by conscription, which he considered a 'violation of [his] liberty'. Nevertheless, the prospect of being ostracised and possibly ruining his future career was daunting. Sandy reflected that, at the beginning, he was not brave enough to make the stand of some of his peers. In 1965, after registering under the NSA, he sought and was granted temporary deferment to complete his studies at the University of Melbourne. By 1968, however, when his studies were completed, he had absorbed ideas ranging from John Stuart Mill on freedom and liberty to Jesus' teaching on responding to violence with gentleness and passivity – compounding his aversion to war and conscription. He had also been exposed to the influences of war resisters, including Vivienne Abraham's sister, Shirley, and the Reverend Terry Lane.

Lane conducted a ministry to young men who faced conscription after being balloted in. Later, Sandy experienced the exhilaration of marching in the May 1970 Moratorium in Melbourne, led by his hero, Dr Jim Cairns, whom he found a 'mesmerising' presence.

Consequently, by the time Sandy graduated with a Bachelor of Commerce and a Diploma of Education in 1968, his views had hardened into resistance. Significantly, too, protesters had grown from the isolated few in 1965 to masses in 1968. Sandy had undergone a medical, was passed fit, and had been advised that he would be called up in January 1969. He decided to apply for registration as a CO. The hearing occurred in Melbourne on 23 January 1969, with an unusual outcome. The magistrate was clearly hostile to both COs and Christians and insisted on establishing that Sandy was opposed to 'all things military' in order to avoid being conscripted as a non-combatant. When the magistrate ruled that he had not made a sufficient case, Sandy recalled:

> The room and its occupants became a blur and whirled around in my head. I felt physically sick and was thinking of what fate was to befall me. There was great fear but also a strong desire to summon the courage to do what my conscience demanded. I was prepared to go to jail.

To his great surprise, both Sandy's lawyer and the state's legal advocate remonstrated with the magistrate, stating that Sandy had proved his case. The magistrate changed his mind, and Sandy walked out of court a free man with a total exemption from military service.[32]

Increasingly, resisters employed the strategy of challenging the NSA's validity. Bruce Palling was sentenced to seven days' imprisonment at Carlton (VIC) Court on 10 August 1970 for refusing to enter into a recognisance to attend a future medical examination. The sentence was not imposed, because Palling challenged a sub-section of the NSA in the High Court. Sub-section 2 of Section 49 became notorious: it gave the prosecutor the power to request the court to:

> ask the person convicted of failing to attend a medical examination if he will enter into a recognisance to attend a future examination,

and if he does not agree, then the Court shall sentence him to imprisonment for 7 days.

Palling challenged on the basis that this sub-section was unconstitutional. A Full Bench of the High Court in Melbourne heard the submission on 13 October 1970 but reserved its decision. In Sydney's Phillip Street Court on 1 October 1970, Michael Jones' lawyer submitted that the entire Act was invalid and unconstitutional – or, at least, the penalty sections of it were. Jones' case was adjourned until 15 October, when Anable SM found the NSA, whether in its original or amended forms, to be a 'direct and true exercise by the Commonwealth Parliament of its legislative powers with respect to defence'. He refused to reveal a basis for his finding; Palling's case had not then been heard before the High Court, and so there was no legal precedent. The magistrate then adjourned the matter until 13 November, when Jones lodged an application to be registered as a CO, which was to be heard on 26 November. Anable again adjourned the prosecution until the day following the hearing.[33]

Jones's decision to change his strategy and apply to be registered as a CO doubtless invoked the criticism of hardline non-compliers and may have been regarded as weakness in the face of a potential two-year prison sentence. A more thoughtful reaction came in a letter from Law Lecturer N. S. Reaburn of the University of Tasmania, who admitted that his first reaction when reading of Jones's application was 'to laugh myself silly'. On reflection, however, he thought that 'the real tragedy of this particular instance has been its highly public nature.' It served to indicate that 'between the intention, the will and the act, there is a long, dark step.' He concluded that a decision to go to jail for two years for disobeying the NSA was personal and deserved 'to be made in the quiet of the soul, as free as possible from irrelevant pressures.'[34] Although the fear of jail had become less effective as a means of discouraging many young men from taking a stand against conscription, Chapter 9 will show that imprisonment was a humiliating and often shattering experience for those who had to endure it.

The most extreme protest against the NSA occurred on 23 August 1972, when a time bomb was left in the offices of the Department of Labour and National Service in Perth. Fortunately, no one was injured, although experts claimed that it was a very powerful bomb. Julian Ripley and Rupert Gerritsen were charged with the offence. Both men were released on bail, and the trial was set for 21 February 1973. Gerritsen failed to appear, having absconded to New Zealand, where he was later arrested. Ripley was sentenced to five years in prison, despite his repeated denial that he had anything to do with planting the bomb. He was convicted largely upon the testimony of the detective who interviewed him. Ripley claimed that he had confessed to the crime because he feared being beaten up by the police. Appearing in court after his extradition from New Zealand, Gerritsen pleaded guilty to the charge of constructing and planting the bomb and was sentenced to six years' imprisonment. Gerritsen served one year of his sentence before being paroled.[35]

By the late 1960s, three choices faced most young men of conscription age who objected to enlisting. They could comply with the Act, register and apply for exemption as a CO. They could register and then refuse to comply with any further summons – to enlist, to attend a medical or to attend court charged with failure to enlist or attend a medical. Lastly, they could refuse to comply with any aspect of the Act, usually by not registering and by writing to the Minister for Labour and National Service stating their intention to disobey the Act. These last men fell into a government category of 'those denied the benefit of the ballot'. They knew that, by taking this stance, they were liable to be convicted and sentenced to two years in prison. Once they had embarked on this road, two further choices were available. One was to go into hiding, or 'underground'; the other was to wait or present oneself for arrest. Chapters 8 and 9 describe the experiences of those who took these paths of resistance.

1970 Moratorium march in Bourke Street, Melbourne.

## CHAPTER 8
# 'Making a monkey out of the cops'

On 8 May 1970, thousands took to the streets of Australian cities to march in protest against continued military involvement in Vietnam. This demonstration and its successors on 18 to 20 September 1970 and 30 June 1971 were known as 'Moratorium marches'. While much publicity was given to the three Moratorium mass marches held across Australia, the Anti-Vietnam War Moratorium Campaign that organised them was ongoing, only suspending its activities late in 1971 after the federal government committed itself to withdrawing the bulk of Australian troops from Vietnam.

The first Moratorium was inspired by international events. Successful Moratorium rallies had taken place in cities across the USA in October 1969. November 1969 brought the revelation that US troops had massacred 500 Vietnamese civilians at My Lai in March 1968, provoking further outrage against the war. The size of the street protests and the lack of violence confounded criticisms that this was merely the communist-inspired, lunatic fringe giving vent to its opinions. Both the CPA and the ALP opposed the war and gave support to the resisters. Over 70 ALP Members of Parliament signed a statement supporting the campaign, which aimed to force the withdrawal of Australian and all other foreign troops from Vietnam and the repeal of the NSA. An estimated 70,000 marched at the largest demonstration in Melbourne. In an act of considerable courage, Labor Member of the House of

The Sydney Moratorium march, 1970.

Representatives Dr Jim Cairns, the Victorian Moratorium Committee chairman, marched in the front row. Cairns risked not only his political career, but also his personal safety, if the march turned violent. The previous year, he and his family had been brutally bashed in their home by intruders because of his anti-war stance; only one of them was tried and found guilty. Addressing the gathering in the Treasury Gardens, Cairns said that the 'sea of upturned faces' gave him 'even greater confidence in the Australian people.' He asked: 'What other issue could have produced a response like this?' After the speeches, the marchers moved, 60 abreast, down Bourke Street. Reaching the intersection with Elizabeth Street, they sat down. The roadway was covered with people for four blocks.[1]

Compared with Melbourne, the Sydney march was surprisingly small. Only about 10,000 took part. There was a heavy police presence after threats of violence, but most violence came from counter protests. John Wilson, who marched, recalled it as 'really impressive with thousands of protesters carrying candles through Kings Cross.'[2] In Brisbane, where an estimated 5,000 people marched, one counter protester, a returned serviceman, was permitted to speak. He told a silent crowd: 'You wouldn't know what it's bloody all about.' He asserted that the allies were right to be fighting in Vietnam and Cambodia.

About 1,000 people marched in Adelaide. Returned Vietnam veterans interrupted the march 20 times and seized and burnt National Liberation Front and pacifist flags. In Hobart, where about 2,000 anti-war protesters

The Sydney Moratorium march, 1970.

Adelaide Moratorium march, 1971 in Rundle Mall.

Adelaide Moratorium march, 1971 at Victoria Square.

turned out, a woman drove her car into the route of the march, but police moved her on. In Perth, where CPA and ALP members were prominent among the organisers, about 10,000 marched – a number comparable with Sydney, despite Perth's much smaller population. Sixty ANU students in Canberra protested at Parliament House, reacting to provocative comments by two federal ministers. Billie Snedden, Minister for Labour and National Service, had raised an outcry by claiming that the Moratorium campaign organisers were 'political bikies pack-raping democracy'. Billy McMahon, then Minister for External Affairs, said that protestors should 'take to heart' the fatal shooting of four students at Kent State University in the USA. This somewhat ambiguous message could have been taken as a threat; but, in 1970, Australian police were not normally armed.[3]

Usually, marchers managed to remain peaceful while suffering extreme provocation. On the day following the 18 September 1970 Moratorium march, the *Canberra Times* reported that demonstrators in Perth were pelted with eggs, lemons and water and were sprayed with fly spray, but resisted retaliating. Demonstrations in Adelaide and Sydney were marred by violent incidents. Campaign organisers reminded participants that violence merely played into the hands of the government and helped to create the kinds of stereotypes bluntly asserted by Snedden.

Other demonstrations followed the initial Moratorium march. In WA, the focus of draft resistance was the UWA campus. Among those who became non-compliers were tutor Gary Cook and students Bill Thomas, Derek Schapper, Peter Vintila, Wayne Henderson, Rene Le Miere, William Lines, Piercy Porter and Vincent Bresland.[4] On 7 August 1970, about 24 students conducted a sit-in against conscription in the National Service Registration Office on St. George's Terrace, Perth. The demonstrators chained themselves across a passageway so that no one could enter or leave the building. Some carried placards showing a child impaled on a bayonet, with the caption: 'Be conscripted. Learn a trade'. Another project, Peace Now, was organised by WA Institute of Technology lecturer Tony Watts, Judy Forsyth and the Reverend Keith Wilson (later a Minister in the Burke-led, state Labor government).

The Act was the focus of much protest. According to Mike Matteson, the NSA had only ever been an 'a-few-troops-for-foreign-wars' Act, for the purpose of winning the friendship of 'Uncle Sam'. He believed that anti-conscription strategies 'based on crippling the Act solely by mass refusal to register' were doomed to fail, because any such refusal did not actually deprive the government of troops. Further:

> The government has no need to prosecute the 11,000 offences at present untouched. They have only to keep enough prosecutions going to answer attacks that they are doing nothing; while they are seriously looking for those of us who are underground, they have issued no more warrants. The government has no need for an ideally functioning National Service scheme – all they need is a working system that gets them what they need while provoking no more opposition than they can finally ignore.

Consequently, only an entirely new strategy – 'mass refusal by people who follow it through to jail' – could defeat the government's purpose. To do this, there had to be a mass issuing of arrest warrants and 'a way to get warrants carried out'.[5] The figure of 11,000 non-compliers was based on Department of Labour and National Service returns, which were among government documents apparently leaked to the DRU. In February 1971, *Resist*, the DRU newspaper, claimed that these 'confidential documents' revealed that 11,500 non-compliers were defying the draft. *Resist* asserted:

> The files, from the national service statistics section, list the number of defaulters – as the department calls them – for the three offences of refusing to register, refusing to attend a medical examination, and refusing to obey a call-up notice… The files recently 'became available' to the Draft Resisters' Union of Victoria, which has evidence to show they are genuine. However, this must be withheld in order to avoid prosecution.

The figures published in *Resist* showed that, up to 31 December 1970, 11,233 people had refused to register for National Service since the scheme's inception. These included 1,659 who could not be traced. Only 1,007 – about 10 percent – of the remaining 8,574 had been prosecuted. In the past six months, this had dropped to around 5 percent. Despite the headline, '11,500 defy draft',

*Resist* revealed that most of the draft dodgers did not make a public stand; they simply didn't register. Much smaller numbers refused to attend medicals (400, of whom 72 had been prosecuted and convicted) or obey call-up notices (90, of whom 35 had been prosecuted and convicted). *Resist* concluded:

> The message of these files for all 20 year olds is quite clear – Don't Register. If you merely want to avoid army service, keep quiet about it. If you want to work for the abolition of conscription, tell the DRU and make your stand a public one.[6]

Matteson appears to have been correct in his assessment of government strategy. A list dated 18 April 1972 shows only 20 names across the whole of Australia for whom arrest warrants were outstanding. Of these, the oldest was for Tony Dalton, dated 18 June 1971.[7] As these chapters show, the government was often very slow to respond to overt law-breaking, even when non-compliers had warned of their intentions in advance. Even so, the strategy did appear to be working towards the end of the conscription period. Michael Hamel-Green has used official figures released during 1971 and 1972 to show that prosecutions of 'those denied the benefit of the ballot' (that is, non-compliers) rose from 12 percent in 1971 to 71 percent in 1972. He estimated that there were 2,738 non-compliers in 1971, and 1,238 in the first half of 1972.[8] These figures are, of course, well short of the DRU's 11,000.

From convincing the authorities of an individual's sincerity in not wishing to kill his fellow man, therefore, the Vietnam era anti-war activists turned to offensive tactics aimed at embarrassing the government and challenging the law's validity. For the strategy to be tested, non-compliers needed to present themselves *en masse* to be arrested. Although some did, many others did not. Instead, they went underground, defying and mocking the police by making appearances at demonstrations, as Cook, Hamel-Green and others did at the last Melbourne Moratorium march; appearing at university rallies; and giving radio and television interviews.

Gary Cook was the highest profile WA draft resister. A UWA graduate who was an Economics tutor in 1969, Cook originated from the rural community of Toodyay. He was one of the first non-compliers in WA – although he, too, initially registered for National Service and applied for deferment during his studies. In 1969, when his call up came through, Cook attended the medical examination, was found fit and was told to report to Irwin Barracks in January 1970. He chose not to comply, instead informing the Department of Labour and National Service that he was not going to attend military training. He published his decision in an article titled, 'Hell no, won't go to Vietnam' in the *Perth Independent* of 4 March 1970. Cook gained the sympathy of a wider public, possibly because he was short-haired, clean shaven and not the bearded, long-haired, hippy stereotype that many people associated with anti-war protesters; later, he grew his hair, then had it forcibly cut in Fremantle Prison (see Chapter 9).

As the previous chapter explained, the August 1970 amendments to the National Service Regulations, empowering the Minister to direct National Service registrars to refer non-compliers to the courts, meant that non-compliers could have objector status bestowed upon them in their absence from court and without their consent.[9] Cook was the first WA non-complier to be referred. He did not attend the hearing on 7 October 1970 but had prepared a statement, which his friend Derek Schapper read to the court on his behalf:

> I refuse to participate in this hearing, just as I will refuse to comply with any procedure which is part of the conscription system, a system which directly contributes to the suffering of the Vietnamese people. This hearing is an attempt by the Government to avoid having to gaol me for two years. The presence of a large number of political prisoners in our gaols is apparently not a pleasant prospect for our Government. I have not applied for CO status and I do not want to be classified as a CO within the terms of the *National Service Act*.[10]

Ansell SM found that Cook 'did not hold beliefs which prevented him from engaging in military service'. After police issued a warrant for his arrest, Cook took refuge with draft resistance groups in Melbourne and joined the DRU.

By 1971, an increasing number of young men were neither awaiting arrest nor presenting themselves for arrest, but actively resisting it by going underground. Their stories are replete with daring escapes from police officers – and none more so than during the Melbourne University Siege. Originally, non-compliers had assumed that their strategy would lead to

Poster in support of Ian Turner, Paul Fox, Tony Dalton, Michael Hamel-Green and Laurie Carmichael, 1969.

mass arrests and imprisonments, but this didn't happen. The government assumed, wrongly, that a token number of imprisonments would intimidate most young men into complying with the NSA. Increasingly aware that only about 10 percent of non-compliers were being pursued through the courts, the DRU sought new ways of drawing attention to the extent of resistance to the war and conscription.

Four underground resisters – Gary Cook, Tony Dalton, Paul Fox and Michael Hamel-Green – appeared at the third Melbourne Moratorium march on 30 June 1971, where about 5,000 demonstrators protected them from arrest. Hamel-Green recalled the atmosphere of the march:

> Joining the march from the beginning, we spoke on the speakers' platform in the middle of the Swanston-Collins Street intersection, surrounded by some 80,000 fellow protesters. At the end of the march, some 20,000 remained to escort us back to Melbourne University. With police buses crawling alongside, it was a tense march before we were back into safety. The Commonwealth Attorney-General, Senator Ivor Greenwood, later revealed in a Channel 7 TV interview that the police did indeed intend to arrest the four resisters as the march dispersed but on seeing 'thousands of people surrounding the men' decided otherwise because of the likelihood of a 'civil disturbance'. At this initial trial of the new approach, it did seem as if the resistance underground had indeed created the intended government dilemma.[11]

As resistance to the NSA hardened, the DRU encapsulated the sentiments of many draft resisters in a statement that was endorsed at the union's conference in Melbourne in September 1971:

> Conscription claims that a man's life is only a tool of the government to be used for the purpose of the government. We hold that the actual lives of men are involved in conscription, that men have a right to complete self-management in all things they are involved in, and that conscription is only a form of pseudo-democratic slavery. We assert the basic right of the individual to act according to his conscience and oppose the authority of the state to conscript for any purpose.

Four draft resisters, Gary Cook, Tony Dalton, Paul Fox and Michael Hamel-Green came out of hiding to march in Melbourne on 30 June 1971.

Conscription in practice must be seen not as a form of home-defence, which it is not, but as a necessary part of Australia's participation in the systems of Imperialism that at present control relations between all countries. Imperialism can be seen as the use of different means, from economic 'aid' to genocide, to secure economic and strategic advantage over a people, to use them as a necessary and depressed part of a system advantageous to a major power.[12]

The idea of a draft resistance commune based in the Student Union building at Melbourne University was born in the wake of the successful appearance of the four underground members at the Moratorium march in Melbourne. Plans were developed at the DRU conference. In September, five resisters – Tony Dalton, Mike Matteson, Paul Fox, Michael Hamel-Green and John Scott – announced publicly that they would come out of hiding and work with other anti-conscriptionists on a resistance campaign, based at the University of Melbourne Student Union building. The students also set up a pirate radio station, as a protest against biased reporting in the mainstream media. The Commonwealth police responded by raiding a number of houses associated with the resisters, but they were unable to make any arrests. The commune began on 27 September when four resisters entered the university with other students arriving for classes. Paul Fox had been unable to take part. Preparations for a speedy exit – if necessary – included stationing scouts around the university and obtaining a siren to warn of police. The press arrived *en masse*, attracted by news of the police raids and revelations about the pirate radio station. The resisters realised that hundreds of police could soon be invading the campus. They prepared to delay police by barricading entries to the building with chains, and by linking arms. They identified a small hiding place in the George Paton room and stocked it with food and a toilet bucket in preparation for a siege.

On the second afternoon, the pirate radio station 3DR (the initials standing for 'Draft Resistance') began broadcasting. Students located a Post Master General (PMG) van parked nearby with a jamming device to intercept 3DR's signal, and they disabled the antenna. By the third day, supporters and resisters were re-evaluating the situation. For two nights, 150 supporters had maintained a presence to deter police; but they were unsure how much longer they could endure. The resisters had organised the anti-conscription campaign freely from the Student Union, and the radio operators had been able to broadcast. Some felt that the point had been made; others wanted to continue as long as possible, because the commune was attracting more and more people each day. It became clear, however, that a major police raid was likely early the next morning. Doubts about hiding four resisters in the George Paton room led to a decision to split them up, with two to remain and the others to go into another hiding place.[13]

Tony Dalton and John Scott left during the night. Mike Matteson and Michael Hamel-Green prepared to hide in a cavity behind the wall, which they had accessed through a lighting grill in the ceiling. At 5 am on 30 September, about 150 Commonwealth police officers descended upon Melbourne University and forced their way into the Student Union building, breaching two barricades and entering the George Paton room. The barricades provided enough delay for Matteson and Hamel-Green to climb into their hiding place behind the wall. Police officers thoroughly searched the room, causing considerable damage to university property. Crouching in the confined space, hardly daring to breathe, Matteson and Hamel-Green heard a police officer ask, 'What's up there?' At that moment, a superior officer called him to remove the doors of a cupboard, and those hiding remained undetected. In an interview later, Tony Dalton stated:

> If [the police'd] gone up through the lighting grill, they'd probably have found the hole and found them. I think it was the only hiding hole that wasn't discovered in the whole operation.

When asked what kept him going while 'hiding inside all day and moving all the time from house to house', Dalton replied that it took a while to adjust, because he had been an active organiser; this was impossible while underground. He felt quite frustrated, but he was able to do more reading and was trying to complete his architecture degree. The things that kept him going were 'a moral commitment [to] opposing the *National Service Act*' and the hope that, if the government accepted the challenge of massive resistance, and large numbers went to jail, 'then we'll have a very good chance of defeating the Act'. And there remained the hope of a Labor victory in the next election.[14] All four of the Melbourne University Commune fugitives remained free, and more daring escapes occurred.

Gary Cook did not take part in the Melbourne University Commune. He had already returned to WA in August 1971 and was arrested when he appeared at a student protest rally in Perth. Demonstrators gathered outside St Mary's Cathedral, initially intending to march to the Commonwealth police offices. When Cook and Bill Thomas (who had also been in hiding) appeared with a statement of resisters' reasons for continuing to oppose the draft – despite the Gorton government's announced withdrawal of combat troops – the marchers went instead to the Department of Labour and National Service. Cook, Staples, Schapper and Thomas were arrested. While the others were released after their fines were paid, Cook was sentenced to two years in prison for his defiance of conscription laws.

During his court appearance, an unruly demonstration erupted outside. Prior to his trial, Cook urged his supporters not to wage a 'free Cook campaign', because he felt it would detract from the anti-conscription campaign. In doing so, he encouraged a departure from established tactics of anti-conscription groups when their members were jailed. His words fell on deaf ears, however. Indeed, given the mood of the crowd, he must have known that no one would take any notice. About 50 supporters accompanied Cook to court, marching with him from Speakers Corner on the Perth Esplanade. They packed the court and began whistling and clapping when Cook appeared at the front of the court. He incited them by walking up to the bench and sitting in the magistrate's chair. Two court attendants lifted him out of the chair and placed him on the floor. The crowd hissed and whistled when Bateman SM entered court. Cook interjected several times during proceedings and was eventually removed from court. When he returned, Cook stated that the penal sections of the NSA were being applied selectively. He claimed that at least 12,000 people had committed offences under the Act, but 'only 9 or 10 percent of these had been prosecuted.'

Cook was asked whether he was prepared to enter into a recognisance that he would comply with the provisions of the Act. When he answered that he would not, Bateman sentenced him to two years in prison. Supporters attempted to block the exits and snatch Cook from the police guard. The police brought in decoy vehicles, but the crowd refused to leave the exits. Cook was finally removed via a Beaufort Street exit. Someone threw an orange smoke bomb at the vehicle as it drove away. The explosion burnt a police inspector's hand. About 10 people climbed onto the car, trying to force it to stop. The driver accelerated and then braked sharply several times to dislodge them; but, as some fell off, more climbed on. The car travelled several blocks before it was finally cleared of all the demonstrators. The crowd marched back to the court and attempted to take over the building, but police held them off. Six people were arrested and charged with disorderly conduct by creating a disturbance and using insulting or obscene language. One 17 year old was charged with aggravated assault.[15]

Those underground members who remained free continued to risk arrest by making public appearances. During Sydney University's Orientation Week in 1972, Mike Matteson appeared on the battlements of the main building with a loud hailer and addressed a large crowd of students. Journalist Peter Galvin reported that 'extraordinary and effective measures' prevented plainclothes police from entering the building and arresting him. These included a DRU member acting as decoy while Matteson made his escape – despite Commonwealth police cars guarding all entrances to the university and officers with 'high-powered binoculars and walkie-talkies' patrolling the roof of the University Motel across Parramatta Road from the campus.[16]

On 24 April 1972, two Commonwealth police officers, Constables Boyle and Veitch, jumped into a car that was waiting at the traffic lights in Parramatta Road, outside Sydney University, and handcuffed themselves to the backseat passenger. The quick-thinking driver, Jim Couch, turned immediately into the university campus. The passenger began shouting, 'Help! Draft resister! I'm Mike Matteson. The police have got me!' and 'Sanctuary!'. Fortunately for him, students nearby acted quickly, surrounding the car as it stopped. Students used the public address system in the adjacent Fisher Library to call for help. Within 10 minutes, up to 1,000 students had gathered, preventing the police from leaving with their prisoner. Someone, somehow, procured a pair of bolt cutters and freed Matteson, who quickly disappeared into the crowd. The police officers departed the campus, the handcuffs still dangling from Boyle's wrist.[17] Twice, Matteson had avoided arrest by the determination of the students to foil the police. In parliament, the Attorney-General, Senator Greenwood, faced embarrassing questions from his own party about the extent to which the University of Sydney was 'co-operating' with police in revealing the identities of the students who released Matteson.[18]

The DRM and the DRU made political use of their underground members. Wayne Henderson featured in a dramatic appearance when he was whisked onto campus at a UWA anti-conscription rally. He arrived riding pillion on a motorbike, jumped off and was shown briefly to the masses before jumping back on the bike and roaring off again. Thomas was similarly 'exhibited'. Filmed by ABC TV, Thomas (disguised in sunglasses) also arrived on the back of a motorbike in front of a huge crowd outside the Reid Library at UWA. 'Bodyguards', carrying walkie-talkies, surrounded him. One bystander carried bolt croppers, reminiscent of Michael Matteson's dramatic escape at Sydney University.[19]

Despite the glamour of such escapades, life underground could be anything but glamorous. Matteson spent 14 months on the run, going into hiding in September 1971 when police issued a warrant for his arrest. While underground, he spoke at Sydney and Melbourne Universities and was interviewed on TV's *This Day Tonight* programme and on ABC radio.[20] In May 1972, a few weeks after his much-publicised escape from the handcuffs of the Commonwealth police, Matteson told *Bulletin* journalist Peter Samuel: 'Yes, I'm tense. I'm tense all the time now. After about three nights in one place I can't sleep. I have nightmares about prison.' He had not seen his mother or sisters for eight months. Police kept a constant watch on his home and followed family members when they left the house.[21]

In Perth, Wayne Henderson's family experienced similar surveillance. Henderson recalled that it was 'pretty scary'. He was always aware of the impact of his decisions on others, trying to avoid causing trouble for family and friends who gave him shelter. The police parked outside his parents' house for weeks at a time, forcing him to climb over the back fence. On the lighter side, sometimes they parked outside the wrong house, and he walked straight past them without being recognised.

Bill Thomas went underground when he was called up, following his release from Fremantle Prison. The Ship Painters' and Dockers' Union Secretary, Paddy Troy, offered him a job, and he worked under a false name. Thomas was sure that the police would have found him 'if they really wanted to' but 'they had Gary Cook in jail and that served the purpose.' He continued his studies

'Making a monkey out of the cops'

Michael Matteson, 1971. He was underground for 14 months before voluntarily surrendering to police. Front cover of the last edition of *The Peacemaker*.

The University of Western Australia was the site of many anti-Vietnam War demonstrations in Perth in the 1960s and 1970s. Winthrop Hall (above), where students sat their end-of-year examinations was the scene of Bill Thomas' daring escape from police in November, 1972. (Below). The Great Court outside the Reid Library, where both Bill Thomas and Wayne Henderson made brief, dramatic appearances in front of crowds of students before being whisked off to safety on motor bikes.

as an external student, using Gary Cook's parents' home in Toodyay as his contact address. Despite the risk of being arrested, in November 1972, he attended the end of year examination at UWA and completed his paper. Another student, David Parker (later Deputy Premier in the Dowding-led, state Labor government), tipped him off that two plain clothed Commonwealth police officers were waiting at the exit to arrest him as he left the examination room. Thomas escaped through a small door next to the pipe organ, which led out onto the roof. From there, he dropped to the ground and eluded the police. Thomas later reflected that 'the cops had the good grace to wait until the exam was finished'. They were perfectly entitled to march into the examination and arrest him. He felt, though, that the officers' zeal was tempered by their knowledge that the anticipated change of government on 5 December would result in the release of all imprisoned objectors and an end to the compulsory National Service scheme.[22]

Ian Davies, convenor of the Sydney DRU, was also avoiding arrest because he couldn't see any 'political effect to be gained by being jailed'. Like Thomas, he was able to continue his studies with the help of 'sympathetic lecturers' who passed material on to him so that he didn't need to attend lectures. Davies said that he would remain active, despite the risk of being arrested. Both Davies and Thomas were in better situations than Matteson, whose public appearances had almost cost him his freedom on several occasions. He was no longer able to study or work and admitted to doing 'precious little' most of the time.[23]

Matteson was still free when he made a statement on 8 November 1972 that he would court arrest. Three draft resisters who had 'undergone various forms of selective prosecution' would accompany him: Peter Gunning had refused to obey a call-up notice five months previously and hadn't yet been prosecuted; Sandy Thomas was also liable for prosecution for refusing to undergo a medical examination; and Graeme Jensen had served 25 days in Long Bay prison in August 1969 for refusing a medical, but had not been prosecuted since.[24] Matteson returned to his family home. His mother phoned police to advise that he wished to surrender, and police arrested him on 9 November. Despite his voluntary surrender, police pinioned his arms and hustled him into a police car. In court that afternoon, he was sentenced to 18 months with hard labour for refusing to comply with the NSA. On 17 November, Matteson was sentenced to another 18 months in prison for resisting arrest at Sydney University, to be served concurrently with the previous sentence.[25] In the ultimate irony for police, Matteson was one of eight prisoners released by the incoming Labor government on 6 December 1972. After being on the run for 14 months, he had spent less than a month in prison.

Throughout 1972, the police continued to issue warrants for some non-compliers and ignore others. One of the former was Malcolm Vick, an Adelaide teacher and Methodist lay preacher who failed to appear in court on 14 July. Supporters distributed circulars bearing his statement of reasons for objecting to the NSA. 'I have been waiting two years for this to happen,' he said:

> A man does not go to gaol for 18 months for fun and needless to say I am not looking forward to it. But I also believe the *National Service Act* is worth resisting, even if the consequences of this action can be fairly drastic.[26]

Another non-complier to fall foul of the NSA in 1972, Mike Payne, had already appeared twice in Perth courts before he was fined $40 for failing to register. He had been fined $20 for obstructing a Commonwealth Officer during the blockade of the National Service Office in 1970 (Chapter 7) and had escaped with a caution for 'disorderly conduct' during another protest the following year. On 29 September 1972, he was convicted and sentenced to seven days in prison for failing to register. He was also fined $50 for attempting to escape legal custody. Payne recalled:

> I tried to enliven the proceedings by, seeing the girth of the officer in charge of me, making a break from captivity – alas, I slipped on loose gravel and was recaptured within minutes. I remember I quoted from Max Stirner that the 'violence of the individual against society is called crime while the violence of society against the individual was called law'. He did not really get it, I think, and he obviously thought me odd.

The following month, Payne was hit with another $50 fine for carrying an offensive weapon, a smoke flare that he planned to use in a demonstration later that day. Finally, he was convicted of failing to register and given an

18-month prison sentence; amendments to the law had reduced two-year sentences to 18 months. He was one of the prisoners pardoned when the ALP was elected to government.[27]

The day after the ALP won the federal election on 5 December 1972, breaking a 23-year period in opposition, *The West Australian* interviewed four WA non-compliers – David Finkelstein, Peter Rattigan, Bill Thomas and Renee Le Miere – about their experiences of resisting the draft. All said that they had led 'normal lives' (unlike Matteson and some others). Le Miere believed that the former government did not want too many in jail 'for political reasons'. He said that the police thought that jailing one or two resisters would frighten the rest into complying: 'Towards the end, many young people were simply not registering because they knew they could break the law with relative immunity.' Rattigan was arrested and taken to the lock-up four days before the election, charged with failing to enlist and ordered to appear in court. Prior to this, he had been living a normal life at his family's home in Claremont for a year without being arrested.[28] In April 1972, the WA Police Commissioner, Mr Wedd, had instructed his officers that executing warrants against draft resisters was a federal police responsibility.[29] This does not explain why federal officers did not arrest those non-compliers, such as Thomas and Rattigan, who were living openly in the community. The next chapter discusses the experiences of those who were arrested and sentenced to months or years in a civil prison.

Protesters outside Long Bay Prison, NSW, where
Lou Christofides spent 51 days in 1970.

## CHAPTER 9
# 'A stinking, rotten hole'

Civilian prisons such as Long Bay, Goulburn and Fremantle, like military prisons, used solitary confinement on bread and water as a punishment; but objectors feared more intensely the psychological effects of being the victims of petty violence and discrimination by prison guards and the possibly of attacks from their fellow inmates. Michael Matteson expected to be 'destroyed' by his jail experience, and he was certainly changed by it. Sentenced in May 1969 to 30 days in Long Bay, he determined that he would defend himself 'with a brick or a club but not a knife' if assaulted in the prison. He admitted that he was 'shaking' as he entered the prison to serve his first sentence; yet, he became so appalled by the treatment of prisoners that, on release after his second term – seven days in Long Bay in October 1970 – he used his high public profile to bring attention to jail conditions.[1]

Not all objectors endured brutal treatment. At the opposite end of the scale from Matteson's treatment was Gordon Reisenleiter's experience. A Jehovah's Witness, sentenced to two years in Townsville's Stuart Prison for refusing to agree to obey a future call-up notice, Reisenleiter received much more humane treatment and was anxious not to become 'a political pawn'. Malcolm Dickson, a Sydney teacher who visited Reisenleiter in prison in January 1969, reported to *The Peacemaker*: 'He appears to be quite well cared for by his friends and relatives and is treated well by the prison authorities.' Reisenleiter

Protester spraying a graffiti message on the wall of Long Bay Jail where Lou Christofides was imprisoned.

was employed in gardens outside the prison compound, was permitted to write one letter a week and received 'unlimited' inward mail. He was allowed five visitors per week. Dickson wrote:

> He seems content to accept the two-year sentence as God's will, and has pledged himself to spread God's work in gaol .... Being a Jehovah's Witness, he does not recognise the *National Service Act* and was anxious that I should not involve his name in any political campaign or in any newspaper.[2]

Despite his humane treatment, however, Reisenleiter was paying the price of his liberty for the sake of his beliefs. On 23 December 1969, Senator Jim Keeffe (ALP) had organised a 24-hour silent vigil outside the Commonwealth Government offices in Townsville, to remind everyone who opposed the Vietnam War in silence 'that one person is suffering while the city enjoys Christmas.' Reisenleiter was released on 27 February 1970, having served 15 months of his two-year sentence. After his release, he said that he had received about 200 Christmas cards from Australia, Britain, Germany, the USA and Canada. He reiterated that he had been 'treated very kindly' and that he would do the same thing again if he was forced to. Prison had not changed his beliefs that killing was wrong.[3]

John Zarb, who was jailed on 14 October 1968, had the option of choosing his prison. He elected to serve his two-year sentence in Pentridge, where he had his own cell and could participate in 'educational and debating' activities. Zarb was studying for Matriculation in Humanities, prior to beginning an Arts course at university. He was released on 28 August 1969 on compassionate grounds, having served almost 11 months of his sentence.[4]

It seemed that even being jailed in the same prison could yield quite different experiences. Michael Hamel-Green's time in Pentridge was quite unlike Zarb's. Hamel-Green served his first sentence, seven days, in September 1969 for refusing to attend a medical examination. He was also fined $40 and costs. Like many other resisters, Hamel-Green feared the prospect of prison: 'physical threats, even the risk of rape (a friend who had been in gaol told me how this had happened to him).' He recalled the humiliations of imprisonment:

As we stood, naked, in a line, the warder said, 'Bend over and spread your cheeks' and proceeded down the line to inspect us one by one. Next, we were made to shower with a group of warders lewdly looking on.

In C-Division, one of the oldest sections of Pentridge, where cells contained nothing but a 'bed and a bucket...the rituals of humiliation and degradation had begun' for Hamel-Green. And yet, a strange thing happened to him:

Whatever the hardships ahead, I remember thinking I had already had a small victory. One less instrument for making war, a particularly indefensible war. I was behind the bluestone walls but, oddly, as I lay on my bunk, I felt freer than ever. The harpoon barb was no longer lodged in me. I had cut the line.[5]

Frances Newell, who was engaged to Hamel-Green, also served several short prison terms for refusing to pay fines resulting from her anti-war protests. She recalled feeling 'powerless and humiliated' by the experience.[6]

In October 1969, Peter Hornby in NSW and Brian Ross, a farmer from Orbost in Victoria, had become the first non-compliers to receive a two-year jail sentence. Hornby did not appear in court but had a statement read out on his behalf. He wrote that, in going to jail, he was following his conscience:

It is wrong to allow young men to be conscripted for military service, to be trained to kill under orders, and to be sent to fight in Vietnam.

Ross, who was convicted and sentenced in the Orbost Court on 29 October 1969, similarly wrote:

Can the state ask people to kill, let alone tell them to kill? And can it ask them to die, let alone tell them to die? To whom does life belong? And to whom does an individual's mind and body belong?[7]

After six weeks in Sale Prison, Ross wrote a rather bemused letter about the unreality of life in jail, which was published in *The Peacemaker*'s

Brian Ross (left) and Peter Hornby (right) were the first non-compliers to receive a 2-year prison sentence.

November–December 1969 issue. He did not mention his treatment, except in passing references – it was hard to watch a lightning storm through '1in. thick glass and bars'; the difficulty of getting used to being locked up; and he referred to prison as 'a stinking, rotten hole'. Ross was able to reflect philosophically on how he might view his jail sentence in the future, unsure whether he would be 'disappointed about the wasted time' or 'glad that I have had the experience'.

In contrast to Reisenleiter's generous allowance of five visitors per week, Ross was permitted visitors only once per fortnight. Just before Christmas 1969, he requested a visit from three members of the ALP, because he was an active member of his local branch. The visit was arranged, but when Dr Jim Cairns, Frank Crean and another ALP member arrived at the prison on 18 December, they were denied entry. *The Peacemaker* did not make the connection, but this may have been because a group of Ross's supporters had demonstrated outside the prison a few days earlier and daubed white paint on the walls.[8]

Ross was released from prison on 21 September 1970, after serving 11 months of his two-year sentence. The circumstances of his release were exceptional. Ten months after his imprisonment, the Minister decided that there should be an inquiry to ascertain whether Ross was a CO to all forms of military service. In order to circumvent the legal provisions, the Attorney-General appointed a Supreme Court judge from the ACT, Mr Smithers, to conduct an inquiry. Ross agreed to participate, and the inquiry was held in an open court at Sale on 24 August. Ross immediately asserted that he was a non-complier, not a CO. He made a statement in court that read like a creed:

> I believe that I can better serve mankind than by killing.
>
> I believe that I can better serve mankind by resisting laws and governments which force me to kill.
>
> I believe that I can better serve mankind by resisting our wrong and cruel invasion of Vietnam and our equally wrong reasons for it.

Ross added that this inquiry was 'serving the interests of the government' and the Act, but was not in his interests, nor those of his cause. He believed that the NSA was 'not being administered, which is the first step towards its repeal.' He refused to answer any questions, beyond reiterating that his course was 'complete non-compliance'. Smithers persevered and later had two private interviews with Ross.[9]

The Governor-General exercised his prerogative of mercy on Smithers' recommendation. Despite Ross reiterating that he was not a CO, Smithers stated that Ross had conscientious beliefs that prevented him from rendering any type of military service. He got no thanks from Ross, who appeared on TV the following day to state that he was a non-complier, not a CO, and that he had never applied for exemption as a CO. Ross said that the NSA would be repealed only when there were large numbers willing to go to jail rather than comply.[10] Ross's constant refusal to take what some may have regarded as the easy way out, especially after having experienced almost a year in prison, illustrates the strength of his resolve. By this late stage, apparently, both government and legal authorities were finally beginning to realise that the young men who determined to take a non-compliant stand would not be swayed by either inducements or prison. This didn't stop magistrates from continuing to sentence non-compliers to prison during the last two years of Australia's involvement in the Vietnam War.

Brian Childs, another non-complier, served 26 days in prison in NSW for refusing to pay a $40 fine. On 20 April 1969, he wrote to Vivienne Abraham that, after a depressing few hours when he arrived in prison, during which he was shorn of his hair and beard, he'd had 'a restful and thoughtful few days'. He was able to read Erich Fromm's *The Sane Society*, which had strongly influenced his thinking. Childs wrote that he was 'treated very well' and that he had 'fitted in quite well with everyone and made some good friends'. He was allowed several visitors at one time. Despite his relatively positive experience, however, he acknowledged that a longer jail term would be harder to endure. He concluded the letter: 'I may as well finish by saying "having a wonderful time; wish you were here".' This optimistic letter was written early in in his jail term. The experience may have soured before he was released, but he was still prepared to risk another term in prison.

After his release, Childs continued to refuse to cooperate. He strongly objected to being referred as a CO, after repeatedly ignoring call-up and medical examination notices and summons to court during 1971. He was arrested on 15 May 1972 and appeared in court on 5 June, where he was granted an adjournment to seek legal advice. He insisted that the only change to his beliefs had been his desire not to go to jail for two years. He wrote that, although he considered himself 'a CO under the meaning of the Act', his revulsion at the Act's 'practical and theoretical meanings' stopped him from opting out by seeking exemption. A hearing to determine whether Childs had a conscientious belief was further delayed; on 15 December 1972, the Deputy Crown Solicitor informed his solicitors, F. W. Jenkins and Co. (Abraham's employers), that the Minister did not wish to proceed with the matter.[11] The change of government on 5 December meant that, along with many other young men, Childs was now free of his obligation under the NSA.

The Minister released figures on 21 April 1970 showing that, in the six months between 1 September 1969 and 28 February 1970, courts had heard 122 cases of failure to register for National Service, resulting in 117 convictions and five dismissed cases. A further 42 cases were listed for hearing. All 10 cases of failure to register for a medical examination had resulted in convictions, and 20 cases were listed for hearing. The one case of failure to obey a call-up notice had also been convicted.[12] These 195 cases were of young men who had either been non-compliers from the time they became liable to register under the NSA or who had adopted a stance of non-compliance after registering. Yet, incredibly, the Minister claimed in parliament in June 1970 that 'fewer than 100 men have failed to report for service since the inception of the scheme in 1965' and that, of 17,000 called up since June 1968, only four had been imprisoned. 'Four gaoled out of 17,000?' ran *The Peacemaker* editor's incredulous footnote:

> Or should it be one out of 15 openly refusing to obey callup notices, now the three who failed to gain total exemption as COs have been released?

Snedden delivered these figures in parliament during a speech in which he claimed that it was impossible to devise a scheme of civilian service that would be 'equitable' and 'practical' compared with army service. He announced further amendments to the NSA. Non-compliers were to be referred to the courts as COs, whether or not they applied for exemption. From September 1970, the birth dates drawn in ballots would be published.[13] These changes indicate that the protesters were making an impact on government policy.

The government didn't want the prisons filled with non-compliers, as the case of Charles Martin in SA shows. Martin's story illustrates a change in the strategy of dissidents; amendments to the laws affecting them; and the department's rethinking of its attitude to non-compliers. Martin had originally complied with the NSA. He registered for National Service in 1966, was balloted in, but was granted a deferment until the end of 1969 to complete his studies. He received a call-up notice for 29 January 1970, by which time he had decided that he could no longer comply with the Act. Summonsed to court on 25 September, charged with failing to obey a call-up notice, Martin complied by attending court. He pleaded guilty and was fined $200. After refusing to enter into a recognisance that he would obey a future call up, Martin was sentenced to two years and was sent to Yatala Prison. Following his imprisonment, the department advised that he could still avoid a jail sentence by either reporting for national service or applying to be registered as a CO. Martin refused both options. In a statement that he prepared prior to imprisonment, he wrote:

Our involvement in Vietnam is the latest manifestation of a persistent trait of Fascism in our society, expressed in racism...obsession with law and order, unquestioning acceptance of authority, a strong belief in the Protestant Ethic (i.e. 'success' and 'wealth' are a sign of goodness), [and] an interpretation of freedom as meaning freedom to exploit. Since compliance with the *National Service Act* is validation of such principles and perpetuates such attitudes I have refused to obey my call-up notice.[14]

Martin continued to refuse any 'deal' whereby the Liberal government – now led by Billy McMahon – would release him from prison. He informed the McMahon administration that he would not ask it or any other Liberal government 'for an early release in any circumstances.' Martin was released on 8 October 1971, in line with the South Australian practice of remitting one-third of the sentence for good conduct. During his imprisonment, parliament passed an amendment to Section 51 of the NSA, shortening sentences for breaches of the Act from two years to 18 months. This meant that the remaining prisoners, Geoff Mullen and Gary Cook, had their two-year sentences shortened to 18 months.[15]

Despite his spirited response to the magistrate during his trial (see Chapter 7), Mullen's third imprisonment, commencing on 22 March 1971, was a wretched experience, starting with his handling by police officers before he left court.[16] Two witnesses, Pat Drummond and Peter Galvin, saw Mullen being brought out to the police vehicle for transportation to Long Bay. They testified that he appeared 'dishevelled', his face was 'severely reddened' and looked as if he had been struck 'with a padded object'. At Long Bay, Mullen was confined to his cell for a weekend after refusing to salute on parade. Then he was taken to Berrima Training Centre, where prisoners were permitted to study. Mullen had completed a university degree in computer science but wanted to undertake postgraduate studies in Arts, so he was trying to arrange a Bachelor of Letters course by extension from the University of New England (Armidale). He had not been at Berrima long, however, before the authorities again transferred him, this time to Newnes Afforestation Camp near Lithgow. They claimed that this move was necessary because they feared demonstrations outside the jail. Mullen was allowed to receive letters and visitors but could write only one letter a week.

This was not the end of Mullen's shifting from prison to prison. His case came up in the NSW State Parliament on 28 September 1971, when the Minister for Justice, John Maddison, was forced to justify Mullen's transfer to five different jails in six months. Maddison claimed that Mullen's removal from Newnes was because 'he [Mullen] was unable to relate in proper ways with the other inmates.' While Maddison wasn't clear what he meant by 'proper ways', he admitted that Mullen was likely to be 'subjected to violence from the other inmates'. He blamed Mullen for this, stating:

> Unhappily, he does not conform with the reasonable and relaxed conditions in which we have tried to place him. This is most unfortunate for him.

This accusation is at odds with Mullen's reactions to his situation, expressed in letters to his mother, of which extracts were published in *The National Times* of 7–12 June 1971. He wrote that transferring from Long Bay to Berrima was like being in heaven after 'a brief visit to hell'. He also found the 'crims' very friendly and interesting. But his mother admitted to being worried; although she could visit him regularly, they were always in the company of a third person, and she did not know how he 'really' felt. He did, however, mention 'culture shock' and 'misery' in relation to his experience. It was likely that Geoff and his mother were each putting on a brave face out of consideration for the other. He also had to be careful what he wrote, because every letter was censored. Mullen was moved in November 1971 to his sixth prison at Emu Plains, where he remained until his release.

Throughout his imprisonment, Mullen corresponded with Vivienne Abraham, but he resented her overzealousness in trying to organise his affairs – including speaking on his behalf. If anyone should do this, he reiterated several times, it would be his mother. In his final letter from prison, dated 20 January 1972, he admitted to sometimes being a 'ferocious' critic of Abraham, and he hoped that there remained 'no ill-will to divide us'. Prisoners who criticised their conditions risked their letters being confiscated – and, indeed, it appears that this happened to two letters Mullen wrote to his mother – but in his last letter to Abraham, he couldn't resist one parting dig:

I'm carefully husbanding all my bile and venom for my release (16th Feb) when I will have a few choice words to say about the prison system.

Whatever the 'choice words' Mullen had, they do not appear to have been reported in the mainstream press. *The Peacemaker* had ceased publication at the end of 1971, thus closing off an alternative avenue of reporting on the words and actions of 'draft dodgers'. Along with Mike Matteson, Charles Martin and Ian Davies, Mullen spoke at an anti-conscription forum during Sydney University's Orientation Week on 1 March. Perhaps he spoke of his prison experiences on that occasion. He may have repeated his earlier advice to a non-complier: 'I wouldn't blame anyone who didn't follow it right through'.

Gary Cook had spent some months underground in Victoria before returning to WA and being arrested (see Chapter 8). When Cook was sentenced to two years in prison on 27 August 1971, he was sent initially to Wooroloo Training Centre in the Perth hills. While at Wooroloo, he was beaten up by other prisoners and lost two front teeth. In February 1972, following his refusal to have a haircut, he was transferred to Fremantle Prison, handcuffed to a chair and shorn of his 'frizzy locks'. In March 1972, he was granted leave to study one day a week at UWA, but this was withdrawn after Cook refused to scrub the floor of his cell. Cook's brother, Peter, complained that he was being punished twice for the same offence, because he had already spent time in solitary confinement.[17]

Possibly the reason for withdrawing Cook's study leave was political, rather than punitive. On 12 April 1972, WA Labor Senator Hartley Cant addressed the Australian Senate on Cook's situation. He accused the Attorney-General, Liberal Senator Ivor Greenwood, of 'a most disgraceful performance by a Minister of the Crown in Western Australia'. Greenwood had complained on television that, in allowing Cook one day's study leave per week, the prison officers had not acted in accordance with the law. Cant disagreed, arguing that there was a standard practice for granting study leave; Cook had to apply for it, like any other prisoner. Not only had Greenwood lacked 'the common decency' to await a reply from Claude Stubbs, the Minister in charge of prisons in the state Labor government, before making a public statement; he had not even advised the Minister that he would be discussing the matter on the

TV programme *Today Tonight*. Cant accused Greenwood of trying to make political capital out of Cook's treatment, 'but I can assure him that he gained no mileage in Western Australia from the way this matter was handled.' Cant said that he had spoken to many Western Australians and found that 'they were completely disgusted' by Greenwood's attitude. He further accused Greenwood of using Cook's case to attack the WA state Labor government and 'draw attention away from the problems of the Liberal Party.' Cant added that, since the change of government in WA in 1971, the Tonkin Labor administration had amended the Regulations concerning granting 'leave of absence of certain prisoners' for their 'welfare or the welfare of the family unit.' He challenged Greenwood:

> or any other legal man in this place to argue that the words 'for his welfare' would not include study leave, or would not include the release of a prisoner to complete his studies or to continue his studies at a university?

Cook had not been given special treatment, Cant argued. He was one of 25 inmates in WA prisons who had been granted study leave to attend courses. The Director of the Corrections Department and the Minister in the State Government were responsible for granting prisoners leave. It was not the responsibility of the federal Attorney-General. In the light of Senator Greenwood's performance, Cant suggested, 'The Prime Minister (Mr. McMahon)...should reconsider [his] appointment [as Attorney-General].'[18]

Despite Cant's stout defence, Cook appeared before a magistrate on 14 April charged with a breach of discipline, and his permission to attend lectures was withdrawn.[19] A further controversy erupted in July, when the Guild of Undergraduates employed Cook as an assistant research officer to undertake a survey of student needs, initially for three months, with the prospect of permanency. He was granted daily leave from the prison to perform his duties. In parliament, the Minister, Claude Stubbs, was forced to justify Cook's appointment (made on the basis of his Economics qualifications) and to deny that it was made 'at the behest of the Labor Party.'[20] Jim McGinty, the Guild of Undergraduates President, also had to justify Cook's appointment. While acknowledging that there were many unemployed graduates, he said that

Cook's experience in statistics and economics made him the best qualified of those who had applied for the position.[21] The constant scrutiny that the federal Coalition government and the state Liberal opposition gave to Cook is particularly odd, considering that others charged with the same offences against the NSA remained underground, free to pursue their studies or work (see Chapter 8), while Cook served his sentence. The most logical conclusion for this scrutiny is that it was political. To mention those still free would be to draw attention to the federal Government's incompetence or inactivity in arresting a growing number of non-compliers.

Cook's sentence, reduced to 18 months, was mostly served in Fremantle Prison. A towering, convict-built edifice dating from the 1850s, it was nearing the end of its life as a prison. Another non-complier, Bill Thomas, described it as '19th century maximum security'. Thomas had a taste of Fremantle Prison when he was given a seven-day sentence early in 1972 for refusing to enter into a recognisance that he would attend a medical examination. He was shocked to discover that Indigenous Australians made up roughly half the prison population. He recalled his boredom in being locked in a cell with one other inmate for 16 hours a day, and his disgust at the primitive conditions:

> In the morning, you'd come down to breakfast, bring your shit bucket [which served as a toilet for two men], collect breakfast, go back to the cell and eat breakfast. Then you had to place your knife and fork in view of the warder, so he'd unlock the door. You'd come out, be marched down to the yard. Marched off to work at 10am. It was supposed to be hard labour. The work was chopping wood. There was a break for lunch by 11am. You'd take the shit bucket up to cell, with your lunch. Eat lunch. Back down to the yard. There would have been 200 guys in the yard at the woodheap, and only one or two axes. You'd look forward to your time on the axe.

By the time Thomas arrived, Cook had served about six months of his sentence. They spent much of their time together in the wood yard, awaiting their turn with the axe. Thomas recalled that 'Gary Cook took it really hard. The treatment was brutal. I was there only seven days. He was there for 18 months.' Thomas avoided an 18-month sentence by going underground until

An ABC news team surrounds Gary Cook (front, left) as he leaves UWA with his welfare officer. Cook's employment by the Student Guild as a researcher, while serving an 18-month sentence in Fremantle Prison, brought bitter criticism from Senator Ivor Greenwood and others in the Federal Coalition government.

the ALP gained government on 5 December 1972 and immediately released all of the imprisoned resisters. He admitted that the police probably knew of his whereabouts but did not arrest him.[22]

Mike Payne served a portion of his 18-month sentence in Fremantle, then at Karnet Prison Farm, south of Perth. He was pardoned and released in December 1972. His description of Fremantle was similar to Thomas': old, overcrowded and tense. At times, three inmates shared a small cell – and the toilet bucket. Although he did not personally experience the 'major worries' that some inmates spoke of (such as rape or beatings), Payne met a fellow prisoner in the yard 'who claimed to be an hermaphrodite and to be the victim of, and fearful of, sexual attack'. Payne was once put in solitary confinement for refusing to call a prison officer 'sir'. In solitary, there was 'a bucket...a mattress on the floor and a Holy Bible. I got to read the Song of Solomon and the Book of Job'. In comparison to Fremantle, life at Karnet was 'fairly laid back'. Payne worked mostly in the pumpkin fields, 'was well fed and slept soundly'; but he was aware of potential violence and sometimes felt that his 'welfare was being watched [over]'. He attributed his safety, at least in part, to the state Labor government and to the prospect of a federal Labor victory – the latter a reason that Thomas gave for the police not arresting him while he was underground. Yet, nothing Payne experienced in prison changed his 'growing Kropotkinite conviction of prisons as protection mechanisms for unjust property divisions and as universities of crime.'[23]

Under a punitive, rather than reformative, system, prison is not meant to be an enjoyable experience. Non-compliers were not classed as political prisoners, so their experiences were the same as those of inmates convicted of violent crimes. It appears that the government aimed to frighten young men into complying with the law, through applying to register as COs or obeying court rulings if their applications were unsuccessful. Despite the humiliation, boredom and, at times, violence experienced in prison, this strategy clearly failed.

The draft officially ended on 6 December 1972, when the new Deputy Prime Minister, Lance Barnard, abolished conscription. Of the remaining National Servicemen serving in the army, 7,000 were to be released by Christmas; the other 3,000 would be demobilised by the beginning of March. All charges against draft resisters were dropped, and the non-compliers who were still serving jail sentences were released within days of the election victory. They were: Mike Matteson and Michael Kocan (both in NSW); Ken McLelland, Ian Turner and Bob Scates (VIC); Robert Martin (SA) and Gary Cook and Mike Payne (WA). Of these, Cook had been imprisoned the longest, having served since 27 August 1971.[24]

The last serving troops departed from Vietnam in December 1972, and the Governor-General issued a proclamation on 11 January 1973, formally declaring an end to the Australian involvement in the war.[25] For Australians, after a decade of division and dissent, the war was finally over.

# Responses to being a dissident

## CHAPTER 10
# 'It made me a left-wing activist for life'

Inevitably, a study of this nature invites many questions. How many objectors and draft resisters were there? What difference did opposition to conscription make? How much were individual dissidents affected by the stance they took, and its consequences? Did their experiences impact on life outcomes, such as their paid employment, charity work or other causes that they became involved in? Official figures have been difficult to obtain. There was no breakdown for each state. As Chapter 2 mentioned, the official total of men who applied for exemption from the 1951-59 National Service scheme was 3,679, while 227,000 had been trained. With regard to the 1965-72 National Service scheme, Senator Wright (the Minister representing the Minister for Labour and National Service) supplied some figures in response to a question from Senator Lawrence Wilkinson (Labor, WA) on 22 February 1971. Up to 31 December 1970, 46,838 National Servicemen had been enlisted in the army; 567 applications had been granted total exemption as COs; and 293 had been exempted from combat duties. There were still 282 applications awaiting determination. These figures indicate that, up to end of 1970, 1,142 men had applied for either total or partial exemption, not including those whose applications had been dismissed.

Senator Wright told parliament that he was unable to provide numbers of non-compliers. Nor was he able to state how many men had been prosecuted by the department for failing to comply with the NSA. Yet, each state was required to send returns to Canberra, initially every six months, later monthly, containing details of 'defaulters' as well as those who registered, enlisted, were deferred or were exempted. As Chapter 8 discussed, Hamel-Green estimated that there were 2,738 non-compliers in 1971 and 1,238 in the first half of 1972. The DRU newspaper, *Resist*, claimed that 11,500 non-compliers were defying the draft. On page 2 of the same issue, *Resist* published a document, reputedly from the Department of Labour and National Service, listing the numbers of 'defaulters' in each state from the commencement of National Service in 1965 until 31 December 1970. I will discuss these further in relation to my own research.[1]

In researching this book, I assembled the names of 530 dissidents and details of their experiences either as COs, who complied with the NSA, or CNCs, who refused to comply (See Appendix 2). Only 16 in my sample applied for exemption just from combat status. It is unknown how many of the 293 in Senator Wright's figures were ordered to perform non-combatant duties when they had applied for total exemption. At least 29 in my sample were thus ordered, after having either applied for total exemption or refused to comply with the NSA.

The sample is indicative of changing methods of dissent. In the later period, more dissidents sought to defy the law, rather than complying with it. CNCs were in the majority (283 of the sample, compared with 227 COs). Some CNCs began by complying with the Act – registering and applying either for a deferment, in order to complete their studies, or to be exempted from military service – and then changed their position to non-compliance. Others were non-compliers from the beginning, advising the Minister for Labour and National Service of their intent.

The very small number (16) in the sample who applied for exemption from combatant duties only contrasts with the 1950s, where about 20 percent of the sample (Appendix 1) were in this category. Some who applied for total exemption were National Servicemen who, having enlisted and commenced training, decided that they could not continue. All these applicants were ultimately successful, with several being ruled medically unfit by the army. Only one (Stead) completed his training, and this was because he decided not to continue with an appeal after the dismissal of his initial application for exemption. In similar cases to his, National Servicemen had either won an appeal or succeeded with a second application for exemption as a CO.

Another major difference between the dissidents in the 1950s and in the 1960s–70s National Service schemes was the number who served prison sentences in civilian prisons. Whereas seven (less than 3 percent) in the 1950s sample were incarcerated, and all were in military detention in Holsworthy or another correctional establishment, most of the 61 prisoners (11.5 percent) in the 1960s–70s sample served their one or more terms in civil jails. These sentences ranged from one day, in lieu of a fine, to two years (later shortened to 18 months). As their stories illustrate, treatment varied enormously from prison to prison. At least eight in the sample also spent time underground, which was not a characteristic of dissent in the 1950s. Lastly, most of the objectors in the first sample belonged to the Christian faith; many in the second sample denied having any religious motive for their opposition to conscription or the Vietnam War. Consequently, I have not included religious belief in the second sample.

In summary, given the limitations of Senator Wright's figures, it is not possible to make direct comparisons with either Hamel-Green's figures or mine. For example, of the 227 applications for total exemption in my sample, only 154 were granted total exemption (including those who appealed a magistrate's decision). This represents less than 68 per cent of applications, but it is less than one-quarter of the number that Wright claimed had been given total exemption up to the end of 1970. Three others in the sample were exempted on referral against their wishes. Hamel-Green's figures indicate that there were 4,076 non-compliers in the 18-month period from January 1971 to mid-1972. My sample of 283 CNCs represents 6.9 percent of that figure, but it represents a longer time frame. Further, as mentioned previously, the DRU claimed that the police were ignoring 11,000 prosecutions. According to the Department of Labour and National Service list published in *Resist*, investigations were proceeding against 10,164 'defaulters' at the end of 1970: 1,007 had been prosecuted and convicted; 62 prosecutions were 'pending'; 52 had been dismissed; and 54 were withdrawn. The department was 'unable to trace' 1,659 'defaulters'. Of the 1,007 who had been convicted, almost half (422) were in Victoria; 174 in SA; 155 in Tasmania; 104 in Queensland; 78 in WA and 74 in NSW. The Tasmanian and NSW figures are particularly surprising, given the difference in population in those two states.[2] In my sample, the combined totals of COs and CNCs were: NSW 145; Victoria 228; Queensland 26; SA 31; WA 64; Tasmania 15; and ACT 15.

A Commonwealth police list dated 18 April 1972 states that warrants were outstanding for only 20 non-compliers. This seems to bear out the DRU's criticism that the authorities were reluctant to prosecute anything like the actual number of offenders, although Hamel-Green suggests that the rise in prosecutions from 1971 to 1972 indicates that Commonwealth police were taking action against non-compliers. Yet, even when the government sought an easy way out by declaring some CNCs COs without their acquiescence ('on referral'), these numbers were very small – only six in my sample. One thing that is evident is that the proportion of the population who resisted conscription was much greater during the Vietnam War period than in the 1950s, despite the much smaller number recruited for the armed services (46,838, compared with 227,000). Undoubtedly, much of this resistance came from Australia's involvement in the war and from the unprecedented use of conscripts as active servicemen in a battle zone.

In assessing the impact of anti-war protest in the 1950s, 1960s and 1970s, it is necessary to take a long-term view. Despite the differences between the Vietnam draft resisters and their predecessors, it is possible to trace a common heritage among all COs and war resisters of the 20th century. They stood up for their principles when those principles were not merely unpopular but completely untenable to a majority. In wartime, objectors were accused of cowardice and of conspiring with the enemy; in peacetime, they were despised as being 'soft' and 'unmanly' because they did not relish military training. Their sacrifices and heroism went unrecognised by a society wedded to the notion that 'sacrifice' and 'heroism' necessarily involved active service overseas, fighting wars that were sometimes only marginally strategic for Australia.

COs had formed small but significant minorities in both World Wars and in the period of National Service examined in Chapters 1 and 2. After World War II, objectors were better prepared to resist when necessary, because of their experiences during the war. The movements that formed or re-formed in the 1950s, in opposition to National Service and to the nuclear arms race, introduced a new generation to concepts of civil rights and what that meant in connection with a citizen's duty. The groundwork was laid for establishing a philosophy of the right of the individual versus the right of the state. By the late 1960s and early 1970s, Australian scholars such as D. H. Monro and Glen Withers were concluding, respectively, that conscription was an unjustifiable abuse of civil liberties, and that conscription is unjust when it is unnecessary (as, arguably, it was in the 1960s, when Australia was not threatened with invasion by a hostile power).[3]

Ultimately, dissidents won the victory initially sought by the Australian Freedom League in 1912: no Australian has been conscripted for military service since 1972. Amendments to the *Defence Act* in 1992 provide for the recognition of 'selective conscientious objection' to particular conflicts and require prior parliamentary approval before conscription can be introduced. Conscription in wartime now also requires the approval of both Houses of Federal Parliament.[4]

Those dissidents who stayed true to their principles believed that they had achieved something. Michael Hyde, a student protester and later a teacher, who 'invested 15 years' of his life in the anti-war movement, believed: 'we did actually help stop the war in Vietnam. We also got people to look at the issue of US bases and how these things are interconnected'. Melbourne University graduate Garrie Hutchinson, who became a media adviser to Bob Hawke, reflected that he:

> would not like to say the Australia we have now is the result of what the anti-war movement did then, but we would not have the Australia we have if it had not happened.

He acknowledged that, as in previous wars, the social divisions continued in the Vietnam War's aftermath. Once, returned servicemen had been the heroes; those who, for whatever reason, did not serve were despised and regarded as having shirked their duty. Post-Vietnam, Hutchinson believed:

> If you didn't go to war, the experience had a positive, liberating effect... If you went to the war, the whole period had a traumatic result. The tragic thing is that a lot of kids went because they didn't think they had a choice.[5]

That may have been the case in the early post-Vietnam War years. More recently, the 'Anzac cult' and, in the 1980s, the 'defence of the digger' have risen in popularity and become again entrenched in society. Opinions remain divided on whether Australia should have been involved in the Vietnam War, and this is reflected in the responses of those surveyed for this book. Geoffrey Sandy believed that the Vietnam War was as divisive as the conscription plebiscites in 1916 and 1917: 'the divisiveness has not healed for many of my generation.' While having 'the greatest respect' for those who 'believed in the rightness of the cause and served in Vietnam', he felt 'less sympathy' towards those 'who blindly accepted whatever the government or military told them to do, or used their family's wealth and influence to avoid call-up.'[6] Others mentioned that they don't discuss their views on the Vietnam War; one stated that 'talking to strangers about my Nasho experience has led me to the belief that it is best to keep quiet about my views.'[7] This reticence indicates that revealing his opinion about the war continues to draw criticism from some quarters – even half a century after the event.

The impact that being a dissident had upon the later lives of individuals, therefore, depended upon many factors. Just a few examples are given here out of the thousands who protested; nevertheless, they show that individual resistance to the *status quo* was not confined to the dissidents' Vietnam War years, nor primarily motivated by self-preservation. A resister's chances of coming through the experience without suffering serious emotional trauma were influenced by support from family, friends and groups. Imprisonment, discrimination, public criticism, exposure to injustice in the courts and prison conditions sometimes changed the direction of later life.

In an era so often characterised by folk singer Bob Dylan's divisive warning to parents, 'don't criticise what you can't understand' because 'your sons and your daughters are beyond your command', many parents supported their sons in court, even when they disagreed with their views. Apart from the mothers who joined Save Our Sons, evidence of parental support emerges as a strong theme in many of the stories of objectors and non-compliers. Bill White's parents supported their son throughout his ordeal, including accepting the protesters who covered their front fence with placards, camped on their front veranda and, presumably, used their facilities. Parents not only appeared in court as witnesses for the sincerity of their sons' beliefs but also pleaded their case with various parliamentarians and wrote to the press expressing disappointment, disgust and anger with the way their sons were treated. The parents of both Leonard Truscott and Frank Tuting expressed their appreciation privately to Vivienne Abraham or publicly to *The Peacemaker* for assisting their sons' stand. They lobbied members of the Federal Cabinet and other influential people. 'Has my son to spend time in gaol to prove his sincerity?' Ronald Tuting wrote to Attorney-General Nigel Bowen. He pointed out that Leonard:

> spends so much of his time in study while other lads roam the streets in mobs...yet for a reward is told that he must engage in something which, as his evidence clearly explains, would cause offence to his God, or else spend time in gaol.[8]

On 16 June 1971, the Melbourne *Herald* published a letter from the Reverend John Graf, whose son, Peter, had been 'unexpectedly transferred from his bed at night to the amenities of Her Majesty's prison'. Graf pointed out that his son was a registered alien and that he could have been:

> *passively* registered by the Government for national service as is done in overseas countries, thereby removing the – to conscientious non-compliers – odious obligation of *active* registration which implies, to them, unacceptable recognition of the Government's right to conscript them.[9]

Gary Cook's father, William Cook, wrote to *The West Australian* complaining about the 'selective nature of National Service' and Senator Greenwood's 'relentless campaign' against his son.[10] Tony Pointon's parents supported him when he sought exemption as a CO. His father and cousins accompanied him to court in 1971. Although his father had been a member of the British Commonwealth Occupation Force in post-war Japan, he taught Tony 'that war was wrong'.[11] Paul McKeich's parents, siblings and friends accompanied him to court, and his parents testified on his behalf.[12]

Some parents were less proactive but still supported their sons. John Wilson remembered that his parents respected his decision and didn't try

Rowan Cahill with his future wife, Pam Dick, c. 1968. She supported him in court, testifying, "He is the most honest person I know".

to persuade him to obey his call up. Family members suffered because of his resistance:

> Mum found it very difficult going into Biloela because people would cross the street to avoid meeting up with her. In a small rural community, this sort of behaviour doesn't get forgotten or forgiven easily… My older brother took some flack at the local football club and my father stopped going to the pub because it became very uncomfortable for him. It was about 20 years later that my uncles Ken and Col and my cousin Franny told me they were proud of what I did.[13]

Parents, siblings and friends visited dissidents in prison. Gary Cook's parents and siblings regularly visited him in Fremantle Prison. David

'It made me a left-wing activist for life' 201

Michael Hamel-Green and Frances Newell at her 21st birthday party at the Melbourne University Bistro, 7 October 1969. Both endured stretches in prison for their principles.

Mowbray's family accompanied him to the Phillip Street Police Station in Sydney when he presented himself for arrest after a court order, having refused to pay his fine. His father complained about the police officers' rough handling of his son, who had merely stopped to answer questions from reporters outside the police station (Chapter 7). Douglas Dawson's friends were very supportive, despite 'not always agreeing' with his stance. Fiancées and girlfriends offered support, too, as in the cases of Rowan Cahill, Bill White and David Mowbray. Cahill's fiancée testified in his CO hearing in court: 'He is the most honest person I have ever met.'[14] Bill White's fiancée, Clare Seale, and his mother visited him in Victoria Barracks. Michael Hamel-Green's fiancée, Frances Newell, was a co-protester, appearing in the Melbourne City Court in March 1969, charged with distributing illegal material on the streets of Melbourne (Chapter 7). Michael and Frances both served short terms in prison. They were married while Michael was underground, and both resorted to wearing disguises so that they could meet in secret.¹⁵

Not all families and friends were so supportive. Chapter 5 noted that Bernard Cannon held a scholarship to train as a teacher, which bonded him to the NSW Education Department for several years after he graduated as a teacher. When he refused to register in 1968, his father informed the Education Department, who advised Cannon that he would lose his scholarship if he didn't register; his bondsmen, who had stood financial guarantors for him, would be financially liable. He was forced to register, because he had no funds with which to reimburse them.

Upon returning to the United Kingdom for a while in the mid-1970s, Mike Payne discovered how deeply his father disliked the actions he had taken:

> He was very disappointed. That was very hard as it was pretty well impossible to explain to him how my actions had been, in my eyes at least, honourable. His position had been that I had known of the Australian involvement in Vietnam before I left the U.K. and therefore should not have acted as I had done when I got here. I felt that I had left the old country for personal reasons, not in order to become a rat-bag, but that wrong was wrong and evil was evil and, if seen in that way, should be opposed without compromise... My mother would always say that she maintained that a dead hero never helped anyone. Increasingly the fact that we never bridged these communication/ philosophical divides is a real hurt.

Peter Webb's parents were 'appalled' at his objection to being conscripted. Although Webb didn't attend street demonstrations, he applied for exemption in 1968 because he believed 'that the objection needed to be publicly registered.' When his birthdate wasn't drawn, his parents showed obvious relief, without saying so:

> They didn't want me to associate myself with 'left-wing trouble-makers'. They were middle-class, religious, and unable to see those prosecuting the war as 'right-wing trouble-makers'. I never suffered the social rejection some of my friends did.

Although Ken Beale's immediate family accepted his decision, one particular cousin was quite hostile to him. Beale was confused when even some members of the church he had attended appeared to support violence and gave him 'a hard time' about his discharge. He was cut dead in the street by a man whom he knew and respected. When he went back home to WA, he was 'in a void'. He didn't think that non-violence was the answer. Beale's girlfriend had an uncle who was a Jehovah's Witness. He started attending Bible studies and discussed Jesus' attitude to war. In 1971, he joined the Witnesses, who provided the answers he had been seeking. Although the Witnesses claimed not to be pacifists, basing their attitude to war on the Old Testament, none was involved in military or police service in modern times. Beale had never heard of any Witnesses entering military service.

Ian Marshall was a pacifist from WA who applied for exemption but was ruled medically unfit as an asthma sufferer prior to the hearing. He experienced prejudice from senior staff in his workplace who were former army or reserve personnel. He believed that his stance as a CO affected his promotion because 'they always mentioned the objection in interviews for promotion.' While 'most friends understood', some of his fellow workers treated him 'like a leper'.

Keith Headland, a railway man from Victoria who was a non-complier and had joined the DRU, similarly experienced discrimination:

> I had a host of experiences, too many to write [about]. They tried [to] set me up to sack me, said that I would not pass my examinations for [locomotive] driver, all deflected by the union and men who supported me. I am the black sheep of the family that are still alive. Lost friends [were] more than made up [for] by some of the blokes from the job I didn't know previously who sought me out to congratulate me for standing on my principles.

Paul McKeich also experienced discrimination. Some of his fellow soldiers called him a 'communist' and a 'coward' when they heard that he was applying for exemption, and similar epithets were cast in the civilian world. When he returned to his position in the Department of Labour and National Service, he applied for the promotion that was due to him as a university graduate. He was told that he had 'missed out on a promotion opportunity because I had been away doing my national service'. He knew that this was illegal, so he appealed successfully to the Public Service Board and received his promotion.[16] He reflected that, in everyday life since being exempted as CO:

> I have never talked much about this chapter of my life. I am very careful of the company I am in as to what I say to whom. Most men today who were called up and went to Vietnam still talk about it (some positively, some negatively). I rarely mention I was called up and on the very rare occasion I have told someone I was a CO, I don't recall ever getting a positive or supportive response.[17]

There is an enduring myth that soldiers who served in Vietnam were denied victory parades, spurned and treated badly on their homecoming,[18] yet little has been written of the ongoing trauma experienced by those who stood up against the war. Geoff Sandy (Melbourne), who was among the first young men to be balloted in 1965, wrote:

> There is no doubt that the Vietnamese war has affected me greatly throughout my life. It has taken me fifty years to get to the position where I could write this personal story. It has taken all this time before I could cope with reading once again the horrors of that immoral war which was perpetrated in my name.
>
> The first time I attended a performance of the musical *Miss Saigon* during the 1990s, I was so overcome with emotion that I could not speak during the interval. I know I am a sucker for a tragic love story but the emotional impact was much more than this. It triggered feelings and experiences from the 1960s about the war and conscription and the tremendous struggle I had with my conscience.[19]

For those who spent time in either civil or military prisons, the experience could be overwhelming and traumatic, especially when the sentence was several months or even years. Rowan Cahill, also among the first to be balloted, later wrote of the lasting impact that confinement in prison had upon some dissidents:

For some, the incarceration changed them forever, having the effect of Post-traumatic Stress. One prominent activist who served the full two years...could never stay in a confined space for any length of time in later life. It was a brutal penal time in many ways, replete with bashings by warders, and before the NSW prison system in particular was reformed following Justice Nagle's Royal Commission into New South Wales Prisons, 1976–78.[20]

Peter Cook reflected that the impact of the prison experience on his brother Gary must have been profound. He could only speculate, however, because Gary never spoke about it afterwards. 'Even good friends that he made later in life were completely unaware of his stance on conscription or his period of imprisonment.'[21] Bill Thomas, who served briefly with him in Fremantle Prison, recalled that Cook 'took it really hard'. Cook passed away in 2019. In his obituary, his brother and sister wrote that, after his release from prison, despite his exceptional academic ability, 'Gary did not seek a high-flying career.' Instead, employed in 'low-level jobs', he devoted his life to study, obtaining several more university degrees:

> Gary's path was one of uncompromising commitment to truth and moral principle. It was a moralism, in the best sense of that word, born of beliefs in anti-authoritarianism, autonomy and sympathy for the underdog.[22]

This understanding of Cook's character helps to explain his motivation for opposing conscription and – perhaps even more – the reason for his return from relative security in Melbourne to present himself at a demonstration in Perth, where he must have known that he would be arrested. Another respondent to my survey, who spent several weeks in prison, testified to the powerful impact of his experience as a war resister when he wrote: 'I hope you understand that it has brought back a lot of memories for me, some "flashbacks" traumatic – others unpleasant.'

When asked, 'how did your stand affect your later life?', Mike Payne, who spent time in Fremantle and Karnak prisons, reflected thoughtfully:

> How can a person say? As time went by, I remained pleased with the stand I had made against things like militarism, the Vietnam war and conscription. I also became rather ashamed of some of the things I had supported such as authoritarian third world governments and parties. I do not beat myself up about it too much – I was after all young, naïve, and working from honest motives. It was a particularly horrible, disgusting war in a century that had seen a lot of them. Still in a way I feel that I am lucky to have lived in a period when there was a real hope of change, when people could read a book and let it change their lives (until the next book). All to no effect in the end perhaps but it was good to have been there and participated in a small way. And who knows how bad things might have got if no one had protested?

But, on a less positive note:

> I never regained any trust in society. Vietnam – and the other military interventions since then – seem to me to have shown an ugly underbelly to the world I live in. I have worked at jobs like agricultural labourer, gardener and cleaner. I think the Vietnam War had an enormous effect on my life – my actions in response to it much less.

David Bisset expressed a similar reaction when stating that his experience as a non-complier gave him 'a profound disrespect for most human societies (particularly that Western society that claimed my allegiance)' because they were based on 'aggression, violence, greed, deception and hypocrisy'. He did maintain a respect for 'scientific, technological and cultural achievements', believing that 'worthwhile change' could be brought about through cooperation. Another respondent believed that Labor being elected to government in December 1972 made war resistance a 'non-issue': 'With the passage of time it has simply become an issue of mild curiosity (to most, but not all).'

In later life, many dissidents worked to reform society in various ways, often through activism, politics, entering the caring professions or charity work. Ken Beale joined the Jehovah's Witnesses and spent 30 years of his working life in the caring professions, including working for Aboriginal communities and in mental health. Paul McKeich joined the Christian ministry, serving as a pastor in various churches in Australia and New Zealand. Peter Webb later became a Quaker, having been brought up as 'loosely Methodist'. He has maintained a pacifist stance throughout his life, although he continues to question his motives in seeking exemption from military service. He wondered whether his 'conscientious objection [was] based on fear alone' or an objection to conscription. Adrian Walker, who was a Quaker before he was called up for the 1950s National Service scheme and who was granted total exemption, believed that his stance reinforced his view 'that war is so needless'. Since making his stand as a CO, he had sometimes experienced prejudice, but he had always stood for his beliefs.

John Wilson entered the nursing profession, moved from Queensland to Tasmania and became an activist in the gay and environmental movements. He was arrested while protesting in the Tarkine wilderness and at Mother Cummings Peak, but police later dropped the charges. Wilson also stood as a Greens candidate in several elections. Keith Headland wrote that the experience made him 'a left-wing activist for life'. He represented his union, the Australian Federated Union of Locomotive Employees (AFULE) at Divisional Council level. Rowan Cahill similarly reflected on the massive change in himself:

> Being conscripted in 1965 changed everything. The rebel in me challenged the system, and as that was a minority position to take at the time, I found solidarity with those who viewed things similarly. And so it was that I moved significantly to the left, and stayed there throughout my life, developing in the process significant leadership, public speaking, writing, publishing, organising skills. The would-be poet and the aspirational solo sailor became instead an enemy of the state, and confirmed as such when ASIO opened its file on me in 1967.

Mike Payne continued his involvement with anarchist and peace groups, including the Indian Ocean Peace Coalition that opposed US warships visiting Fremantle. Increasingly, these protests included environmental actions 'as it began to look as though the main war was the one by capitalism against the biosphere'. In the early 21st century, in Albany, Payne organised protests against Australia's military involvement in Afghanistan and Iraq. Tony Pointon also felt that his stand as an objector politicised him. Afterwards, he was involved in several green and pacifist ventures, including a housing cooperative and the Peace Fleet, a fleet of yachts owned by people who opposed the US Navy ship visits to Fremantle. As a student at Murdoch University in the 1980s, Pointon was arrested during a protest against a road being built through the Murdoch wetlands. Stephen Meredith, a Tasmanian Quaker who was granted total exemption from military service on the grounds of conscientious objection in 1970, believed that his experience of campaigning against the war in sit-ins and street marches made him 'more committed to social justice issues' than he might otherwise have been.

Some dissidents, appalled by the prison experiences that they or their friends had endured, including violence by warders, sought prison reform. Michael Matteson had already voiced his abhorrence of the system when being interviewed during his period underground. Bill Thomas was appalled by the high number of Indigenous prisoners in the Fremantle Prison population. Rowan Cahill, while not having first-hand experience of prison, was shocked by stories of brutality in Long Bay prison in NSW. Later, while teaching in a 'soft educational unit of the NSW prison system', Cahill found that many prisoners:

> were afraid, correctly or not, of both the Long Bay and Goulburn jails, cultures and environments they variously associated with homosexual rape, inmate brutalities, abnormalities like human faeces in servings of prison food, even the odd, unexplained suicide.[23]

Others, such as Michael Hamel-Green, sought to improve society through academic careers or by entering politics. Bill Thomas, who represented the ALP in the WA Legislative Assembly for 15 years (1986–2001), strongly believed that the action in Vietnam constituted a war crime but spoke of reconciliation between Vietnam veterans and anti-war dissidents as a positive sign, healing some of the divisions in society. Thomas travelled to Vietnam with Graham Edwards, a Vietnam veteran and a Labor member of the Legislative Council. He obtained funding for a men's retreat at Woodman Point, which the Vietnam Veterans' Association organised to help former servicemen struggling with issues of domestic violence. Funerals, too, have brought together groups that were once totally opposed to each other. Vietnam veterans were present at

the funerals of Gary Cook and Chuck Bonzas (a veteran who later became a 'peacenik' and protested against the US warship visits).
Sympathy for soldiers is also evident in Ken Beale's comments. He reflected on the lack of concern about how war experience affected soldiers:

> There is no thought about how those soldiers with the guns will feel after the battle when they become an individual again.

What bothered me was that National Service in Australia in the 1960s and 1970s was for the purpose of sending inexperienced 20-year-old rookies to Vietnam. I did not know much of the history of Vietnam but I felt very uneasy about the reports that were coming from Vietnam in the early years of the war. We were expected to go to a country and deal with a people and a culture vastly different from ours. We were not familiar with the culture. We were not familiar with the customs. The climate and the country's topography contained threats we were not prepared for. It was like Gallipoli all over again. It was a badly thought out political situation. It was not something that Australia should be involved in.[24]

In the light of revelations in 2020 about the actions of some Special Air Service (SAS) troops serving in the war in Afghanistan, this reflection remains tragically relevant.

Has the influence of the rebellious Vietnam generation extended into the 21st century? I believe that it has. Challenging the status quo is perhaps the greatest legacy that the Vietnam War generation has bequeathed to its successors. There were objections to the National Service scheme of the 1950s and, indeed, to military conscription before and during two World Wars; but protest during the Vietnam War was appreciably different. It evolved from the individual's ethical objection to military service – usually based on Christian teachings against killing one's fellow human beings – to a questioning, not merely of the government's right to conscript its citizens for military service, but also of Australia's involvement in overseas wars and of the morality of particular wars. Rather than complying with the NSA through seeking exemption, dissidents challenged its legality and sought to have it rescinded. For the first time in history, large numbers of Australians wilfully disobeyed the law. In doing so, they forged a generation of people who were prepared to take to the streets to voice their dissent in far larger numbers than ever before, not merely in lawful protests, but in unlawful actions such as sit-ins. Street protest is far from dead. Successors to the anti-Vietnam War protests extend from those of the feminist and Aboriginal and Torres Strait Islander movements, through the campaigns against Australian involvement in wars in Iraq and Afghanistan, to the Occupy protests and, more recently, the Climate Change actions. All of these involve young people, including those of school age.[25] Taking to the streets educated protesters in methods of dissent and removed the fear of arrest and imprisonment. The anti-Vietnam War campaigns not only radicalised a generation but also passed on a legacy of protest that is strongly evident today.

## APPENDIX 1
# Sample of 258 Objectors and non-compliers, 1951–59

This list comprises 258 objectors who applied for full or partial exemption from military service in 1951–59. They represent 7 percent of the official figure of 3,679 applicants. The information is from official government figures, *The Peacemaker*, mainstream and alternative press from around Australia, and survey responses and interviews collected between 1996 and 2021.

**ABBREVIATIONS**

**Religions**

| | |
|---|---|
| Breth. | Brethren |
| CA | Christian Assembly |
| Christad. | Christadelphian |
| CI | Christian Israelite |
| JW | Jehovah's Witness |
| ND | Non-denominational Christian |
| SDA | Seventh Day Adventist |

Column 2 gives demographic details, where known. These may include religion, age (in parentheses), occupation, town and state.

Column 3 gives details of court appearances, where known. These may include the name of the magistrate, the court, town and state, and the date of the hearing.

| | |
|---|---|
| CPS | Court of Petty Sessions |
| J | Judge |
| Mag. Crt | Magistrates' Court |
| NSA | National Service Act 1951 |

| | |
|---|---|
| PM | Police magistrate |
| RM | Resident Magistrate |
| SM | Stipendiary Magistrate |
| Appl. TE | Applied for total exemption from any form of military service |
| Appl. ECD | Applied for exemption from combat duties |

Column 4 gives the outcome of the application.

| | |
|---|---|
| Order NCD | Ordered to perform non-combatant duties. |
| Med. Corps | Medical Corps |

Column 5 includes details of any appeal and resultant sentence and other details where known. These may include the name of the judge, the court, town and state, date of hearing and outcome.

| | |
|---|---|
| J | Judge |
| Dist. Crt | District Court |
| Qtr. Sess. | Quarter Sessions |
| Order Med. Corps | Ordered to serve in Medical Corps |

Appendix 1    213

**SUMMARY**

| Total in sample | 258 |
|---|---|
| **State** | |
| ACT | 3 |
| NSW | 78 |
| Queensland | 81 |
| SA | 22 |
| Tasmania | 10 |
| Victoria | 18 |
| WA | 44 |
| Unknown | 2 |
| **Religion** | |
| Brethren | 8 |
| Christadelphian | 34 |
| Christian Assembly and other sects | 16 |
| Christian Israelites | 4 |
| Jehovah's Witnesses | 69 |
| Mainstream Christians (Anglican, Methodist, etc) | 6 |
| Non-denominational Christian | 29 |
| Quaker | 7 |
| Seventh Day Adventists | 53 |
| Unknown | 27 |
| No religion | 1 |

| **Total exemption** | |
|---|---|
| Applications | 198 |
| Granted | 81 |
| Ordered to perform non-combatant duties | 59 |
| Dismissed | 52 |
| Outcome unknown | 6 |

| **Non combatant duties** | |
|---|---|
| Applications | 56 |
| Granted | 52 |
| Dismissed | 4 |
| | |
| Non-compliers | 5 |
| Committed to Holsworthy Military Correctional Establishment | 18 |

| Name | Details | Court Appearance | Outcome | Appeal/Sentence |
|---|---|---|---|---|
| Abell, Frederick Thomas | Christian Mackay Qld | Appl. TE Baker SM CPS Mackay 22/4/54 | Granted | |
| Anderson, Kenneth Brian | SDA Wee Waa NSW | Appl. TE Ward SM Police Crt Narrabri 9/4/53 | Order NCD Appealed | Storkey J Qtr. Sess. 14/7/53 Appeal dismissed |
| Anderson, Ronald | CI SA | Appl. TE Adelaide Mag. Crt 1954 | Dismissed | Sent to Holsworthy In military hospital May 1954 |
| Arblaster, Cyril Harold | CI (19) Motor mechanic Cessnock NSW | Appl. TE C.H. Blackmore SM Maitland 28/4/53 | Dismissed Appealed | O'Sullivan J Maitland Dist. Crt 29/10/53 Appeal upheld |
| Aussel, James Bernard | Christian (22) Fitter & machinist Griffith ACT | Appl. TE R.A. McKillop SM Canberra Date unknown | Order NCD | |
| Bailey, Warren William | SDA WA | Appl. ECD Taylor RM Court details unknown Perth 10/10/53 | Granted | |
| Barlow, Stanley | Unnamed Christian sect (18) Yeppoon Qld | Appl. TE N.F. Applin SM CPS Rockhampton 20/2/53 | Dismissed Appealed | Sheehy J Brisbane 21/6/53 Decision reserved |
| Barrett, Phillip Martin | JW (19) Bulimba Qld | McKenna SM Brisbane 18/1/52 | Granted | |
| Barrie, Geoffrey Phillip | Christad. Newcastle NSW | Appl. TE Court details unknown 1953 | Dismissed Appealed | Unknown |
| Batterham, Alan | SDA Kelmscott WA | Appl. ECD Wallwork SM Perth Police Crt 20/2/1953 | Granted | |
| Beaven, Lawrence Alexander | JW Singleton NSW | Appl. TE Court details unknown | Dismissed | Amsberg J Newcastle Dist. Crt 27/10/53 Order Med. Corps |

Appendix 1    215

| Name | Details | Court Appearance | Outcome | Appeal/Sentence |
|---|---|---|---|---|
| Beck, John Victor | CA (18) Pine faller Mt Gambier SA | Appl. TE D.C. Williams SM Mount Gambier Police Crt July 1954 | Granted | |
| Beel, Geoffrey John | Methodist VIC | Appl. TE Court details unknown | Order NCD Appealed | Read J Melbourne 2/10/53 Appeal upheld |
| Bennett, Stanley Robert | JW (18) Colac VIC | Appl. TE Court details unknown 21/11/54 | Granted | |
| Berry, Peter Edward | Christian (19) Uni Student Eastwood NSW | Appl, TE Meagher SM Court details unknown Sept. 1952 | Order NCD Appealed | Redshaw J Sydney Sept. 1953 Appeal dismissed |
| Bethel, John Frederick | JW Minister Townsville Qld | Appl. TE Keleher SM Townsville CPS July 1952 | Granted | |
| Blakeney, Glenn Alexander | JW Log hauler Mt Hawthorn WA | Appl. TE A.G. Smith SM Perth Police Crt 29/7/53 | Granted | |
| Bond, George Robert | Christian Grazier Mackay Qld | Appl. TE J.C. Baker SM Mackay CPS 28/4/53 | Granted | |
| Booth, Ivor Graham | SDA Railway porter Qld | Appl. ECD N.F. Applin SM Rockhampton 20/1/54 | Dismissed | |
| Borodale, Neville | SDA WA | Appl. ECD Taylor RM Perth 0/10/53 | Granted | |
| Boyle, John | Christad. Inglewood WA | Appl. TE W.J. Wallwork SM Perth Police Crt 27/2/53 | Order NCD Appealed | Dwyer J Supreme Crt 23/7/53 Appeal upheld |
| Brimsmead, Robert Daniel | Mena Creek Qld | Appl. TE A. Schwarten SM Innisfail CPS 24/11/53 | Granted | |

| Name | Details | Court Appearance | Outcome | Appeal/Sentence |
|---|---|---|---|---|
| Bromwich, Clyde William | JW Dubbo NSW | Appl. TE Stapleton SM Dubbo Crt June 1954 | Order NCD | |
| Broun, Noel Francis | Quaker (18) Farmer Coorow WA | Appl. TE Smith SM Perth Police Crt 25/2/54 | Granted | |
| Brown, Robert James | JW Painter Geelong VIC | Appl. TE Steedman SM Geelong City Crt? 1953 | Granted | |
| Brunsden, Stanley Raymond | Non-denom. Christian NSW | Appl. TE Blackmore SM Wagga Wagga CPS 13/5/53 | Order NCD | |
| Bundesen, Keith John | Christad. (18) Sawmill worker Rockhampton Qld | McLean SM Brisbane Summons Crt 15/8/52 | Dismissed Fined Sent to Holsworthy Appealed | Sheehy J Supreme Crt Brisbane 26/6/53 Appeal upheld |
| Bundesen, Neville McLeod | Christad. Farm worker Mackay Qld | Appl. TE Baker SM Mackay CPS 28/4/53 | Granted | |
| Burgess, Kenneth | SDA (18) Timber truck driver Mackay Qld | Appl. ECD J.C. Baker SM Mackay CPS Date unknown | Granted | |
| Butcher, Ronald Robert | Breth. Leeton NSW | Appl. ECD Blackmore SM Narrandera CPS Date unknown | Granted | |
| Byriel, Francis Conrad | JW (18) Apprentice plasterer Qld | Appl. TE Fowler SM Cairns 28/8/55 | Granted | |
| Cameron, James | JW State unknown | Appl. TE Court details unknown | Order NCD Appealed | Appeal dismissed Sent to Holsworthy |

Appendix 1    217

| Name | Details | Court Appearance | Outcome | Appeal/ Sentence |
|---|---|---|---|---|
| Cameron, John Douglas | New Lambton NSW | Appl. TE Court details unknown | Order NCD Appealed | Amsberg J Newcastle Dist. Crt 27/10/53 Order Med. Corps |
| Carr, Ronald Douglas | JW Vic Park WA | Appl. TE Wallwork SM Perth Police Crt 20/2/53 | Dismissed | |
| Carrell, Geoffrey | SDA Southgate NSW | Appl. ECD Blackmore SM Grafton Special Crt 6/5/54 | Granted | |
| Cawse, David | SDA Trainee school teacher Qld | Appl. TE Court details unknown | Dismissed Appealed | Andrews J Qld Dist. Crt Oct. 1959 Appeal upheld |
| Chard, Robin George | JW Labourer Murwillumbah NSW | Appl. TE J.R. Scarlett SM Lismore CPS 31/8/54 | Order NCD | |
| Clanahan, Arthur Gordon | Breth. Railway apprentice Annerley Qld | Appl. TE Burchill SM Summons Crt 18/11/52 | Dismissed | |
| Clarke, Brian James | JW Wembley Park WA | Appl. TE F.E.A. Bateman SM Perth Police Crt 21/10/53 | Granted | |
| Clarkson, Stanley Reginald | Non-complier NSW | Charge of failing to comply with NSA McCaulay SM Sydney 27/6/56 | Fined £25 Committed to army custody | |
| Clements, Victor Paul | JW (18) North Hobart TAS | Appl. TE Turner PM Hobart Police Crt 28/9/53 | Granted | |
| Cocking, Noel Anderson | Methodist NSW | W.E. McAndrew SM Newcastle NSW 30/12/94 | Order Med. Corps | |

| Name | Details | Court Appearance | Outcome | Appeal/Sentence |
|---|---|---|---|---|
| Connell, Desmond | CA SA | Appl. TE Kangaroo Island SA Mag. Crt 1954 | Order NCD | Did not appeal Summonsed Fined £10 Sent to Holsworthy |
| Constantine, John George | JW (19) Devonport TAS | Appl. TE Court details unknown | Order NCD Appealed | Gibson J Burnie Sept. 1953 Appeal upheld |
| Cooper, Warren Richard | SDA Wembley WA | Appl. ECD Wallwork SM Perth Police Crt 20/2/53 | Granted | |
| Corker, Arthur William | SDA (18) WA | Appl. ECD Stotter SM Bridgetown WA Police Crt 28/10/53 | Granted | |
| Corker, Edward Albert Garth | SDA (19) WA | Appl. ECD Stotter SM Bridgetown WA Police Crt 28/10/53 | Granted | |
| Cox, Geoffrey Frederick | Christian Farmer Hillside VIC | Appl. TE Cuthill SM Sale CPS 3/6/52 | Granted | |
| Cox, Lester Grant | Non-denom. Christian Farmer Hillside VIC | Appl. TE Cuthill SM Sale CPS 3/6/52 | Granted | |
| Davies, Edward Hamilton | WA | Applied for exemption from remainder of military service: change of religious belief Smith SM Perth Police Crt 11/1/55 | Granted | |
| Dell, Ronald Keith | Christad. Morningside Qld | Appl. TE Court details unknown | Order NCD Appealed | Skerman, Acting J Supreme Crt Brisbane 11/6/53 Appeal upheld |

Appendix 1     219

| Name | Details | Court Appearance | Outcome | Appeal/ Sentence |
|---|---|---|---|---|
| Deutscher, Maxwell John | Christian (18) uni student Adelaide SA | Appl. TE Scales SM Adelaide 6/7/55 | Adjourned Changed application to non-comb. duties | Order Med. Corps (SA policy for all non-combatants) |
| Dowsett, Roy Peters | SDA Nedlands WA | Appl. ECD Wallwork SM Perth Police Crt 20/2/53 | Granted | |
| Earl, Jared Charles | Christian (18) Clerk Deakin ACT | Appl. ECD R.A. McKillop SM Canberra Date unknown | Granted | |
| Eaton, James Charles | SDA (18) WA | Appl. ECD Stotter SM Bridgetown WA Police Crt 28/10/53 | Granted | |
| Ellice, Rodney Eason | JW Post official Manjimup WA | Appl. TE Smith SM Perth Police Crt 29/7/53 | Granted | |
| Elliott, Norman James | SDA Dairy farmer Dungog NSW | Appl. ECD Blackmore SM Dungog CPS 8/5/53 | Granted | |
| Euston, John Stanley | (18) Salesman Kangaroo Point Qld | Appl. TE Moore SM Court details unknown 6/9/54 | Granted | |
| Fatnowna, Matthew Fitzmaurice | SDA Qld | Appl. ECD Baker SM Mackay CPS 21/7/53 | Granted | |
| Fennell, Kevin John | SDA Nambucca Heads NSW | Appl. ECD Tyler SM Kempsey CPS 7/7/54 | Granted | |
| Fenton, Nevil John | SDA Timber worker Armidale NSW | Appl. ECD Armidale CPS 5/8/54 | Granted | |

| Name | Details | Court Appearance | Outcome | Appeal/ Sentence |
|---|---|---|---|---|
| Fildes, Lex | JW<br>Carpenter<br>Speers Pt NSW | Appl. TE<br>R.A. Hardwicke SM<br>Newcastle<br>18/11/53 | Dismissed | |
| Finney, Raymond Frank | JW (18)<br>Sunnybank Qld | Appl. TE<br>Smith SM<br>Mag. Crt<br>16/11/53 | Granted | |
| Fisher, Frederick John | ND<br>Student<br>Muresk College WA | Appl. TE<br>K.H. Parker SM<br>Northam Police Crt<br>16/7/52 | Order NCD | |
| Fletcher, Douglas Alexander | Christian<br>Glen Innes<br>NSW | Appl. ECD<br>McDonald SM<br>Glen Innes Crt<br>30/3/53 | Granted | |
| Ford, Gordon Arthur Samuel | Christian<br>Truck driver<br>Drake NSW | Appl. TE<br>J.R. Scarlett SM<br>Lismore CPS<br>31/8/54 | Order NCD<br>Appealed | Fitzpatrick J<br>Lismore Qtr. Sess.<br>28/10/54<br>Appeal upheld |
| Fox, Robert | Christad. (19)<br>Bulldozer driver<br>Nanango Qld | Appl. TE<br>Kingaroy Mag. Crt<br>5/6/53 | Dismissed<br>Appealed | Mansfield J<br>Supreme Crt<br>Brisbane<br>9/7/53<br>Appeal upheld |
| Gale, James Arthur | JW<br>Cairns Qld | Appl. TE<br>Had completed some army service<br>Smart SM<br>Cairns<br>28/8/55 | Granted total exemption | |
| Gare, John Edward | Quaker<br>Student<br>Maylands WA | Appl. TE<br>Court details<br>unknown 19/8/52 | Granted | |
| Gilson, Leslie James | JW (19)<br>Dairy farmer<br>Branxton NSW | Appl. TE<br>C.H. Blackmore SM<br>Maitland<br>28/4/53 | Order NCD<br>Appealed | Amsberg J<br>Newcastle Dist.<br>Crt 27/10/53<br>Order Med. Corps |
| Gordon, John Alexander | Christian (18)<br>The Caves Qld | Appl. TE<br>N.F. Applin SM<br>Rockhampton CPS<br>28/6/53 | Order NCD | |

Appendix 1     221

| Name | Details | Court Appearance | Outcome | Appeal/Sentence |
|---|---|---|---|---|
| Gould, Colin | CI (18) Radio mechanic Whittingham NSW | Appl. TE Ward SM Singleton Crt Date unknown | Granted | |
| Gould, Jeffrey | CI (19) Welder Whittingham NSW | Appl. TE CK Ward SM Singleton Crt Date unknown | Granted | |
| Gray, Walter Henry | SDA (19) Motor mechanic Innisfail Qld | Appl. TE Schwartzen SM Innisfail Crt 8/7/1954 | Granted | |
| Green, Clifford James | Methodist Uni student Strathfield NSW | Appl. TE Court details unknown | Granted | |
| Grondal, Donald | JW WA | Appl. TE Court details unknown | Order NCD Appealed | Dwyer J Perth 11/9/53 Appeal upheld |
| Grosser, Llewellyn James | SDA Millicent SA | Appl. ECD D.C. Williams SM Mt. Gambier Mag. Crt 14/1/53 | Granted | |
| Grosser, Terence | SDA Millicent SA | Appl. ECD Williams SM Mt. Gambier Mag. Crt 14/1/53 | Granted | |
| Grundy, Eric Sydwin | JW (18) apprentice fitter Gladesville NSW | Appl. TE Meagher SM Sydney 19/11/52 | Granted | |
| Haggarty, Colin | ND Farm worker Rockhampton Qld | Appl. TE Brisbane CPS Date unknown | Dismissed Appealed | Sheehy J Supreme Crt Brisbane 27/6/53 Appeal dismissed Sent to Holsworthy |
| Hamilton, William Macarthur | SDA NSW | Appl. ECD Smith SM Griffith Crt 6/8/53 | Granted | |

| Name | Details | Court Appearance | Outcome | Appeal/Sentence |
|---|---|---|---|---|
| Hann, John William | SDA Dairy farmer Mt Gambier SA | Appl. ECD Williams SM Mt Gambier 16/9/53 | Granted | |
| Harrison, Edmund | Christian Michelton Qld | Appl. TE Court details unknown | Outcome unknown | |
| Haskins, John Leslie | JW Qld | Appl. TE Baker SM Mackay CPS 21/7/53 | Granted | |
| Hatter, John Francis James | Christad. Granville NSW | Appl. TE Court details unknown 1953 | Dismissed | Appeal dismissed |
| Havelberg, Noel | JW Menindee NSW | Appl. TE Garnesy SM Broken Hill CPS 14?/4/53 | Order NCD | |
| Heldt, Arthur Roderick | Anglican storeman South Grafton NSW | Appl. TE Blackmore SM Grafton Special Crt 6/5/53 | Dismissed | |
| Henig, Ian Reece | SDA (18) Wongulla SA | Appl. TE Williams SM Swan Reach 27/7/53 | Dismissed Appealed | Mayo J Adelaide 28/9/53 Appeal upheld |
| Hildebrandt, Frederick John | Ayr Qld | Appl. TE Baker SM Ayr CPS 19/10/53 | Granted | |
| Hill, Colin | Christad. (19) Apprentice Rockhampton Qld | Appl. TE Court details unknown Aug. 1952 | Dismissed Appealed | Appeal dismissed ?/6/53 Sent to Holsworthy Released 10/10/54 |
| Hill, Kenneth Alexander | SDA Student Armidale NSW | Appl. ECD Armidale CPS 5/8/54 | Granted | |
| Hinks, Raymond John | (19) Farmhand Diamond Creek VIC | Appl. TE Court details unknown | Order NCD Appealed | Book J Melbourne County Crt 1/7/53 Appeal dismissed |

Appendix 1  223

| Name | Details | Court Appearance | Outcome | Appeal/Sentence |
|---|---|---|---|---|
| **Hoppe, Kevin Cleve** | JW (18) Largs Bay SA | Appl. TE Johnston PM Port Police Crt July 1954 | Granted | |
| **Horig, Carl Leslie** | JW Bus conductor Rocklea Qld | Appl. TE Court details unknown | Rejected No appeal | George SM Brisbane Summons Crt 4/5/54 Fined for failure to reg. |
| **Horn, C.** | JW Qld | Court details unknown Qld | | Sent to Holsworthy Released Dec.? 1954 |
| **Hosking, Trevor John** | Woodville West SA | Appl. TE Court details unknown 27/9/55 | Granted | |
| **Hoult, Lindsay Roy** | Christian Farmer Antigua Qld | Appl. TE Ward SM Maryborough CPS 17/11/54 | Granted | |
| **Howe, Eric Roy** | Deloraine TAS | Appl. TE Court details unknown | Dismissed Arrested for ignoring call up | Sorrell PM Burnie Police Crt 24/9/52 Fined Taken into army custody |
| **Howe, Jack** | JW TAS | Appl. TE Crisp PM Launceston Police Crt 10/1/55 | Dismissed | |
| **Humphrey, Franklin Mark** | JW Tile fixer Cannington WA | Appl. TE Smith SM Perth Police Crt 29/7/53 | Granted | |
| **Irvine, John Charles** | Church of God junior clerk Willoughby NSW | Appl. TE Meagher SM Sydney 30/6/53 | Order NCD | |

| Name | Details | Court Appearance | Outcome | Appeal/Sentence |
|---|---|---|---|---|
| Irwin, Dale Courtney | JW (18) Preacher Qld | Appl. TE Noyes SM Chermside Summons Crt Date unknown | Granted | |
| Johannesen, Alvan Glen | Christian (18) Cane cutter Oakwood Qld | Appl. TE Will SM Maryborough CPS 22/9/54 | Dismissed | |
| Johnson, Brian James | JW Bench hand Dundurrabin NSW | Appl. TE Blackmore SM Coffs Harbour CPS 14/5/53 | Dismissed | |
| Johnson, Frederick John | Christian (18) Plasterer's apprentice Enmore Qld | Appl. TE Smart SM Cairns CPS 10/11/53 | Granted | |
| Johnston, James Henry | JW (18) Cairns Qld | Appl. TE Smart SM Cairns 28/8/55 | Granted | |
| Jones, John Lee | Anglican (SDA beliefs) Elect. apprentice Brisbane Qld | Appl. TE NS trainee changed mind about war Taylor SM Court details unknown 30/10/53? | Granted | |
| Kay, William Kenneth | Christad. Burragorang Valley NSW | Appl. TE Court details unknown 1953 | Dismissed Appealed 1954 | Outcome unknown |
| Kemp, Douglas Victor | ND Mackay Qld | Appl. TE Baker SM Mackay CPS 28/4/53 | Granted | |
| Kilpatrick, S. | JW Qld | Appl. TE Court details unknown | | Sent to Holsworthy Released Dec.? 1954 |
| King, Charles | Christad. SA | Appl. TE Court details unknown | Order NCD Appealed | Ross J Adelaide Sept. 1953 Appeal upheld |

Appendix 1   225

| Name | Details | Court Appearance | Outcome | Appeal/ Sentence |
|---|---|---|---|---|
| King, Reginald Charles | Christad. Dismissed from Commercial Bank when he wouldn't enlist Largs Bay SA | Appl. TE Court details unknown 23/5/52 | Order NCD Failed to comply with Act | Johnson SM Adelaide Police Crt 29/9/52 Adjourned Ross J Supreme Crt Adelaide 20/7/53 Decision reserved |
| Kingsmill, Richard | Non-Biblical beliefs NSW | Appl. TE McCaulay SM Martin Place Sydney CPS Date unknown | Unknown | |
| Kirk, James William B. | student Paddington Qld | Court details unknown 28/8/55 | Exempted from combatant service | |
| Knight, Alan Gilbert | (17) Forth TAS | Appl. ECD Wilson PM Burnie Police Crt 18/10/54 | Granted | |
| Knight, Athol | True Followers of Christ Ipswich Qld | Appl. TE Innes, Acting SM Ipswich 31/1/52 | Order NCD | |
| Knight, Owen | True Followers of Christ Ipswich Qld | Appl. TE Innes, Acting SM Ipswich 31/1/52 | Order NCD | |
| Lague, Eric John | JW Subiaco WA | Appl. TE Bateman SM Perth Police Crt 21/10/53 | Granted | |
| Lapham, Ross Eric | Christad. Apprentice fitter Punchbowl NSW | Appl. TE Meagher SM Sydney Special Crt 19/11/52 | Granted | |
| Latter, Alan Avery | Farmhand Maison Dieu NSW | Appl. TE Ward SM Singleton Crt 3/7/54 | Dismissed | |

| Name | Details | Court Appearance | Outcome | Appeal/Sentence |
|---|---|---|---|---|
| Leadbetter, Arthur | Christad. farmer Alstonville NSW | Appl. TE Anderson SM Lismore CPS 8/12/52 | Granted | |
| Leppard, E. | Christad. NSW | Court details unknown NSW | Dismissed Sent to Holsworthy | Released Dec.? 1954 |
| Lockyer, John Barry | SDA Farmer Wellington Mills WA | Appl. TE Stotter RM Bunbury Crt Aug. 1952 | Order NCD | |
| Lyell, Ronald William | Nambour Qld | Appl. TE Court details unknown 1953 | Order NCD Appealed | Stanley J Supreme Crt Brisbane 9/6/53 Appeal dismissed |
| MacDonald, Archibald Norman | Qld | Appl. ECD Fowler SM Brisbane 9/5/55 | Granted | |
| MacMillan, Leslie John | Christian (18) Farmer Qld | Appl. TE N.F. Applin SM Rockhampton CPS 20/1/54 | Order NCD | |
| Mansfield, John | Christad. Enfield NSW | Appl. TE Court details unknown | Dismissed 1953 Appealed | 1953 Appeal dismissed |
| Marshall, Stuart James | (18) Apprentice fitter North Rock Qld | Appl. TE N.F. Applin SM Rockhampton CPS Sept. 1954 | Dismissed Appealed | Supreme Crt 16/11/54 Order NCD |
| Mason, Brian Keith | Quaker SA | Appl. TE Court details unknown Nov. 1951 | Order NCD He refused to enlist | No right of appeal May 1952 Fined £10 Sent to Holsworthy |
| Mason, Harleigh Cecil (or Harley) | CA SA | Appl. TE Court details unknown | Order NCD Appealed | Mayo J Supreme Crt Adelaide 28/9/53 Appeal disallowed Sent to Holsworthy 1954 |

Appendix 1    227

| Name | Details | Court Appearance | Outcome | Appeal/Sentence |
|---|---|---|---|---|
| Mathews, Donald Arthur | Christian Trainee teacher Port Pirie SA | Appl. TE Richards SM Port Pirie Crt 12?/1/54 | Granted | |
| Mauderer, Conrad G. | Apprentice plumber St. Kilda VIC | Appl. TE Army training revolted him Moore J Melbourne County Crt 30/4/57 | Total exemption; German immigrant, had been in war as a child | |
| Maxwell, Bruce Rodford | Christad. Newcastle NSW | Appl. TE Court details unknown | Order NCD | Newcastle Police Crt Failure to enlist 30/12/54 Fined Committed to army custody |
| Maxwell, Morton Raymond | JW cleaner Leederville WA | Appl. TE Smith SM Perth Police Crt 29/7/53 | Granted | |
| McCamley, Maurice Cecil | SDA (18) Charters Towers Qld | Appl. ECD Verry SM Charters Towers CPS 22/8/1952 | Granted | |
| McClure, Noel | Christad. Marrickville NSW | Appl. TE Court details unknown | Order NCD | Refused call up Fined Sent to Holsworthy |
| McCombe, Donald | Christad. (18) Camp Mountain Qld | Appl. TE McKenna SM Summons Crt Brisbane 14/2/52 | Granted | |
| McDonald, Austin | ND VIC | Appl. TE Court details unknown | Order NCD Appealed | Dethridge J Wangaratta County Crt 4/10/55 Appeal upheld |
| McGonigal, Colin | Christad. NSW | Appl. TE McCaulay SM CPS 3/3/55 | Dismissed Appealed | Clegg J Sydney Qtr. Sess. 5/5/55 Appeal upheld |

| Name | Details | Court Appearance | Outcome | Appeal/Sentence |
|---|---|---|---|---|
| McIntosh, Regan | CI (18) mechanic Plenty VIC | Appl. TE Court details unknown | Dismissed Appealed | Book J Melbourne County Crt 1/7/53 Appeal upheld |
| McKinlay, D. | Christad. NSW | Court details unknown | | Sent to Holsworthy Released ? 1955 |
| McNaughton, Brian Keith | Exclus. Breth. (17) Jackeroo Warwick Qld | Appl. TE Elte SM Warwick CPS 11/3/53 | Dismissed | |
| McRae, Eric Douglas | Cleveland Line Qld | Appl. TE Court details unknown | Order NCD Appealed | Stanley J Supreme Crt Brisbane 9/6/53 Appeal dismissed |
| Meech, Kevin George | Minden Qld | Appl. TE Fowler SM Rosewood CPS 3/6/52 | Granted | |
| Morgan, Malcolm Edwin | Non-complier NSW | Charge of failing to comply with NSA McCaulay SM Sydney 27/6/56 | Fined £25 Committed to army custody | |
| Morgan, Richard Alan | JW (17) Collie WA | Appl. TE Rodriguez SM Collie Crt 16/11/55 | Granted | |
| Morgan, Robert Harper | JW Dairyhand Donnybrook WA | Appl. TE Stotter RM Bunbury Crt Date unknown | Order NCD | |
| Morris, Barry | SDA Warrell Creek NSW | Appl. ECD Tyler SM Kempsey CPS 7/7/54 | Granted | |
| Morrisby, Donald Stanley | JW (18) North Hobart TAS | Appl. TE Turner PM Hobart Police Crt 28/9/53 | Granted | |
| Mouritz, Douglas. | JW NSW | Court details unknown | Appealed | Clegg J Sydney Qtr. Sess. 5/5/55 Appeal dismissed |

Appendix 1    229

| Name | Details | Court Appearance | Outcome | Appeal/Sentence |
|---|---|---|---|---|
| Nash, Charles Alan | SDA Qld | Appl. ECD Keleher SM Townsville CPS July 1952 | Granted | |
| Nash, Malcolm James | SDA Townsville Qld | Appl. ECD Keleher SM Townsville CPS 21/12/54 | Granted | |
| Nilon, Robert McDonald | SDA Farm labourer Bexhill NSW | Appl. ECD Scarlett SM Lismore CPS 31/8/54 | Granted | |
| Nixon, Thomas George | Qld | Appl. TE Keleher SM Townsville 20/4/55 | Dismissed | |
| Noack, Nigel Leonard | JW Storeman Townsville Qld | Appl. TE Keleher SM Townsville 1/9/53 | Granted | |
| Nockolda, Brian | Amer. religious sanctuary UWA student WA | Appl. TE Court details unknown WA Oct. 1959 | Granted | |
| Norman, David Alexander | JW fitter and turner South Perth WA | Appl. TE Smith SM Perth Police Crt 29/7/53 | Granted | |
| Norman, Raymond | JW Mt Gambier SA | Appl. TE Williams SM Mt. Gambier Mag. Crt 14/1/53 | Dismissed | |
| Osborne, Leslie Warren | JW (18) Labourer Granville NSW | Appl. TE Meagher SM Court details unknown | Order NCD Appealed | Curlewis J Sydney 11/2/54 Appeal dismissed |
| O'Hern, George Ernest | SDA Motor mechanic NSW | Appl. ECD Armidale CPS 5/8/54 | Granted | |
| O'Toole, Robert Archer | Christad. (18) Church would expel him Qld | Appl. TE N.F. Applin SM Rockhampton CPS 20/2/53 | Granted | |

| Name | Details | Court Appearance | Outcome | Appeal/Sentence |
|---|---|---|---|---|
| Oxenbridge, David | CA NSW | Appl. TE Court details unknown 8/5/54 | Order NCD | Enlisted but refused to wear uniform Sent to Holsworthy |
| Parkes, Eric Victor | JW (18) Mechanic's asst Coopers Plains Qld | Appl. TE Taylor SM Brisbane Mag. Crt 10/11/54 | Granted | |
| Parnell, John Albert | SDA Jackadgery NSW | Appl. TE Blackmore SM Grafton Special Crt 6/5/54 | Order NCD | |
| Phillips, Adrian | Portland VIC | Appl. ECD Prowse SM Portland Police Crt Date unknown | Dismissed | |
| Phillips, Graeme | Methodist VIC | Appl. TE Court details unknown | Order NCD Appealed | Read J Melbourne 1/10/53 Appeal upheld |
| Phillips, Kevin | Portland VIC | Appl. ECD Prowse SM Portland Police Crt Date unknown | Dismissed | |
| Pilcher, John Hamilton | Breth. Bendigo VIC | Appl. ECD Marwick SM Bendigo CPS 20/10/53 | Granted | |
| Plunkett, Stephen | Christad. (18) Apprentice printer Arncliffe NSW | Appl. TE Meagher SM Special Federal Crt 26/8/52 | Granted | |
| Pogson, David | Christad. Bellfield NSW | Appl. TE Court details unknown 1953 | Dismissed Appealed | 1953-4 Court details unknown Appeal dismissed |
| Pratt, Allan Henry | SDA Mt. Hawthorn WA | Appl. ECD Bateman SM Perth Police Crt 21/10/53 | Granted | |
| Pratt, Walter Keith | Church of Christ Station hand Mt Gambier SA | Appl. ECD Williams SM Mt Gambier 16/9/53 | Granted | |

Appendix 1    231

| Name | Details | Court Appearance | Outcome | Appeal/ Sentence |
|---|---|---|---|---|
| Prestidge, Leslie John | Breth. NSW | Appl. ECD McCaulay SM Sydney 16/2/55 | Dismissed | |
| Pusey, Barry Max | JW NSW | Appl. TE McAndrew SM Newcastle 30/12/54 | Order Med. Corps | |
| Raven, John William | Christad. WA | Appl. TE Smith SM Perth Police Crt 21/2/57 | Granted | |
| Roberts, Donald George | SDA (18) Clerk Maryborough Qld | Appl. TE Maryborough CPS 22/9/54 | Granted | |
| Roberts, Reginald William | Christad. Farmer Yeppoon Qld | Appl. TE N.F. Applin SM CPS 15/10/53 | Dismissed | Sent to Holsworthy Released 10/10/54 |
| Rogers, Norman John | Breth. (19) Apprentice carpenter Telopea Park ACT | Appl. ECD McKillop SM Canberra 13/2/57 | Granted | |
| Roos, Harold Raymond | JW Glen Innes NSW | Appl. TE McDonald SM Glen Innes Crt 30/3/53 | Order NCD | |
| Ross, Amos | JW Glen Innes NSW | Appl. TE McDonald SM Glen Innes Crt 30/3/53 | Order NCD | |
| Ross, Donald James | Christad. Urangan Qld | Appl. TE Ward SM Maryborough CPS 17/11/54 | Granted | |
| Ross, William James | Christad. Scarborough Qld | Appl. TE McKenna, SM Court details unknown 24/4/52 | Granted | |

| Name | Details | Court Appearance | Outcome | Appeal/ Sentence |
|---|---|---|---|---|
| Salmond, Ronald Hume | SDA South Lismore NSW | Appl. ECD K. Anderson SM Lismore CPS 8/12/52 | Granted | |
| Saxon, Samuel Raymond | Christad. Dairy farmer Tarcutta NSW | Appl. TE Blackmore SM Wagga Wagga CPS 13/5/53 | Dismissed Appealed | Brennan J Wagga Wagga Qtr. Sess. 14/8/53 Appeal upheld |
| Schirmer, Glen Ian | Christian (18) Farmer Mackay Qld | Appl. TE Baker SM Mackay CPS 3/11/54 | Granted | |
| Schultz, Ronald Herman | JW North Ipswich Qld | Appl. TE C. Innes, Acting SM Ipswich 31/1/52 | Dismissed | |
| Scott, Dereham Lloyd | Non-complier TAS | Refusal to register Sorell PM Hobart 28/3/52 | Fined £2 + costs | |
| Searle, John Wesley | SDA New Lambton NSW | Appl. ECD McAndrew SM Newcastle 30/12/54 | Order Med. Corps | |
| Seymour, Alan | Wodonga VIC | Registered Appl. TE Court details unknown 22/8/52 | Order NCD Appealed | Wangaratta County Crt 12/8/53 Appeal dismissed Seymour refused medical exam Prosecuted Fined Applied for re-hearing |
| Sharpe, Philip James | Christian Ipswich Qld | Appl. TE Fowler SM Ipswich CPS 8/7/52 | Dismissed | |
| Shepherd, Peter Maxwell George | SDA Millicent SA | Appl. ECD Williams SM Mt Gambier Mag. Crt 14/1/53 | Granted | |

Appendix 1    233

| Name | Details | Court Appearance | Outcome | Appeal/ Sentence |
|---|---|---|---|---|
| Shields, Graham Alwyne | SDA Maylands WA | Appl. ECD Wallwork SM Perth Police Crt 20/2/53 | Granted | |
| Shipard, Carl Edwin | SDA Mt Gambier SA | Appl. ECD Gordon SM Mt Gambier Mag. Crt 14/7/58 | Dismissed Appealed | Reed J 22/9/58 Appeal upheld |
| Sholz, John Clyde | SA | Appl. TE Court details unknown | Order NCD Appealed | Mayo J Supreme Crt Adelaide 28/9/53 Appeal dismissed |
| Silver, George Bernard | Christian Qld | Appl. TE H.B. Carney SM Brisbane 9/11/56 | Dismissed Appealed | Matthews J Supreme Crt Brisbane 11/3/57 Order NCD |
| Sleigh, Adrian | Details unknown | Court details unknown | | |
| Smith, Norman James | JW Shop asst Maryborough Qld | Appl. TE Ward SM Maryborough CPS 17/11/54 | Granted | |
| Smith, Raymond Robert | Christad. (18) Hawthorne Qld | Appl. TE McKenna SM Brisbane Summons Crt 14/2/52 | Granted | |
| Smith, William Henry | (17) Port Pirie SA | Appl. TE Richards SM Port Pirie 18/11/53 | Order NCD | |
| Southon, Donald Edward | SDA Murwillumbah NSW | Appl. TE J. Scarlett SM Lismore CPS 31/8/54 | Granted | |
| Staib, Donald Arthur | Assembly of Good Faith (twin) Farmer Qld | Appl. TE Carney SM Gympie 25/1/1952 | Granted | |
| Staib, Noel Francis | Assembly of Good Faith (twin) farmer Qld | Appl. TE Carney SM Gympie 25/1/1952 | Granted | |

| Name | Details | Court Appearance | Outcome | Appeal/ Sentence |
|---|---|---|---|---|
| Staier, Allen Charles | Believers of Christ Farmer Maryborough Qld | Appl. TE Ward SM Maryborough 18/3/53 | Granted | |
| Stephens, David George | Apostolic Church Apprentice mechanic Bunbury WA | Appl. ECD Stotter RM Bunbury Police Crt 23/4/54 | Granted | |
| Stephens, R. | JW NSW | Court details unknown | | Sent to Holsworthy Released 1955? |
| Stewart, Milton Sandeman | SDA Millicent SA | Appl. ECD Williams SM Mt Gambier Mag. Crt 14/1/53 | Granted | |
| Strahan, Robert Samuel | Breth. Farmhand Bentley NSW | Appl. TE Anderson SM Lismore CPS 8/12/52 | Order NCD | |
| Strahan, Stanley Harold | JW Welshpool WA | Appl. TE Smith SM Perth Police Crt 29/7/53 | Order NCD | |
| Strange, David | SDA Hobart TAS | Appl. ECD Turner PM Hobart Police Crt 30/6/52 | Granted | |
| Sutherland, George Forbes | JW Mackay Qld | Appl. TE Baker SM Mackay CPS 22/4/54 | Granted | |
| Sutton, Carl Laurie | Christad. (20) Dental tech. Elwood VIC | Appl. TE Hill SM Melbourne Feb. 1953 | Dismissed Appealed | Melbourne County Crt 31/3/54 Appeal upheld |
| Symes, David James | SDA (18) Townsville Qld | Appl. ECD Hart SM Townsville CPS Date unknown | Granted | |

Appendix 1    235

| Name | Details | Court Appearance | Outcome | Appeal/ Sentence |
|---|---|---|---|---|
| Thomas, John Douglas | SDA Northam WA | Appl. ECD Parker SM Northam Police Crt 16/7/52 | Granted | |
| Thomas, Norman Arnold | SDA Northam WA | Appl. ECD Parker SM Northam Police Crt 16/7/52 | Granted | |
| Thompson, Alleyne James | SDA Banana grower Brunswick Heads NSW | Appl. ECD Scarlett SM Lismore CPS 31/8/54 | Granted | |
| Thompson, Cyril | Christian (18) Stanthorpe Qld | Appl. TE Knowles, Acting SM Stanthorpe CPS 27/7/53 | Granted | |
| Thorniley, Kenneth | JW South Perth WA | Appl. TE Smith SM Perth Police Crt 29/7/53 | Granted | |
| Till, Donald Lance | SDA WA | Appl. ECD Taylor RM Perth 10/10/53 | Granted | |
| Tilley, Leonard Keith | VIC | Appl. ECD Hayes SM Mildura 12/5/55 | Granted | |
| Tomlin, Alan Arthur | Christad. Linesman Lakemba NSW | Appl. TE Meagher SM Sydney Special Crt 23/7/53 | Order NCD | |
| Topley, Norman David | JW NSW | Appl. TE Solling SM Sydney 30/7/52 | Dismissed | |
| Townsend, John Raymond | Christad. (18) Dairy hand Dayboro Qld | Appl. TE Mansell SM Brisbane Summons Crt 29/9/52 | Order NCD | |
| Trewarn, Lawrence | JW Mechanic Bedfordale WA | Appl. TE Smith SM Perth Police Crt 29/7/53 | Order NCD | |

| Name | Details | Court Appearance | Outcome | Appeal/Sentence |
|---|---|---|---|---|
| Trickett, Allen James | JW Farm worker Launceston TAS | Appl. TE PM Launceston 1/12/52 | Dismissed Appealed | Green J Supreme Crt Launceston 12/8/53 Appeal upheld |
| Troy, Rodney Sydney | JW WA | Appl. TE Taylor RM Perth 10/10/53 | Granted | |
| Tubman, Peter Laurence | Christian (19) Farmer Rollands Plains NSW | Appl. TE Tyler SM Kempsey CPS 7/7/54 | Granted | |
| Tubman, William Lindsay (brother of Peter) | CA Rollands Plains NSW | Appl. TE Court details unknown 8/5/54 | Order NCD | Enlisted but refused to wear uniform Sent to Holsworthy |
| Turner, John Patrick | No religion Fairfield NSW | Appl. TE Sydney Special Crt 4/12/52 | Order NCD | |
| Twine, Donald Frank | Christad. (18) Trainee tech. Moggill Qld | Appl. TE Moore SM Brisbane Summons Crt 6/9/54 | Granted | |
| Vollrath, Robin Rodney | SDA WA | Appl. ECD Taylor RM Perth 10/10/53 | Granted | |
| Waddy, Ronald | Quaker WA | Appl. TE Perth Police Crt Aug. 1951 | Order NCD (ambulance corps) | Perth Police Crt 8/7/52 Fined £10 for not registering Refused to enlist Military detention |
| Wakefield, Ashley James | School teacher Hobart TAS | Appl. TE Brettingam-Moore SM Hobart Police Crt 31/3/52 | Order NCD | |
| Wakefield, John James | Qld | Appl. TE Noyes SM Chermside Summons Crt Date unknown | Granted | |

Appendix 1     237

| Name | Details | Court Appearance | Outcome | Appeal/ Sentence |
|---|---|---|---|---|
| Wakefield, William Hubert | JW North Mackay Qld | Appl. TE Baker SM Mackay CPS 22/4/54 | Granted | |
| Walker, Adrian | Quaker Farmer Morwell VIC | Appl. TE Morwell Gippsland VIC Date unknown | Granted | |
| Ward, Graeme Francis | SDA Bowraville NSW | Appl. ECD Tyler SM Kempsey CPS 7/7/54 | Granted | |
| Watson, John McPherson | SDA WA | Appl. ECD Smith SM Perth Police Crt 25/2/54 | Granted | |
| Watson, Trevor Roland | JW (18) Case repairer Sunshine VIC | Appl. TE Court details unknown | Dismissed Appealed | Mulvaney J Melbourne County Crt 2/2/54 Appeal upheld |
| Welch, Noel Clyde, | JW South Grafton NSW | Appl. TE Blackmore SM Grafton Special Crt 6/5/54 | Dismissed | |
| Welch, Wilbur E. | JW South Grafton NSW | Appl. TE Capp SM Grafton CPS 22/6/54 | Order NCD | |
| Wells, George Edward | JW Ipswich Qld | Appl. TE Innes, Acting SM Ipswich 31/1/52 | Dismissed Appealed | Full Crt Brisbane 21/3/52 Appeal dismissed |
| Wendt, Donald Herbert | CA Qld | Appl. TE Appeared in court charged with refusing to obey orders (?) Qld Mag. Crt Date unknown | Order NCD Refused to wear uniform Sent to Holsworthy 1954 Appealed | Stanley J Supreme Crt Brisbane 9/6/53 Appeal dismissed |
| Westley, James | Christian (20) Dairy farmer Gloucester NSW | Appl. TE Tyler SM Gloucester CPS 9/3/54 | Order NCD Appealed | Stephen J Taree Dist. Crt 22/6/54 Appeal dismissed |

| Name | Details | Court Appearance | Outcome | Appeal/ Sentence |
|---|---|---|---|---|
| Whitehead, Wilfred L. | JW Watchtower Bible & Tract Society Glen Innes NSW | Appl. TE McDonald SM Glen Innes Crt 30/3/53 | Order NCD | |
| Wibberley, Mervyn | Breth. Mt. Lawley WA | Appl. ECD Bateman SM Perth Police Crt 21/10/53 | Granted | |
| Wilkinson, Harold | Quaker UWA student WA | Appl. TE Court details unknown WA Oct. 1959 | Granted | |
| Wilkinson, Robert William | Orchardist Medowie NSW | Appl. TE Wood SM Maitland Crt July 1954 | Order NCD | |
| Williams, Ronald Lindsay | JW Donnybrook WA | Appl. TE Bateman SM Perth Police Crt 21/10/53 | Granted | |
| Willis, D. | Quaker NSW | Court details unknown | Order NCD Refused to serve | Sent to Holsworthy Released 1955? |
| Wode, Herbert Clive | JW Warwick Qld | Appl. TE Eite SM Warwick 30/1/52 | Granted | |
| Woodard, Norman John | Christian Farm labourer Alligator Creek Qld | Appl. TE J. Baker SM Mackay CPS 26/2/53 | Granted | |
| Woolacott, Ray | CA Qld | Appl. TE Qld. Mag. Crt Date unknown | Order NCD | Did not appeal In Holsworthy 1954 |
| Wright, Arthur William | Christad. Auburn NSW | Appl. TE Court details unknown 1953 | Dismissed Appealed | Appeal dismissed |

Appendix 1  **239**

| Name | Details | Court Appearance | Outcome | Appeal/ Sentence |
|---|---|---|---|---|
| **Wrigley, Kenneth William** | JW (formerly Methodist) Served in RAAF when a Methodist, then became JW Qld | Appl. TE McKenna SM Brisbane Mag. Crt 13/9/53 | Granted | |
| **Wyborn, Kevin Ronald** | SDA Apprentice Lismore NSW | Appl. TE Scarlett SM Lismore CPS 31/8/54 | Granted | |
| **Young, H.F.** | Anglican Gladstone Qld | Appl. TE Hickey SM Gladstone 12/5/52 | Dismissed | |
| **Youngman, Ian** | JW WA | Appl. TE Taylor RM Perth 10/10/53 | Granted | |

## APPENDIX 2
# Sample of 530 Objectors and Non-Compliers, 1965–72

This list comprises 530 dissenters (objectors and non-compliers) to the 1965–72 scheme. It is impossible to ascertain how representative this list is, because of inadequate official figures. The information is from official government figures, *The Peacemaker*, mainstream and alternative press from around Australia and survey responses and interviews collected between 1996 and 2021.

### ABBREVIATIONS

| | |
|---|---|
| applic. | application |
| AWL | Absent without leave (from the Army) |
| CNC | Conscientious Non-complier (didn't register) |
| CO | Conscientious Objector (registered, applied for exemption) |
| FPC | Federal Pacifist Council |
| FTC | Fail to comply (*National Service Act 1951*) |
| med. | medical |
| NC | Non-combatant (applied for and/or granted non-combat duties) |
| NSA | *National Service Act 1951* |
| NS/AWL | Enlisted as a national serviceman, then went absent without leave |
| NS/NC | Enlisted as a national serviceman, then applied for exemption from combat duties |
| NS/TE | Enlisted as a national serviceman, then applied for total exemption |
| Referral | Where CO status is granted on referral by Minister or court, without the CNC's application for CO status or his attendance in court |
| TE | Total exemption from any form of military service |

Prison sentences are indicated by length of sentence, e.g. 7 days, 18 months.

**SUMMARY**

| | |
|---|---:|
| Applied for total exemption (including applications after enlisting) | 227 |
| Failed to comply with NSA | 283 |
| Applied for NC duties (including applications after enlisting) | 16 |
| Other/unknown | 4 |
| **Sample total** | **530** |
| Granted total exemption (including on appeal, non-compliers on referral and medical grounds) | 154 |
| Granted NC duties | 49 |
| Fined | 91 |
| Prison (one or more terms) | 61 |

Appendix 2  **243**

| Name | State | Action | Stance | Outcome |
|---|---|---|---|---|
| Abraham, Harry | NSW | Applied for TE | CO | Exempt 21/2/69 |
| Abrahamson, Larry | VIC | FTC NSA | CNC | |
| Acland, Brian | NSW | FTC NSA | CNC | |
| Acton, Geoff | VIC | FTC NSA | CNC | |
| Adams, John P. | VIC | FTC NSA | CNC | 4 days; 7 days CO on referral |
| Adamson, Lindsay | VIC | FTC NSA | CNC | |
| Aitken, Max | NSW | Applied for TE | CO | Exempt 19/11/65 |
| Alberica, Anthony James | | Applied for TE | CO | Exempt 1968 |
| Ames, Gordon W. | VIC | Applied for TE | CO | Exempt 19/8/65 |
| Anderson, John L. | NSW | Applied for TE | CO | |
| Anderson, Juris | NSW | Applied for TE | CO | NC 17/3/69 |
| Anderson, Kevin C. | NSW | FTC NSA | CNC | |
| Anderson, Peter | VIC | Applied for NC | NC | NC 12/8/71 |
| Anderson, Peter R. | VIC | FTC NSA | CNC | Fine $40 30/10/69 |
| Anderson, Robert Desmond | WA | Applied for TE | CO | Exempt 16/1/71 |
| Archer, Kevin E. | NSW | FTC NSA | CNC | Warrant issued 14/2/72 |
| Armand, Chris | NSW | Applied for TE | CO | Deferred |
| Armitage, David A. | VIC | Applied for TE | CO | Exempt 5/12/66 |
| Armstrong, Karl R. | VIC | FTC NSA | CNC | Fines; 8 days; 7 days |
| Aukett, William J.L. | SA | Applied for TE | CO | Exempt 24/4/70 |
| Backman, Clyde | VIC | Applied for TE | CO | Exempt 20/5/69 |
| Baillieu, James George | VIC | Applied for TE | CO | Exempt 15/4/71 |
| Bain, Kevin | VIC | FTC NSA | CNC | |
| Ball, John Richard | WA | Applied for TE | CO | Exempt 13/7/71 |
| Bannon, Kevin | VIC | FTC NSA | CNC | |
| Barnes, Paul | NSW | FTC NSA | CNC | |
| Barry, Ronald J. | WA | NS/TE | CO | Exempt 15/4/71 |
| Bartimote, Bruce J. | VIC | FTC NSA | CNC | Conviction? |

| Name | State | Action | Stance | Outcome |
|---|---|---|---|---|
| Barczak, George | VIC | Applied for TE | CO | |
| Bastian, Paul G. | WA | Applied for TE | CO | Exempt 5/1/70 |
| Beasley, Colin | QLD | FTC NSA | CNC | |
| Beaton, Brian M. | WA | Applied for TE | CO | Rejected Appealed 1971 |
| Beaver, Robert | NSW | FTC NSA | CNC | |
| Beckett, Brian L. | NSW | Applied for TE | CO | Exempt 1970 |
| Beddow, Maxwell | NSW | FTC NSA | CO | 2 years Exempt on 2nd applic. |
| Bell, John | VIC | Applied for TE | CO | Exempt 28/11/66 |
| Bender, Robert | VIC | Applied for TE | CO | TE on appeal |
| Benjamin, Ian | NSW | Applied for NC | NC | NC 1971 |
| Best, Johnnie | VIC | Applied for TE | CO | Exempt 13/5/69 |
| Bignall, Robert | SA | FTC NSA | CNC | Fine; 10 days |
| Bissett, David | ACT | FTC NSA | CNC | Fine 4/5/71 |
| Bissett, Robert A. | VIC | FTC NSA | CNC | Fine Warrant issued 14/3/72 10 days |
| Bisson, Michael Le Grand | SA | Applied for NC | NC | NC 1965 |
| Black, Ralph | VIC | Applied for TE | CO | Dismissed 24/3/70 |
| Blackman, Alan D. | VIC | Applied for TE | CO | Exempt 12/2/70 |
| Blake, John | VIC | Applied for TE | CO | NC 1966 |
| Blundell, Adrian | WA | FTC NSA | CNC | Fine; 7 days 15/4/71 |
| Bock, Stephen C. | NSW | FTC NSA 1969 | CNC | |
| Bolton, Matthew | VIC | FTC NSA | CNC | |
| Booker, Keven | WA | FTC NSA 1970 | CNC | |
| Boucher, John | NSW | Applied for TE | CO | Exempt 30/10/69 |
| Bowen, John | NSW | Applied for TE | CO | Exempt 1970 on appeal |
| Boyd, Thomas B. | VIC | FTC NSA | CNC | |

Appendix 2    245

| Name | State | Action | Stance | Outcome |
|---|---|---|---|---|
| Breen, Shane | VIC | FTC NSA | CNC | |
| Brennan, Garry | VIC | FTC NSA | CNC | Fine 29/6/71 |
| Breuer, David | SA | FTC NSA 1971 | CNC | |
| Bright, Robert | SA | Applied for TE | CO | Dismissed 10/11/66 |
| Broadbent, John | VIC | FTC NSA 1967 | CNC | |
| Brooks, Chris | NSW | FTC NSA | CNC | |
| Brown, Chris | VIC | FTC NSA | CNC | |
| Brown, Paul Stuart | VIC | Applied for TE | CO | Exempt 1967 on appeal |
| Brown, Peter F. | VIC | FTC NSA | CO | NC 19/8/65 |
| Bruce, Michael D. | WA | Applied for TE | CO | Dismissed |
| Buchanan, Noel J. | NSW | Applied for TE | CO | Exempt 29/1/69 |
| Buckle, David W. | VIC | FTC NSA | CNC | Warrant issued 2/2/72 |
| Buggins, Dennis John | WA | Applied for NC | NC | NC 20/12/66 on appeal |
| Burcher, George | WA | FTC NSA | CNC | Fine 27/10/72 |
| Burdon, Philip O. | TAS | Applied for TE | CO | NC 26/10/65 on appeal |
| Burgess, Paul | NSW | FTC NSA | CNC | |
| Burns, Jonathan | ACT | Applied for TE | CO | Exempt 10/12/71 |
| Burns, Michael | NSW | FTC NSA | CNC | |
| Burstin, Graeme R. | VIC | Applied for TE | CO | Exempt 16/5/67 on 2nd appeal |
| Butler, Mark | NSW | Applied for TE | CO | Dismissed Medically unfit |
| Bye, Leo | NSW | FTC NSA | CNC | Twice adjourned 1972 |
| Byrne, Ian K. | NSW | FTC NSA | CNC | Warrant for arrest (?) |
| Cahill, Rowan J. | NSW | Registered/ Applied for TE | CNC/CO | Exempt 1969 on appeal |
| Calinan, Paul John | VIC | Applied for TE | CO | Exempt 12/2/70 |
| Callahan, Rex Francis | VIC | Applied for TE | CO | Appeal rejected NC |

| Name | State | Action | Stance | Outcome |
|---|---|---|---|---|
| Cameron, Glen | VIC | FTC NSA | CNC | |
| Cameron, Laurie R. | VIC | Applied for TE | CO | Exempt 26/7/? |
| Campbell, Alan | NSW | FTC NSA | CNC | |
| Campbell, Christopher R.P. | NSW | FTC NSA | CO | Fine Left Australia 1968 |
| Campbell, Kevin A. | WA | Applied for TE | CO | Exempt 20/1/67 |
| Cannell, Ian G. | | Applied for TE | CO | Exempt 1968 |
| Cannon, Bernard | NSW | FTC NSA | CO | |
| Carmichael, Laurie | VIC | FTC NSA | CNC | Fine x 2; 7 days Exempt |
| Carroll, Denys Edward John | | Applied for TE | CO | Exempt 1969 |
| Carroll, Ian R. | VIC | Applied for TE | CO | Exempt 10/6/71 |
| Cash, Gregory | QLD | FTC NSA | CNC | |
| Cathcart, Graham | QLD | FTC NSA | CNC | |
| Caudrey, Denis W. | VIC | Applied for TE | CO | Exempt 19/8/65 |
| Champion, Norman Dennis | NSW | Applied for TE | CO | NC 31/8/65 Appeal 21/12/65 Judgement reserved Outcome unknown |
| Childs, Brian O. | NSW | FTC NSA | CNC | Fine; refused to pay; 26 days |
| Childs, Michael | NSW | FTC NSA | CNC | |
| Christofides, Louis | NSW | FTC NSA | CNC | Fine 51 days; 3 months' bond |
| Chu, Benedict B.G. | NSW | Applied for TE | CO | Exempt 1/6/66 on appeal |
| Clark, Peter | VIC | FTC NSA | CNC | Fine; 8 days |
| Clark, Renfrey | ACT | FTC NSA | CNC | |
| Clarke, John Faris | WA | Applied for TE | CO | Exempt 11/5/70 |

Appendix 2  247

| Name | State | Action | Stance | Outcome |
|---|---|---|---|---|
| Cliffa, John Felix | WA | NS/TE (originally wanted NC but was asked to do rifle drill) | CO | AWOL during training 1970 |
| Clifton, Michael | SA | FTC NSA | CNC | Summonsed |
| Cochrane, Thomas | QLD | FTC NSA | CNC | Fine $50 plus costs |
| Cochrane, William | QLD | FTC NSA | CNC | Fine x 2 1971 |
| Coffey, Tim | VIC | Applied for TE | CO (66) | |
| Coleman, Ronald | NSW | Applied for TE | CO | Dismissed 5/10/67 |
| Collett, Noel Edgar | QLD | Applied for NC/TE | CO | Exempt on 2nd applic. 1966 |
| Colman, Ronald L. | ACT | Applied for TE | CO | Exempt 13/5/69 |
| Comey, Cliff | SA | FTC NSA | CNC | Fine; 7 days Fasted Exemption granted |
| Cook, David F. | WA | Applied for TE | CO | NC 31/5/66 |
| Cook, Gary James | WA | FTC NSA | CNC | Underground 2 years 1971; reduced to 18 months; pardoned 1972 |
| Cook, Murray C. | VIC | NS/TE | CO | Exempt on appeal 1971 |
| Cornwell, Bruce G. | VIC | FTC NSA | CNC | Fine plus prison 1971 |
| Covich, Danilo | WA | Applied for TE | CO | Rejected on appeal 1966 |
| Cowley, John | VIC | FTC NSA | CNC | Fine 17/5/71 |
| Cowrie, John A. | SA | Applied for TE | CO | Exempt 1970 |
| Craven, Robert | NSW | FTC NSA | CO | Exempt 5/5/69 |
| Crosling, Timothy | VIC | FTC NSA | CNC | |
| Cumberland, C.R.S. | NSW | FTC NSA | CNC | Court 10/5/67 & 22/5/67 |

| Name | State | Action | Stance | Outcome |
|---|---|---|---|---|
| Cutrupi, Michael | NSW | FTC NSA | CNC | Kapooka/ Holsworthy 1967 |
| Dalton, Anthony | VIC | FTC NSA | CNC | Fines Warrant issued 18/6/71 Underground |
| Dalton, Kim | SA | FTC NSA | CNC 1971 | |
| Darby, Rodney M. | VIC | Applied for TE | CO | NC 24/8/65 |
| Davies, Brian | NSW | Applied for TE | CO | Exempt 1969 |
| Davies, Ian | NSW | FTC NSA | CNC | Fine 1972 |
| Dawson, Douglas | NSW | Applied for TE | CO | Exempt May 72 |
| Day, David | VIC | FTC NSA | CNC | Fine $40 plus costs 1969 |
| De Lisseo, Gerardo | NSW | FTC NSA | CNC | |
| Dolk, Tony | NSW | FTC NSA | CNC | |
| Domazetis, George | VIC | Applied for TE | CO | Exempt 15/12/66 |
| Drummond, Neville | VIC | Applied for TE | CO | Exempt 28/11/66 |
| Drummond, Patrick | NSW | FTC NSA | CNC | |
| Duck, Kevin W. | NSW | Applied for TE | CO | NC 18/4/66 |
| Ducray, Robert | VIC | FTC NSA | CNC | Fine 10/5/71 |
| Duncum, Paul | NSW | FTC NSA | CNC | Fine |
| Easton, Brian Robert (Bob) | SA | FTC NSA | CNC | Fine plus 7 days Warrant issued 7/1/72 22 days 1972 |
| Ebel, John | VIC | FTC NSA | CNC | Fines x 2 1969 |
| Ebrail, Phillip | TAS | Applied for TE | CO | Exempt 14/9/71 |
| Erftemeyer, Joseph | VIC | FTC NSA | CNC | Fine Exempt by referral 1972 |
| Ernst, Martin Walter-Heinz | VIC | Applied for TE | CO | Exempt 17/6/65 |
| Farrell, John James | NSW | FTC NSA 1971 | CNC | |
| Fell, John | | | CNC | Fine plus 25 days; fine |

Appendix 2    249

| Name | State | Action | Stance | Outcome |
|---|---|---|---|---|
| Ferguson, Anthony | VIC | Applied for TE | CO | Seeking advice from FPC |
| Fetherston, Adrian | VIC | Applied for TE | CO | Awaiting call-up |
| Field, Gregory | NSW | FTC NSA | CNC | Fine |
| Finch, Wayne | VIC | FTC NSA | CNC | |
| Finkelstein, David | WA | FTC NSA | CNC | |
| Fisher, Ian | VIC | Applied for TE | CO | |
| Fletcher, David | VIC | FTC NSA | CNC | |
| Foley, A.J. (Tony) | NSW | FTC NSA | CNC | Court 1972? |
| Foley, Jeffrey Ross | VIC | Applied for TE | CO | Exempt 17/6/65 |
| Foley, Sean | NSW | FTC NSA | CNC | Fine; 29 days |
| Forster, Rowan | VIC | FTC NSA | CNC | Exempt on referral |
| Foster, Rodney L. | VIC | FTC NSA | CNC | |
| Fox, Paul | QLD | FTC NSA Burnt papers | CNC | Underground Prison 18 months Exempt 1972 |
| Franken, David | QLD | FTC NSA | CO | Fine; prison |
| Frazer, John Laurie | VIC | Applied for TE | CO | Exempt on appeal 6/5/69 |
| Fremlin, Alan | VIC | FTC NSA | CNC | |
| French, Bruce R. | TAS | Applied TE/NC | CO | NC duties |
| Fulton, Patrick | ACT | FTC NSA | CNC | Fine $40; $100 7 days 1970 |
| Galvin, Peter | NSW | FTC NSA | CNC | |
| Galvin, Richard | NSW | FTC NSA | CNC | |
| Garner, Roy R. | NSW | Applied for TE | CO 1967 | Exempt on appeal |
| Garrick, Robert J. | NSW | Applied for TE | CO 1970 | Exempt on appeal |
| Geelan, Terrence S. | NSW | Applied for NC | NC | NC 1967 |
| Gerrand, Christopher | NSW | FTC NSA | CNC | Deceased 1969 |
| Gerritsen, Rolf | WA | FTC NSA | CNC | Charge dismissed |

| Name | State | Action | Stance | Outcome |
|---|---|---|---|---|
| Gerritsen, Rupert | WA | FTC NSA | CNC | 6 years for planting bomb 1971 |
| Gilbert, Robert F. | ACT | Applied for TE | CO | Exempt 17/3/70 |
| Giles, Greg | NSW | FTC NSA | CNC | |
| Gillies, John D. | QLD | Applied for TE | CO | Dismissed 1971 |
| Gilling, Jeremy | NSW | FTC NSA | CNC/CO | Fined; arrested; exempted |
| Ginter, Laurie | VIC | FTC NSA | CNC | |
| Glare, Stewart A. | VIC | Applied for TE | CO | NC (on appeal) |
| Glover, Brian | NSW | FTC NSA | CNC | 7 days; exempted on referral 1971 |
| Godfrey, James W. | QLD | Applied for TE | CO | Dismissed |
| Golding, Philip J. | SA | FTC NSA | CNC | Fine; 7 days; 99 days 1972 |
| Goudie, Gavin D. | VIC | Applied for TE | CO | TE (2nd applic.) |
| Goutty, David | VIC | Applied for TE | CO | Dismissed 1968 |
| Graf, Peter John | VIC | FTC NSA | CO | Fine; 8 days 1971 |
| Graham, James K. | WA | Applied for TE | CO | TE 20/1/67 |
| Grant, Trevor | VIC | FTC NSA | CNC | |
| Gray, Brian | VIC | Applied for TE | CO | NC; appeal rejected |
| Gray, Walter | NSW | Applied for TE | CO | Exempt on appeal 1969 |
| Green, Stephen | QLD | FTC NSA | CNC | |
| Gross, William | SA | FTC NSA | CNC | Fine |
| Gubbins, Richard S. | VIC | Applied for TE | CO | NC Duties 1965 |
| Gudgeon, Mac Irwin | NSW | FTC NSA | CNC | Fine; 51 days 1969 Warrant issued 24/3/72 |
| Gunning, Peter | VIC | FTC NSA | CNC | Fine |
| Gunter, Warren L. | NSW | Applied for TE | CO | NC 1970 |
| Hall, Robert (Bob) | SA | FTC NSA | CNC | 7 days plus 7 days |
| Hall, Wayne Ernest | ACT | Applied for TE | CO | TE 23/7/69 |

Appendix 2    251

| Name | State | Action | Stance | Outcome |
|---|---|---|---|---|
| Hallworth, Richard | NSW | FTC NSA | CNC | |
| Halpin, John | VIC | FTC NSA | CNC | Appeal? |
| Hamel-Green, Michael | VIC | FTC NSA | CNC | Fine; 7 days; 16 days (for sit-in); 7 days plus fine Underground |
| Handbury, Mathew | VIC | FTC NSA | CNC | |
| Hankin, Adam N. | VIC | Applied for NC | NC | NC 12/8/71 |
| Harding, T.J. (Jim) | VIC | FTC NSA | CNC | Fine |
| Hargreave, Chris | TAS | FTC NSA | CNC | |
| Harris, Geoffrey | VIC | FTC NSA | CNC | |
| Harris, Peter | VIC | FTC NSA | CNC | |
| Hart, Gregory | NSW | FTC NSA | CNC | |
| Hartley, George | VIC | FTC NSA | CNC | |
| Harwood, Robin | SA | Applied for TE | CO | Exempt 29/7/66 |
| Havenhand, Bryan | ACT | FTC NSA | CNC | |
| Hay, Trevor | ACT | Applied for TE | CO | Exempt 23/12/68 |
| Haysom, Paul G. | VIC | FTC NSA | CNC | Warrant issued 4/8/71 |
| Head, Bruce D. | VIC | Applied for TE | CO | NC 23/1/67 |
| Headland, Keith R. | VIC | FTC NSA | CNC | Fined |
| Hearsch, Bernard | WA | NS/NC | NC | Granted 15/4/71 |
| Hearsch, Jack | WA | NS/TE 1971 | CO | |
| Heinrich, Leslie Charles | WA | FTC NSA | CNC | Charge of disorderly conduct dismissed 10/8/66 |
| Heldzingen, Errol | VIC | FTC NSA | CNC | Fine |
| Henderson, Alwyn | VIC | Applied for TE | CO | NC Appealed 1968 |
| Henderson, Michael | VIC | FTC NSA | CNC | |
| Henderson, Wayne | WA | FTC NSA | CNC | Fine $40 Underground |
| Hewett, Rex | NSW | Applied for TE | CO | Dismissed |

| Name | State | Action | Stance | Outcome |
|---|---|---|---|---|
| Hicks, Jonathan | VIC | FTC NSA | CNC | Fine $40 plus costs 27/4/71 |
| Higgs, David | VIC | FTC NSA | CNC | |
| Hill, Ian | VIC | FTC NSA | CNC | |
| Hill, Mark Patrick | TAS | Applied for TE | CO | Exempt 2/12/70 |
| Hill, Peter John | | NS/TE | CO | Dismissed. Puckapunyal 2 x 7 days; Holsworthy 10 days. Discharge medically unfit |
| Hill, Robert | VIC | FTC NSA | CNC | |
| Hills, Gary | NSW | FTC NSA | CNC | |
| Hince, Ken W. | VIC | FTC NSA | CNC | |
| Hocking, Ross | VIC | FTC NSA | CNC | |
| Holliday, Chris | VIC | FTC NSA | CO | |
| Hood, John A. | WA | Applied for TE | CO | Exempt 24/6/71 |
| Hooeyberg, Edo | WA | Applied for TE | CO | Exempt on appeal 18/8/70 |
| Hornby, Peter | NSW | FTC NSA | CNC | Fine; 22 days Fine; 2 years |
| Hovey, Roland J. | QLD | Applied for TE | CO | Exempt 7/8/67 |
| Howard, Ian Robert Leslie | VIC | Applied for TE | CO | Dismissed 29/9/66 |
| Howard, Ken | VIC | FTC NSA | CNC | |
| Howie, Ian | NSW | Applied for TE | CO | Exempt 5/11/71 |
| Hubbard, Victor A. | QLD | Applied for NC | CO | Exempt 10/5/71 |
| Hughes, David R. | VIC | Applied for TE | CO | Dismissed 2/10/68 |
| Hulsinga, Tjerk A. | SA | Applied for TE | CO | Exempt 15/9/69 |
| Hunt, David | NSW | FTC NSA | CNC | |
| Hurley, Michael J. | VIC | Applied for TE | CO | Exempt 28/11/66 |
| Hutchinson, Fabian | TAS | FTC NSA | CNC | Fine |
| Ihlein, Graham | VIC | FTC NSA | CNC | |
| Jacona, John C. | VIC | Applied for TE | CO | Exempt |

Appendix 2   253

| Name | State | Action | Stance | Outcome |
|---|---|---|---|---|
| Jedryka, John | SA | FTC NSA | CNC | Fine plus 7 days Exempt |
| Jensen, Graham | NSW | FTC NSA | CNC | Fines; 25 days; 7 days |
| Jessup, John | VIC | Applied for TE 1967 | CO | |
| Jiggins, John | QLD | FTC NSA | CNC | |
| Johansen, Chris | WA | Applied for TE? | CO | |
| Johnston, Barry | VIC | FTC NSA | CNC | Fines, 7 days Warrant issued 7/2/72 8 days |
| Jones, David G. | ACT | FTC NSA | CNC | Fined |
| Jones, Michael C.H. | NSW | FTC NSA | CNC | Fined Warrant Bailed 1970 |
| Joyce, Christopher K. | NSW | FTC NSA | CNC | Warrant issued 2/2/72 |
| Kalkman, Robert J. | VIC | FTC NSA | CNC | Fined 1971 |
| Kapaufs, Alfred | VIC | FTC NSA | CNC | |
| Keane, David | NSW | FTC NSA | CNC | Fined; 31 days; 7 days |
| Kelly, Bruce R. | QLD | Applied for TE 1966 | CO | NC |
| Kelly, Peter | NSW | FTC NSA | CNC | |
| Kelly, Roger | NSW | FTC NSA | CNC | Medically unfit 1969 |
| Kelton, Jim | SA | FTC NSA | CNC | Remanded FTC NSA |
| Kennard, Howard | VIC | Applied for TE | CO | NC 1965 |
| Kennedy, George | VIC | FTC NSA | CNC | |
| Kent, Glen Mercer | WA | FTC NSA | CNC | Fine |
| Kentish, Duncan | SA | Applied for TE | CO | Exempt 1966 |
| Keon, Robert Brian | VIC | Applied NC | NC | NC Duties |
| Kerin, David J. | VIC | FTC NSA | CNC | |
| Kilby, Brian | NSW | Applied for TE | CO | Dismissed 1970 |

| Name | State | Action | Stance | Outcome |
|---|---|---|---|---|
| King, Brian Denis | NSW | Applied for NC/TE | CO | Court-Martial; 70 days |
| Kinsey, Gordon | QLD | NS/TE | CO | Med. discharge |
| Kirk, Warren | VIC | Failed to comply NSA | CNC | |
| Kitching, Robin P. | NSW | Applied for TE | CO | TE on appeal 1965 |
| Knight, Christopher | TAS | Applied for TE | CO | Dismissed |
| Kobelke, John C. | WA | Applied for TE | CO | Exempt 1970 |
| Kochan, Michael | NSW | FTC NSA | CNC | Summonsed S51 NSA Arrested Prison (assault & obstruct) |
| Korobacz, Konrad. | TAS | FTC NSA | CNC | |
| Krepp, Laurie | VIC | FTC NSA 1972 | CNC | |
| Kruszewski, David | VIC | FTC NSA 1971 | CNC | |
| Lamon, John C. | WA | Applied for TE 1965 | CO | |
| Landau, John | NSW | FTC NSA | CNC | Fines; 7 days Medically unfit 1970 |
| Langford, Keith A. | VIC | FTC NSA | CNC | Warrant issued 6/4/72 |
| Langford, Mervyn | QLD | FTC NSA 1971 | CNC | |
| Langrish, Roy A. | WA | Applied for TE | CO | Exempt 14/5/70 |
| Lascars, Ronald | NSW | Applied for TE | CO | Exempt |
| Lavis, Roger Frank | WA | Applied for TE | CO | Exempt on appeal 1966 |
| Law, Anthony H. | SA | FTC NSA | CNC | Exempt 1971 |
| Lawry, Stanley J. | NSW | Details unknown | | Case adjourned |
| Le Breton, Peter | VIC | FTC NSA 1970 | CNC | |
| Lees, John Boyd | VIC | FTC NSA | CNC | Fine 1971 |
| Le Miere, Rene | WA | FTC NSA | CNC | Undergound 1972 |
| Lewis, Gregory D. | NSW | NS/TE | CO | Exempt on appeal |
| Lin, David | WA | Applied for TE | CO | Exempt 1971 |

Appendix 2     255

| Name | State | Action | Stance | Outcome |
|---|---|---|---|---|
| Lockwood, David | VIC | FTC NSA | CNC | Liable 2 years 1970 |
| Lovelock, C. | VIC | FTC NSA 1971 | CNC | |
| Lovett, Michael | VIC | FTC NSA 1970 | CNC | |
| MacDonald, Ian | VIC | FTC NSA 1969 Burnt draft card | CNC | |
| MacDonald, Mark | NSW | Applied for TE | CO | Exempt 1971 |
| Madden, Leonard G. | NSW | FTC NSA | CNC | Warrant issued 14/2/72 |
| Mallem, Peter G. | VIC | Applied for TE | CO | Exempt 1971 |
| Marr, Ronald B. | VIC | Applied for TE 1965 | CO | Exempt 1965 |
| Marginson, Simon | VIC | FTC NSA | CNC | |
| Martin, Charles E. | SA | FTC NSA 1966 | CNC | 11 months |
| Martin, David F. | QLD | FTC NSA | CO | Fines; 14 days Exempt |
| Martin, Robert W. | SA | FTC NSA | CNC | Fine; 18 months |
| Martinson, Paul | VIC | FTC NSA | CNC | |
| Mason, Kenneth | NT | Applied for TE | CO | Exempt |
| Mason, Ronald J. | WA | Applied for TE | CO | Exempt |
| Matteson, Michael C. | NSW | FTC NSA | CNC | Fines Warrant issued 30/8/71 3 prison sentences Underground 14 months Pardoned 1972 |
| Maxwell, John | VIC | Applied for TE | CO | Exempt |
| McCawley, Douglas Ross | NSW | Applied for TE 1967 | CO | NC |
| McCutcheon, Peter | | FTC NSA | CO | Exempt |
| McDermott, Brian | SA | FTC NSA | CNC | |
| McDonald, Ian D.N. | VIC | Applied for TE | CO | NC |
| McDougall, Garry | NSW | FTC NSA 1971 | CNC | |
| McGregor, David | NSW | Applied for TE 1965 | CO | |
| McKeich, Paul | WA | NS/TE | CO | Exempt 16/8/71 |

| Name | State | Action | Stance | Outcome |
|---|---|---|---|---|
| McLean, Neil K. | VIC | FTC NSA | CNC | |
| McLelland, Ken | VIC | FTC NSA | CNC | 18 months 1972 |
| McMullan, Ian | VIC | FTC NSA | CNC | Fine |
| McMullan, Robert | WA | Applied for TE | CO | Exempt 1968 |
| McPharlane, Anthony | NSW | Applied for TE | CO | Dismissed 1967 |
| McPhie, Bruce | VIC | FTC NSA 1967 | CNC | |
| McQuilton, Gordon A. | VIC | Applied for TE 1968 | CO | Exempt 19/10/68 |
| McQuirk, Jim | NSW | FTC NSA | CNC | NC Appeal 28/8/72 |
| Melamid, Sam | VIC | Applied for TE | CO | Exempt |
| Mercer, Kent Glen | WA | FTC NSA | CNC | Fined |
| Meredith, Stephen | TAS | Applied for TE | CO | Exempt 1970 |
| Miles, David | NSW | FTC NSA | CNC | |
| Millichamp, Brian | VIC | Applied for TE 1970 | CO | Exempt |
| Mitchell, Ronald | NSW | Applied for TE 1971 | CO | |
| Mitzkewitsch, Jim | VIC | Applied for TE | CO | Exempt 1970 |
| Moment, George | WA | Applied for TE 1970 | CO | Exempt on appeal 1970 |
| Monaghan, David | VIC | Applied for TE | CO | Exempt 1967 |
| Monro, Leonard J. | NSW | Applied for TE | CNC | Fine, 7 days Exempt (on appeal) |
| Monteri, Joseph | VIC | FTC NSA | CNC | |
| Moody, Stephen J. | QLD | Applied for TE | CO | Exempt 1967 |
| Moore, Darcy | QLD | FTC NSA | CNC | Fine |
| Morey, David | VIC | FTC NSA 1971 | CNC | |
| Morgan, Christopher R. | VIC | Applied for TE | CO | TE 1968 |
| Morris, Stuart | NSW | FTC NSA 1970 | CNC | |
| Mortimer, Peter | NSW | Applied for TE | CO | Exempt on appeal 1971 |
| Mowbray, David | NSW | FTC NSA | CNC | Exempt on referral 1971 |

Appendix 2  **257**

| Name | State | Action | Stance | Outcome |
|---|---|---|---|---|
| Mowbray, Graham | NSW | FTC NSA | CNC | 7 days Exempt on referral 1971 |
| Mowbray, Robert | NSW | FTC NSA | CNC | 26 days TE on referral 1971 |
| Muir, John | VIC | FTC NSA | CNC | |
| Mullen, Geoffrey | NSW | FTC NSA | CNC | Fined; 18 months |
| Muller, David | VIC | FTC NSA Burnt draft card | CNC | |
| Mulvey, Howard | NSW | FTC NSA 1970 | CNC | |
| Muntz, Robert | VIC | FTC NSA | CNC | Fine; 7 days |
| Murray, Neil Irvine | VIC | Applied for TE | CO | Adjourned 1968 |
| Napthine, Roger | VIC | FTC NSA Burnt draft card | CNC | Warrant issued 27/3/72 |
| Nayton, Jonathan F. | WA | Applied for TE | CO | Exempt 1971 |
| Neeme, Aarne O. | NSW | Applied for TE | NS/CO | Exempt on appeal 1971 |
| Nelms, Christopher | VIC | Applied for TE | CO | Exempt on appeal 1966 |
| Nicholls, Gary | NSW | FTC NSA | CNC | Fine 22/12/71 |
| Nixon, Darryl | QLD | FTC NSA | CNC | |
| Nolan, Darrell | VIC | NS/TE 1968 | CO | Dismissed |
| Nore, David L. | WA | Applied for TE 1966 | CO | Exempt on appeal 1966 |
| Norman, Kim R. | NSW | FTC NSA | CNC | Warrant issued 18/2/72 |
| Nott, Peter John | | Applied for TE | CO | Dismissed |
| Noyes, John | VIC | FTC NSA | CNC | |
| O'Donnell, Denis J. | VIC | Applied for TE | CO | 48 days Holsworthy 1967 |
| O'Donnell, Roderick | WA | Applied for TE | CO | Permanently deferred 1965 |
| Olsen, John | QLD | FTC NSA | CNC | |
| Onsman, Harry | VIC | FTC NSA | CNC | |

| Name | State | Action | Stance | Outcome |
|---|---|---|---|---|
| Onstenk, Peter | ACT | Applied for NC | NC | NC |
| Osborrn, Wayne G. | VIC | FTC NSA | CNC | |
| O'Sullivan, Brendon | VIC | FTC NSA | CNC | Fine |
| Overton, Kenneth | TAS | Applied for TE | CO | Exempt 1971 |
| Padgham, Ian R. | VIC | Applied for TE | CO | Exempt 1968 |
| Padgham, Stephen | ACT | FTC NSA | CNC | Fine; 7 days 1970 |
| Page, Gary Albert | VIC | Applied for TE | CO | Exempt 1966 |
| Page, James M. | VIC | FTC NSA Burnt draft card | CNC | |
| Page, John N. | NSW | FTC NSA | CNC | Fine 1971 |
| Pakavakis, Constantine | VIC | FTC NSA | CNC | |
| Palling, Bruce | VIC | FTC NSA | CNC | Fine; 7 days 1969 |
| Panter, Frank J. | VIC | Applied for TE | CO | Rejected on med. grounds |
| Park, Colin Neville | QLD | Applied for TE | CO | NC TE on appeal |
| Parnaby, Oliver | VIC | FTC NSA | CNC | Fine |
| Parsons, Michael | NSW | FTC NSA | CNC | Fine (or 13 days) 1971 |
| Pasco(e), John | WA | FTC NSA | CNC | |
| Paterson, Garry R.J. | VIC | Applied for TE | CO | Exempt 1968 |
| Paull, John | VIC | FTC NSA | CNC | Went to live in NZ 1967 |
| Pavlovic, Milorad | NSW | FTC NSA | CNC | |
| Payne, Michael | WA | FTC NSA | CNC | Fine; 7 days, 18 months Pardoned 1972 |
| Payton, Rodney J. | WA | Applied for TE | CO | Exempt 1966 |
| Pearce, Ian | VIC | FTC NSA 1970 | CNC | |
| Peck, Anthony | VIC | FTC NSA | CNC | |
| Pekkinen, Erki T. | ACT | Applied for TE | CO | NC 1969 |
| Perry, William | NSW | Applied for TE | CO | NC Court-martial |
| Pettit, Richard John | NSW | Applied for TE | CO | NC TE on appeal 1967 |

Appendix 2   259

| Name | State | Action | Stance | Outcome |
|---|---|---|---|---|
| Phillipson, Desmond | WA | NS/TE 1968 | CO | Puckapunyal; Holsworthy Appeal dismissed Med. unfit 1968 |
| Plane, Terry | VIC | Applied for TE 1970 | CO | Exempt 1970 |
| Plant, Rodney | VIC | FTC NSA | CNC | Fine 1971 |
| Plecas, Michael J. | WA | Applied for NC | NC | Decision reserved 1970 |
| Plusch, Alexander | NSW | FTC NSA | CO | Summons invalid? 1971 |
| Pointon, Tony | WA | Applied for TE | CO | Exempt 1971 |
| Poole-Johnson, John | WA | NS/TE | CO | AWL Arrested Discharged med. unfit 1968 |
| Potter, Graham | NSW | NS/AWL | CO | AWL Arrested Exempt 1971 |
| Praed, Clive L. | NSW | FTC NSA | CNC | Prosecution dismissed 1972 Joint citizenship |
| Priest, Lawrence J. | WA | Applied for TE | CO | NC Duties 1971 |
| Pye, John | NSW | FTC NSA 1971 | CNC | |
| Ramsden, Philip D. | VIC | Applied for TE | CO | Exempt 1970 |
| Rattigan, Peter | WA | FTC NSA | CNC | Underground until December 1972 |
| Reed, Peter Hugh | WA | Applied for TE | CO | Exempt 1971 |
| Reeves, Robert K. | VIC | Applied for TE | CO | Exempt 1965 |
| Reisenleiter, Gordon | QLD | FTC NSA | CNC | 2 years |
| Rendevski, Jim | VIC | FTC NSA | CNC | |
| Reynolds, William James | VIC | FTC NSA | CNC | Fine plus 7 days 1971 |
| Rhodes, Alan | VIC | FTC NSA | CNC | |
| Rice, Michael | VIC | FTC NSA 1970 | CNC | |
| Richardson, Dick | ACT | FTC NSA 1971 | CNC | |

| Name | State | Action | Stance | Outcome |
|---|---|---|---|---|
| Ridley, James P. | WA | Applied for TE | CO | Exempt on appeal 1966 |
| Roberts, Leonard | VIC | Applied for NC | NC | NC Duties 1969 |
| Robertson, Ian | NSW | Applied for TE | CO | Hearing 16/12/71. Result unknown |
| Robertson, John | NSW | FTC NSA | CNC | Fine (3 months to pay) 1972 |
| Robertson, Trevor | WA | Applied for TE | CO | Exempt 1970 |
| Robson, Kevin G. | QLD | Applied for NC | NC | NC on appeal 1971 |
| Rodenburg, Robert | VIC | Applied for TE | CO | Exempt 1970 |
| Rodgers, William A.C.R. | VIC | Applied for TE | CO | Exempt 1970 |
| Rodwell, Brian S. | ACT | Applied for NC | NC | NC 1969 |
| Rookes, Ken | VIC | FTC NSA | CNC | |
| Rooney, Stephen | VIC | FTC NSA | CNC | |
| Ross, Brian | VIC | FTC NSA | CNC | Fine; 1 day; 11 months 1968-69 |
| Rowe, John | SA | Applied for TE | CO | Exempt 1969 |
| Rowland, Melville | VIC | Applied for TE 1965 | CO | |
| Rozenthals, John | NSW | FTC NSA 1970 | CNC | |
| Saggers, Raymond John | VIC | Applied for TE | CO | Deferred 1965 |
| Sandy, Geoffrey Allen | VIC | Applied for TE | CO | Exempt 1969 |
| Sanger, Robert L. | VIC | Applied for TE | CO | Exempt 1970 |
| Saunders, Phil | SA | FTC NSA | CNC | |
| Saxton, Gordon Richard | SA | Applied for TE | CO | NC 1966 Appeal dismissed 2nd applic. dismissed |
| Scates, Robert G. | VIC | FTC NSA | CNC | Warrant issued 14/3/72 80 days 1972 |
| Schambre, Edward | VIC | FTC NSA 1970 | CNC | |
| Schanka, Peter | NSW | FTC NSA 1971 | CNC | |

Appendix 2    261

| Name | State | Action | Stance | Outcome |
|---|---|---|---|---|
| Schapper, Derek | WA | FTC NSA | CNC | |
| Scott, A.J.A. (John) | SA | FTC NSA | CNC | Underground 1971–72 |
| Scougall, David | SA | FTC NSA | CNC | |
| Scurrah, Barry John | VIC | Applied for TE | CO | NC Appeal dismissed Exemption on appeal 1970 |
| Shanley, Chris | NSW | FTC NSA | CNC | |
| Shaw, David L.J. | VIC | Applied for NC | NC | Awaiting result 14/9/65 |
| Sills, Alan | NSW | FTC NSA | CNC | |
| Silson, Robert | SA | Applied for TE | CO | Exempt 2nd applic. 1968 |
| Simpson, Daniel J. | QLD | Applied for TE | CO | Exempt 1966 |
| Smalley, Douglas | VIC | Applied for TE | CO | Exempt 1965 (1st hearing) |
| Smith, Geoffrey | NSW | Applied for TE | CO | Exempt 1971 |
| Smith, Gregory O. | WA | Applied for TE | CO | Exempt 1967 |
| Smith, Martin | VIC | FTC NSA | CNC | |
| Smith, Peter Scott | WA | Applied for TE | CO | Exempt 1970 |
| Smith, Philip Douglas | TAS | Applied for TE | CO | Exempt 1969 |
| Soames, Christopher | NSW | Applied for TE (3 times) | CO | Third attempt 1971 |
| Spillane, Brian William | NSW | Applied for TE | CO | NC 1965 |
| Sprod, Timothy James | TAS | FTC NSA | CNC | Fined; 3 months to pay 1971 |
| Stead, Robert | NSW | NS/TE | NS/CO | Dismissed Decided not to appeal Served 2 years Army |
| Steele, George | VIC | FTC NSA | CNC | Liable to 2 years 1970 |

| Name | State | Action | Stance | Outcome |
|---|---|---|---|---|
| Steele, Terence Oliver | VIC | FTC NSA | CNC | NC Fine Arrested, taken to Kapooka Agreed to train 1967 |
| Stephens, Gregory D. | NSW | Applied for TE | CO | NC 1967 |
| Stephens, William Francis | NSW | FTC NSA | CNC | NC 1967 |
| Stephenson, Geoffrey | VIC | FTC NSA | CNC | |
| Stephenson, William | NSW | FTC NSA 1970 | CNC | |
| Stevenson, Peter | VIC | FTC NSA 1971 | CNC | |
| Stewart, Robert | NSW | Applied for TE | CO | NC |
| Stroud, Brian E. | VIC | Applied for TE | CO | NC Appeal dismissed 1968 |
| Sweet, Jeffrey L. | NSW | Applied for TE 1971 | CO | Dismissed |
| Symons, Michael | NSW | Applied for TE | CO | Exempt 1966 |
| Taft, Mark | VIC | FTC NSA | CNC | Fine 1971 |
| Talbot, Gregory R. | VIC | Unknown | | NC 1969 |
| Tarrant, Joe (John) | NSW | FTC NSA 1969 | CNC | |
| Tate, Aaron | NSW | Deferred FTC NSA 1971 | CNC | |
| Taylor, Ian R. | VIC | Applied for TE 1968 | CO | |
| Taylor, Michael Z. | TAS | Applied for TE 1967 | CO | Exempt on appeal 1967 |
| Taylor, Nicholas | NSW | Applied for TE 1970 | CO | 2 appeals dismissed 1970 |
| Taylor, Phillip | VIC | Applied for TE | CO | Exempt |
| Temple, Geoffrey | NSW | Applied for TE | CO | Exempt 1969 |
| Thiele, Robert W. | SA | Applied for TE 1968 | CO | Exempt 1969 |
| Thomas, Alexander John (Sandy) | VIC | FTC NSA | CNC | Warrant for arrest 1972 Underground 1972 |

Appendix 2   263

| Name | State | Action | Stance | Outcome |
|---|---|---|---|---|
| Thomas, William Ian (Bill) | WA | FTC NSA | CNC | 7 days Underground 1972 Warrant issued 3/3/72 |
| Thorp, Douglas H. | WA | Applied for TE | CO | Exempt 1967 |
| Townsend, Simon P. | NSW | Applied for TE twice | CO | 31 days Exempt on 2nd applic. |
| Townsend, Stephen | NSW | FTC NSA | CNC | Fine; 29 days; 2 years |
| Tropp, Fred | VIC | FTC NSA | CNC | |
| Trotter, Gerard R. | WA | FTC NSA | CNC | Warrant issued 23/7/71 |
| Truscott, Leonard | NSW | FTC NSA | CNC | Fine; 29 days Medical exemption |
| Tuck, Martin John | NSW | FTC NSA | CNC | Fine; warrant; adjourned; withdrawn |
| Turner, Ian | VIC | FTC NSA | CNC | Warrant Applic. dismissed Prison; released Dec. 1972 |
| Tuting, Frank | NSW | Applied for TE | CO | NC; appeal dismissed 1965 |
| Tyas, Brian John | NSW | Applied for TE | CO | Dismissed 1965 |
| Valada, Dominic | WA | Applied for TE | CO | Exempt 1966 |
| Van de Klooster, Willy | NSW | Applied for either TE or NC duties | | NC 14/4/69 |
| Van de Wiel, Stanislas J. | VIC | Applied for TE | CO | Dismissed; med. exempt 1965 |
| Varley, John | VIC | FTC NSA | CNC | Fine x 2 1970, 1971 |
| Vergunst, Robert | VIC | FTC NSA | CNC | |
| Vick, Malcolm | SA | FTC NSA 1972 | CNC | |
| Waite, Paul Ernest | VIC | Applied for TE | CO | Exempt 1965 |
| Walker, Alan | VIC | FTC NSA | CNC | Fine 1971 |

| Name | State | Action | Stance | Outcome |
|---|---|---|---|---|
| Wall, Peter K. | VIC | Applied for TE 1968 | CO | Exempt on appeal 1968 |
| Wallace, Donald I. | VIC | Applied for TE 1965 | CO | Exempt 1965 |
| Wallace, Robb | VIC | Applied for TE 1970 | CO | Exempt 1970 |
| Waller, Paul | NSW | FTC NSA 1970 | CNC | |
| Walpole, Christopher | VIC | FTC NSA | CNC | |
| Warren, Geoff | VIC | FTC NSA | CNC | Fine 1970 |
| Waters, Nicholas | VIC | FTC NSA | CNC | |
| Watson, Colin | VIC | FTC NSA | CNC | Fine 1971 |
| Watson, Ian | VIC | Deferred until 1969 | | |
| Webb, Peter | VIC | Applied for TE | CO | Not balloted in 1968 |
| Weir, Michael G. | WA | FTC NSA | CNC | |
| Wellington, Graham Ralph | VIC | Applied for TE | CO | NC 1968 |
| Welsh, James K. | VIC | Applied for TE | CO | Exemption 1968 |
| Wettenhall, Simon C. | VIC | Applied for TE | CO | Exemption on appeal 1969 |
| Wheelwright, Brian D. | WA | Applied for TE | CO | Exempt 1967 |
| Wheelwright, P.V. | VIC | FTC NSA 1970 | CNC | |
| Whisson, Stanley | WA | Applied for TE | CO | NC 1966 |
| White, Alan | VIC | Applied for NC | NC | NC on appeal 1969 |
| White, Michael | VIC | FTC NSA 1971 | CNC | |
| White, William Phillip Orrick | NSW | Applied for TE | CO | Appeal dismissed NC Refused to serve Exemption on 2nd applic. 1965–6 |
| Wickes, Ronald J. | WA | FTC NSA | CNC | Warrant issued 28/3/72 |
| Wickham, Peter | NSW | FTC NSA 1969 | CNC | |

| Name | State | Action | Stance | Outcome |
|---|---|---|---|---|
| Wilkes, Ken | VIC | FTC NSA | CNC | |
| Wilson, Geoffrey | NSW | FTC NSA 1969 | CNC | |
| Wilson, John R. | QLD | FTC NSA | CNC | 2 x 14 days 1972 |
| Wolfram, Malcolm | NSW | Applied for TE | CO | Dismissed 1971 |
| Wollin, John | VIC | FTC NSA | CNC | |
| Wood, Alan John | SA | Applied for TE | CO | Exempt 1966 |
| Wood, Michael | VIC | FTC NSA 1970-71 | CNC | |
| Wood, W. Robert | NSW | FTC NSA 1969 | CNC | |
| Woods, Robert (Bob) | | FTC NSA | CNC | Fine; 33 days 1972 |
| Woolnough, Rodney G. | TAS | Applied for TE 1970 | CO | Exempt 1970 |
| Wray, Simon A. | TAS | NS/TE | CO | Exempt 1970 |
| Wright, Ian M. | NSW | Applied for TE | CO | Appeal dismissed 1969 |
| Wyatt, David | SA | Applied for TE 1966 | CO | Exempt 1966 |
| Yates, Ian | SA | FTC NSA 1970 | CNC | |
| Yates, Thomas J. | VIC | Applied for TE | CO | NC 1967 |
| Ysendoorn, Robert | NSW | Applied for TE | CO | Exempt on appeal 1966 |
| Zarb, John Francis | VIC | FTC NSA | CNC | 2 years 1968 |

# Endnotes

**CHAPTER 1** - 'History shows no certain evidence that preparation for war ensures peace'

1. The statement that forms the title of this chapter comes from the Religious Society of Friends (Quakers), *The Peacemaker*, August 1950, p. 1.
2. Office of the Historian, 'The Australia, New Zealand and United States Security Treaty (ANZUS Security Treaty), 1951', [website] https://history.state.gov/milestones/1945-1952/anzus (accessed 9 January 2020). SEATO = the South East Asia Treaty Organisation.
3. Commonwealth of Australia. Department of Defence, 'National Service Training. Reasons for Introduction of National Service Training', n.d. (1967?), in National Archives of Australia (NAA) Series A1946/15, item 1967/2659.
4. V.G. Abraham, 'National Service Act – Conscription', *The Peacemaker*, May 1951, p. 1.
5. 'A Blow for Human Decency', Editorial, *Sydney Morning Herald*, 6 April 1954, p. 2; Readers' Letters, 'Objectors', *Sun* (Sydney), 9 April 1954, p. 20.
6. Commonwealth of Australia. Department of Defence, 'Defence Committee Minute No. 30/1950 of 16th March, 1950: Conscientious Objectors' in NAA Series A1945 T3, item 182/1/12. The Act also exempted 'persons subject to a prescribed physical or mental disability'.
7. Second Reading of National Service Bill, 5 December 1950, *Historical Hansard*, https://historichansard.net/senate/1950/19501205_senate_19_211/#subdebate-20-0-s0 (accessed 3 February 2020).
8. Commonwealth of Australia. National Service Regulations. Extract from Part IV, 'Conscientious Objectors' in NAA Series A1945 T3, item 182/1/12.
9. Commonwealth of Australia. Department of the Army, Minister for the Army to Rev. E.H. Woollacott, 3 August 1955, in NAA Series A1945 T3, item 182/1/12.
10. Commonwealth of Australia. Department of the Army, Secretary, Department of the Army to Secretary, Department of Defence, 17 January 1956 in NAA Series A1945 T3, item 182/1/12.
11. 'A General on COs', *The Peacemaker*, July 1956, p. 2.
12. 'Conscience has not made cowards of these', *The Peacemaker*, June 1954, p.1.
13. Rev. E.E.V. Collocott, Open letter to Prime Minister Robert Menzies, 23 April 1951, in NAA Series A462/8, item 430/2/1.
14. WILPF to Menzies, 12 September 1951, and reply 16 November 1951 in NAA Series A 462/5, item 430/2/14, folios 30, 31.
15. S. Blackburn Abeyasekere, 'Blackburn, Maurice McCrae (1880–1944)', *Australian Dictionary of Biography*, National Centre of Biography, Australian National University, http://adb.anu.edu.au/biography/blackburn-maurice-mccrae-5258/text8861, published first in hardcopy 1979 (accessed online 1 December 2020).

16  'Boy-conscription' in *Anti-Militarist News*, a circular of the League for Freedom, March 1951, no. 7 in Abraham Papers (collection held by the author at the time of writing). For an account of conscientious objectors to 'boy conscription', see B. Oliver, *Peacemongers, Conscientious Objectors to Military Service in Australia, 1911-1945*, Fremantle, Fremantle Arts Centre Press, 1997, chapter 1.
17  Mason family to Menzies, 2 October 1951, and Department of Labour and National Service Memorandum to Secretary of Prime Minister's Department, 26 October 1951, in NAA Series A462/5, item 430/2/14, folios, 20, 28; Australian Christadelphian Central Standing Committee to Menzies, 29 April 1952 in item 430/2/14.
18  K.D. Howard, *Political Benefit, Defence Burden: the Australian National Service Training Scheme of 1950-1960*, MA diss., Crawley, University of Western Australia, 1992, pp. 210-214. See also *Morning Bulletin* (Rockhampton, Q), 13 March 1953, p. 4.
19  *The Peacemaker*, June 1951, p. 1.
20  Secretary, Department of Labour and National Service to Hasluck, 8 March 1952, and Holt to Hasluck, 10 April 1952, in NAA Series A462/5, item 430/2/11, folios 68 and 69; Gare to Fadden, 10 June 1952, in item 430/2/11, folio 97.
21  *Anti-Militarist News*, no. 11, pp. 13-15.
22  Ashby to Fadden, 4 June 1952, and Drummond to Fadden, 14 June 1952, in NAA Series A462/5, item 430/2/11, folio 93. The Sydney meeting of the Quakers, WILPF and the NSW Peace Council also protested (see item 430/2/11, folios 119, 120 and 139); *Tribune*, (Sydney), 20 August 1952, p. 11.
23  F.R. Sinclair to the Secretary, Prime Minister's Department, 30 September 1952, in NAA Series A462/5, item 430/2/11, Part 1, folio 163.
24  Unidentified newspaper clipping, n.d, enclosed with letter Gospel Publicity League to Menzies, 2 August 1952, in NAA Series A462/5, item 430/2/11, folio 118.
25  The Australian Christadelphian Central Standing Committee to Menzies, 31 August 1953, enclosing unidentified newspaper clipping, dated 8 August 1953, in NAA Series A462/5, item 430/2/1, Part 2, folio 46.
26  Garrett to Menzies, 15 August 1952 in NAA Series A462/5, item 430/2/11, folio 126.
27  Davies to Menzies, 29 April 1952 in NAA Series A462/5, item 430/2/11, folio 133; also Davies to Menzies, 28 July 1952 (folio 144) and 25 August 1952 (folio 128).
28  Decision no. 519 of 19 August. See Memorandum from Department of Labour and National Service to Secretary Prime Minister's Department, 25 August 1952. See also information about the dismissal of Arthur Wright's application by Solling on 31 July 1952, in the same document, folio 144. Regarding media reports and comment, see, e.g., *Advocate* (Burnie, Tasmania), 4 September, 1952, p. 4; *Goulburn Evening Post*, 4 September 1952, p. 3; *The Advertiser* (Adelaide), 4 September 1952, p. 1; *Mercury* (Hobart), 4 September 1952, p. 4; *Argus* (Melbourne), 4 September 1952, p. 14; Letters to the Editor, *News* (Adelaide), 9 September 1952, p. 10.
29  '[Church of Christ] Seek Exemption from Military Service', *Daily Examiner* (Grafton, NSW), 25 March 1952, p. 1.
30  Anti-Conscription Council of Victoria, 'Reports of CO Hearings, Melbourne 1951-8', typewritten report, n.d., (c. December 1951) from Papers of Vivienne Abraham 1938-1989, NLA Accession no. MS 9152/5/3.
31  V. Abraham to K. Kenafick, 18 August 1953, and Pacifist Movement of Victoria, notice of meeting, 26 August 1953, in file 'Victoria 1953', folder no 2; 'PMV Conference - 5th & 6th April 1957: Topics for discussion' in file 'Victoria 1957', folder no 3, Abraham Papers.
32  These examples were taken from *Warwick Daily News*, 3 April, 1952, p. 2; *Townsville Daily Bulletin*, 2 August 1952, p. 1; *The West Australian*, 5 September 1952, p. 4. *Brisbane Telegraph*, 10 June 1954, p. 3; *Morning Bulletin* (Rockhampton), 11 June 1954, p. 1.
33  *Border Watch* (Mount Gambier, SA), 15 January 1953, p. 4.
34  *The West Australian*, 21 February 1953, p. 7.
35  See, for example, the testimony of Neville McLeod Bundesen in the Mackay (Qld) Court of Petty Sessions on 28 April 1953, *Daily Mercury* (Mackay, Qld), 29 April, 1953, p. 3.

Endnotes   269

**CHAPTER 2 -** 'I do not feel satisfied that he holds a conscientious belief'

1   'Youths seek training exemptions,' *The Peacemaker,* August 1953, p. 2.
2   'CO Appeals', *The Peacemaker,* September 1953, p. 2.
3   'Conscientious Beliefs as seen by Judges,' *The Peacemaker,* November 1953, p. 2.
4   *Evening Advocate* (Innisfail, Qld), 8 July 1954, p. 4.
5   *Morning Bulletin* (Rockhampton), 21 February, 1953.
6   *Warwick Daily News,* 18 November 1954.
7   *The Peacemaker,* March 1955, p. 2.
8   Ellen Star Brinton, 'How Peace Groups Defeated Universal Military Training in USA', *The Peacemaker,* January 1954, p. 2. Unfortunately, this did not spell the end of conscription in the USA. *The Peacemaker,* March 1955, p. 1, reported that the US House of Representatives had voted 'overwhelmingly' in favour of extending conscription for another four years.
9   *Age* (Melbourne), 14 April 1954; 'Cobalt bomb only for madmen', *The Peacemaker,* May 1954, p. 1. The Manhattan Project was the code name for the project that developed the nuclear bombs that devastated the Japanese cities of Hiroshima and Nagasaki in August 1945; also 'Atomic Scientists debate moral issues', *The Peacemaker,* April 1954, p. 1.
10   *The Peacemaker,* December 1953, p. 4; Jan–February 1954, p. 4; March 1954, p. 4; April 1954, p. 4.
11   *The Peacemaker,* June 1954, p. 2.
12   VGA [Vivienne Grace Abraham], 'Conscientious Objectors', *The Peacemaker,* September–October 1954, p. 2.
13   *The Peacemaker,* December 1955, p. 1.
14   *Canberra Times,* 2 May 1957, p. 6; 7 June 1957, p. 5.
15   *Canberra Times,* 27 November 1959, p. 1.
16   B. Oliver, '"What Kind of Democracy is This?". Conscientious objectors to the National Service Schemes, 1950-1972' in B. Oliver and S. Summers (eds.), *Lest we Forget? Marginalised aspects of Australia at war and peace,* Bentley, WA, Black Swan Press, 2014, p. 90.
17   Reed, J, judgement, 'Shipard v The Minister of State for Labour and National Service, 22nd September 1958', in Abraham Papers.
18   Christadelphian Standing Committee (NSW) to Menzies, 31 August 1953 and 4 January 1953, in NAA Series A462/5, item 430/2/11, Part 2.


**CHAPTER 3 -** 'War begins in the minds of men'

1   P. Edwards, *A Nation at War: Australian politics, society and diplomacy during the Vietnam War, 1965-1975,* Canberra, Allen & Unwin in association with the Australian War Memorial, 1997, pp. 52-76.
2   *The West Australian,* 19 March 1965, p. 2.
3   *The West Australian,* 24 and 31 March 1965.
4   'National Service Prosecutions', *The Peacemaker,* April–May 1971, p. 11.
5   *The West Australian,* 7 May 1965, p. 1.
6   High Court of Australia, Principle Registry, Canberra, Correspondence files, NAA Series A432, item 1184204, Commonwealth of Australia, National Service Bill, No. 126 of 1964, Section 16 (a), p. 7; also National Archives Fact Sheet, No. 164, 'National Service, 1965-72', http://www.naa.gov.au/collection/fact-sheets/fs164.aspx (accessed 15 June 2012).
7   Edwards, *A Nation at War,* pp. 23, 26, 27.
8   G. Stone, *War Without Honour,* Brisbane, Jacaranda Press, 1966, pp. 39-40.
9   For a description of how the National Service Scheme 1964-72 was conducted, including the 'birthday ballot' and a full list of the birthdays drawn, see S. Langford, 'Appendix: The national service scheme, 1964-72' in Edwards, *A Nation at War,* pp. 355-380.
10   'Australian Casualties in the Vietnam War, 1962-72', Australian War Memorial, https://www.awm.gov.au/articles/encyclopedia/vietnam/statistics (accessed 10 February 2020).
11   'Draft Resistance Movement' leaflet, n.d. [1968?], announcing formation of the movement and

planned activities, emphasis in the original, in Abraham Papers.
12   *The West Australian*, 12 May 1965, p. 22.
13   SOS Newsletter no. 1, September 1965; ASIO minute, dated 9 February 1966, ASIO field officer's report, n.d., and copies of SOS leaflets, in ASIO File, 'Associations – Individual – Save Our Sons – New South Wales, vol. 2, 1865-1966', NAA Series A6122, item 1668; also SOS letter to supporters, 29 June 1965 in NAA Series A6122/1, item 1813, folio 1.
14   M. Henderson, 'Notes on the formation of Save Our Sons, Perth'; also Anon, 'Save Our Sons [obscured] conscription and Vietnam', n.d., report of a meeting at Trades Hall, Perth on 2 April 1966, NAA Series A6122/1, item 1682, folio 15; *The West Australian*, 22 April 1966, p. 1 and 23 April 1966; Joan Davies [interviewed by Bobbie Oliver], Cottesloe, WA, November 2000.
15   J. Knott, 'Noack, Errol Wayne (1945-1966)', *Australian Dictionary of Biography*, National Centre of Biography, Australian National University, http://adb.anu.edu.au/biography/noack-errol-wayne-11249/text20065 (accessed 8 June 2012).
16   *The Spectator*, 19 March 1966, p. 4; 'Church against conscripts', *Age*, 6 May 1966.
17   *Catholic Worker*, no. 362, April, 1966, pp. 3-4; 'Letters', *The Advocate*, 24 February 1966, n. p. The Democratic Labour Party formed from the right wing of the ALP in the 1950s, when the Party split over the role and influence of the anti-Communist Industrial Groups. See, for example, R. McMullin, *The Light on the Hill: The Australian Labor Party 1891-1991*, Oxford University Press, 1991, chapter 11.
18   'Bishop J.S. Moyes applies the criteria of a "just war"', *The Anglican* (Sydney), 7 April 1966, p. 1.
19   'Discussion grows over Viet Nam', *The Anglican*, 14 April 1966, p. 3.
20   *The Australian*, 13 October 1967, p. 3.
21   'Chronology of Australian military involvement in the Vietnam war: 1962-1973', http://www.awm.gov.au/exhibitions/impressions/Chronology.pdf (accessed 13 June 2013).
22   *The Peacemaker*, January-February 1966, p. 1.
23   *The West Australian*, 18 May 1965, p. 2.
24   *Tribune*, 26 May 1965; also 'Vietnam War', *New Zealand History*, https://nzhistory.govt.nz/war/vietnam-war (accessed 22 July 2020).

**CHAPTER 4 - 'Why me?'**

1   R. Cahill, 'Crucible Days: Memoirs of a Cold War Kid', unpublished memoir, n.d., n.p, quoted with the author's permission.
2   M. Hamel-Green, 'Wanted for War: A memoir', *Southerly*, vol. 75, no 3, 2015, pp. 113-120.
3   Ken Mansell, 'Ballads, Ballots and Bureaucratic Balderdash: How I Coped with Conscription', unpublished memoir, quoted with the author's permission.
4   Hamel-Green, 'Wanted for War', n.p.
5   *The West Australian*, 2 July 1965, p. 1; 13 July 1965; 19 July 1965; 20 July 1965, p. 26; 26 July 1965; 27 October 1965, p. 18; 28 July 1965, p. 20.
6   'Robin Peter Kitching. Report of appeal before Judge Monahan in the District Court, Sydney, from decision of Rodgers, SM, sitting in special Court of Petty Sessions, 119 Phillip St, that he be registered as a person whose conscientious beliefs do not allow him to engage in combatant duties', pp. 1, 15; 'Statement from the Bench, dated 26 July 1965' in Abraham Papers, file: 'R.P. Kitching'.
7   *Daily News* (Perth), 17 June 1965, p. 11.
8   N. Mitchell to R.P. Kitching, 24 July 1965, in Abraham Papers, file: 'R.P. Kitching'.
9   'Notes of appeal before Judge Head, District Court, Holden, Sydney, 1 June 1966', in Abraham Papers, file 'Chu'.
10   'Notes of Court Appearance of Stanislas Johannes Van de Wiel, City Court, Melbourne, 16 June 1965', in Abraham Papers, file 'Van de Wiel'; *Daily News*, 17 June 1965, p. 11; *The Peacemaker*, May-June 1966, p. 3.
11   RSL, cited in *The Peacemaker*, September-October 1965, p. 3.
12   The following is drawn from Abraham Papers, file 'Max Beddow'. The only public reference to

Beddow's case found in the press was *Tribune*, 18 December 1968, pp. 1, 12. The photograph on page 12 shows a demonstration held at Sydney Town Hall, protesting against the jailing of John Zarb and Max Beddow.
13 Press Release from the Department of Labour and National Service, 9 March 1966, cited in *The Peacemaker*, March–April 1966, p. 3.
14 Abraham Papers, file: 'Max Beddow'.
15 J. Wilson [letter to B. Oliver and response to survey questions], 12 November 2000.

**CHAPTER 5** - 'What kind of democracy is this?'

1 'Judgment given by N.J. Hunt, Stipendiary Magistrate, in the Court of Petty Sessions, Phillip Street, Sydney, in the case of the conscientious objector Simon Patrick Townsend, 14 June 1968', in Abraham Papers, file: 'Simon Townsend'; also 'Private Simon Townsend' NAA Series M1369/2, item 'Townsend'.
2 'William Phillip Orrick White, Application for Registration as a Conscientious Objector, 5 November 1965; Transcript of Court proceedings of Application for Registration as a Conscientious Objector: William Phillip Orrick White (Applicant), 20 December 1965', p. 7; E.J. Bunting, Secretary, Prime Minister's Department, to F.E. Brown, Camberwell, Vic, 19 August 1966; Sworn Affidavit, signed W.P.O. White, 23 July 1966; circular letter from the Bill White Defence Committee, 8 August 1966; circular 'Bill White Conscientious Objectors' Defence Committee (formerly Bill White Defence Committee)', News Sheet no. 1, April 1967; Owen Webster, 'Bill White and the Power of Intransigence', typescript, May 1967, pp. 16–17, 19, in Abraham Papers, file: 'William White'; *Sydney Morning Herald*, 18 November 1966.
3 *Sun Herald*, 20 November 1966; *Sydney Morning Herald*, 22, 24 and 26 November, 1966, 3 December 1966; *Daily Telegraph*, 30 November 1966; *Australian*, 30 November 1966.
4 *The Peacemaker*, January 1967, p. 1.
5 *Sydney Morning Herald*, 20 December 1966 and 24 December1966; *Herald* (Melbourne), 25 February 1967.
6 *The Peacemaker*, February 1967, p. 3; March 1967, p. 3.
7 M. Dennison, 'The Trials of William White. In the Courts of Conscience', *Bulletin*, 26 November 1966, p. 24.
8 *The Peacemaker*, January–February 1966, p.1;
9 Edwards, *A Nation at War*, pp. 126–7.
10 *Sunday Times*, 11 June 1966.
11 B. Laufer, *All who do not resist participation are guilty': Draft resistance in Western Australia between 1970 and 1972*, Hons diss., UWA, 2006, p. 19.
12 *The Peacemaker*, April–May 1967, p. 1.
13 Typed draft of Federal Pacifist Council press release, n.d., Abraham Papers, file: 'Christopher Richard Paul Campbell'.
14 Typed draft of Federal Pacifist Council press release, n.d., Abraham Papers, file: 'Christopher Richard Paul Campbell'; Christopher Campbell to Vivienne Abraham, 5 March 1968, in Abraham Papers, file: 'Christopher Richard Paul Campbell'; *The Australian*, 13 March 1968.
15 Handwritten note in Abraham Papers, file: 'Laurie Carmichael'.
16 *The Peacemaker*, September–December 1971, vol. 33, nos 9–12, p. 12.
17 B. Cannon to V. Abraham, 31 March 1969 and 2 January 1970, in Abraham Papers, file: 'Bernard Cannon'.

**CHAPTER 6** - 'Under this government, it takes courage to be a conscientious objector'

1 Except where otherwise indicated, Stead's story draws on Abraham's hand-written notes and on correspondence between Stead and Abraham (1966–67), in Abraham Papers, file: 'Robert Stead'.
2 Probably formerly Thistle Harris, a member of the peace movement during World War II; see

Oliver, *Peacemongers*, p. 103.
3   *The Peacemaker*, February 1967, p. 1.
4   *The Peacemaker*, April–May 1967, p. 1.
5   'Prison Letters', *National U*, vol. 4, no. 5, 10 June 1968, p. 2.
6   Leaflet issued by the Melbourne University Labour Club and the Melbourne University Pacifist Club, n.d., c. April 1968, http://www.reasoninrevolt.net.au/bib/PR0001714.htm (accessed 15 June 2020).
7   Australia, House of Representatives, Debates, *Hansard*, 28 May 1968, <http://historichansard.net/hofreps/1968/19680528_reps_26_hor59/> (accessed 28 January 2021).
8   Parliament of Australia, House of Representatives, *Hansard*, 28 May 1968, pp. 1607–09.
9   *Pelican*, 2 May 1968, in Abraham Papers, file: 'John Poole-Johnson'. An NCO is a non-commissioned officer.
10  Notes in Abraham Papers, file: 'John Poole-Johnson'.
11  Desmond Phillipson, 'Statement to the Court, Supreme Court of Western Australia, Appeal No. 51 of 1968, 24 September 1968', in Abraham Papers, file: 'Desmond Phillipson'.
12  Typed notes, 'Desmond Phillipson – 5715736 – 30 days leave without pay from 30/5/68' in Abraham Papers, file: 'Desmond Phillipson'.
13  *The Peacemaker*, January–February 1968, p. 3.
14  Ken Beale's story is drawn from a telephone interview with B. Oliver, 8 September 2020, an email to B. Oliver, dated 12 November 2020, and Ken Beale, 'Turning Point', unpublished memoirs, quoted with the author's permission.
15  Glen Huxley to the author, 18 February 1994.

**CHAPTER 7 -** 'Not to oppose conscription, but to wreck it'

1   'A.S.C.M. meeting in Sydney calls for end to war', *The Anglican*, 18 January 1968, n.p.
2   David Bisset, survey response, 2001.
3   Draft Resistance Movement' leaflet, n.d. [1968?], announcing formation of the movement and planned activities, in Abraham papers.
4   M. Collins, 'If you have no objection – don't bother going to this meeting ..', *The Australian*, 23 March 1968, p. 38.
5   'Canberra sit-in: protesters to ignore fines?' *National U*, vol. 4, no. 5, 10 June 1968, pp. 1–2.
6   *Farrago*, vol. 44, no. 4, 1 April 1966, p. 1; *Tribune* (Sydney), no. 1566, 10 July 1968, pp. 1, 5; *The Australian*, 4 July 1968, n.p.
7   *Tribune*, 10 July 1968, p. 1.
8   'Draft Resistance Movement' leaflet, n.d. [1968?], announcing formation of the movement and planned activities, in Abraham papers.
9   Mike Payne, survey response, 2020.
10  Ken Mansell, 'The Ballad of Urquhart Street', unpublished memoir, cited with the author's permission.
11  *The Peacemaker*, January–February 1969, p. 1
12  'Close to treason', *Advocate* (Burnie, Tas.), 2 July 1968, n.p.
13  *The Peacemaker*, March–April and May–June, 1969. The names included: Brian Currie, Michael Hamel-Green, Frances Newell (Victoria) and Michael Matteson, David Mowbray, Pat Ruffels and Philip West (NSW). Pat Ruffels was an 'elder stateswoman' of the movement who had campaigned against conscription in World War II. See Oliver, *Peacemongers*, pp. 91, 120, 122.
14  Geoff Mullen, statement to electors, 17 September 1969, in Abraham Papers, file: 'Geoffrey Mullen'. The following account of Mullen's court case is from typed notes of court proceedings, n.d., draft of press release relating to Mullen's case in the Phillip Street Court in Sydney on 22 March 1971, and a typed press release in file 'Geoffrey Mullen'.
15  'Biographical Note. Michael Christopher Matteson' and typed notes in Abraham Papers, file: 'Michael Matteson'.
16  P. Manning, 'Portrait of a CO', *Bulletin*, 10 April 1971, p. 23.

17  Matteson to Minister, Labour and National Service, December 1967, p. 1., in Abraham Papers, file: 'Michael Matteson'.
18  Michael Matteson, statement issued on 5 May 1969, prior to entering Long Bay prison, in Abraham Papers, file: 'Michael Matteson'.
19  '23 Conscientious non-compliers', *The Peacemaker*, January–February 1969, p. 6.
20  G. Williams, 'Triplets want to help Vietnamese, not shoot them', *The Australian*, 13 October 1967, p. 3.
21  Graham Mowbray, Robert Mowbray, David Mowbray, 'Statement on National Service', 12 October 1967 and 11 April 1969, in Abraham Papers, file: 'Mowbrays: Joint Statements'. The following statements are all from this file.
22  'Good Friday sit-in', and 'Anzac Day sit-down', *The Peacemaker*, May–June 1969.
23  *The Peacemaker*, July–August 1969, p. 5.
24  'R. v. Graham Albert Mowbray: Court of Petty Sessions, Armidale, 23/5/69. Transcript of judgment by K.R. Webb, S.M.'; undated, unheaded, typed notes (by VA); *Armidale Express*, 23 May 1969, p. 2, all in Abraham Papers, file: 'Graham Mowbray'.
25  *The Peacemaker*, January–February 1970, p. 1.
26  David Mowbray, poem titled 'Resist', dated September 1970, and David Mowbray to Abraham, 18 August 1970, offering the poem for publication in *The Peacemaker*, in Abraham Papers, file: 'David Mowbray'.
27  'Conscientious objector is exempted from military service', *Armidale Express*, 22 March 1971, p. 10.
28  Australia, Senate, Debates, Hansard, 29 October 1970, <http://historichansard.net/senate/1970/19701029_senate_27_s46_c1/> (accessed 22 January 2021).
29  'National Service Figures', *The Peacemaker*, September–October 1969, p. 9.
30  Pearce to Snedden, 22 January 1970, *The Peacemaker*, January–February 1970.
31  See, for example, *The Peacemaker*, March–April 1970; May–June 1970.
32  G. Sandy, *Conscientious Objection: A Personal Story. The Vietnam War Years*, Montmorency: Busybird Publishing, 2018, pp. 4–5, 7-11, 14.
33  *The Peacemaker*, September–October 1970.
34  N.S. Reaburn, letter, *The Peacemaker*, January–February 1971.
35  *The West Australian*, 22 February, 29 and 30 March 1973; *Daily News*, 21 February, 19 September, 1973; *Weekend News*, 28 April 1973; ASIO Memorandum, 'Rupert Gerritson (WPF 17715)', dated 6 September 1974, in NAA Series A 6119, item 4148, 'Gerritson, Rupert'.

## CHAPTER 8 - 'Making a monkey out of the cops'

1  *The Peacemaker*, March–April, 1970; *Canberra Times*, 9 May 1970, p. 1. For the attack on Cairns and his family, see McMullin, *The Light on the Hill*, pp. 323-4; also P. Strangio, *Keeper of the faith: a biography of Jim Cairns*, Melbourne University Press, 2002 (ibook version), pp. 267-8.
2  John R. Wilson, survey response, 2000.
3  *Canberra Times*, 9 March 1970, pp. 1, 3.
4  Laufer, '"All who do not resist participation are guilty"', pp. 28-33; P. Cook, [email B. Oliver], 5 December 2020.
5  Australian Draft Resistance and the Vietnam War - statements by Michael Matteson and Geoff Mullen', *Radical Tradition*, http://www.takver.com/history/matteson.htm (accessed 1 July 2020).
6  '11,500 Defy Draft', *Resist: official organ of the Draft Resisters' Union*, vol. 3, no. 1, 10 February 1971, p. 1.
7  'Outstanding Warrants. National Service Act, as at 18.4.72', in ASIO File, 'Michael Christopher Matteson', vol. 1, NAA series no A6119, control no. 3455, item 138.
8  M. Hamel-Green, 'The Resisters: a history of the anti-conscription movement 1964-1972' in P. King (ed.), *Australia's Vietnam: Australia in the Second Indo-China War*, Sydney, Allen & Unwin, 1983, quoted from p. 121.
9  'Editorial', *The Peacemaker*, August–September 1970, pp. 1-2.

10   'Statement read by Derek Schapper for Gary Cook', unsigned, dated 7 October 1970, Abraham Papers, file: 'Gary Cook'.
11   M. Hamel-Green, 'The Melbourne University Draft Resistance Siege', unpublished essay, quoted with the author's permission.
12   'Australian Draft Resistance and the Vietnam War – statements by Michael Matteson and Geoff Mullen', *Radical Tradition*, http://www.takver.com/history/matteson.htm (accessed 1 July 2020).
13   Hamel-Green, 'The Melbourne University Draft Resistance Siege', n.p.
14   'Conversation with a Draft Dodger: an interview with Tony Dalton by the High Times Super Scooper', n.d., in Abraham Papers, file 'Anthony Dalton'; also, Hamel-Green, 'The Melbourne University Draft Resistance Siege', n.p.
15   *The West Australian*, 28 August 1971.
16   P. Galvin, 'Resisters' hectic week', newspaper cutting, unidentified, n.d., ASIO File, 'Michael Christopher Matteson' item 126. Also reported in *Canberra Times* and other newspapers, 2 March 1972.
17   *Canberra Times*, 25 April, 1972, p. 1.
18   Commonwealth of Australia, Senate, *Hansard*, 24 April 1972, p. 1360.
19   Laufer, '"All who do not resist participation are guilty"', p. 38.
20   'Biographical Note. Michael Matteson' in Abraham Papers, file: 'Michael Matteson'.
21   P. Samuel, 'Making a monkey of Canberra's cops', *Bulletin*, 6 May 1972, p. 19.
22   Laufer, '*All who do not resist participation are guilty*', p. 39; Bill Thomas [interviewed by B. Oliver], 11 September 2020.
23   Samuel, 'Making a Monkey of Canberra's Cops', p. 19.
24   'Statement by Michel Matteson', date 8 November 1972, in Abraham Papers, file: 'Michael Matteson'.
25   *Canberra Times*, 18 November 1972, p. 8; 10 November 1972, p. 7.
26   *The Australian*, 15 July 1972, n.p.
27   Mike Payne, survey response, 2020.
28   'Resisters say they led normal lives', *The West Australian*, 6 December 1972, p. 3.
29   Editorial 'N.S. warrants', *The West Australian*, 7 April 1972.

**CHAPTER 9 -** 'A stinking, rotten hole'

1    P. Manning, 'Portrait of a CO', *Bulletin*, 10 April, 1971, pp. 23–24; also Statement by Lou Christofides, n.d., Abraham Papers, file: 'Louis Christofides'.
2    'Visit to Gordon Reisenleiter', *The Peacemaker*, January–February 1969, p. 2
3    *The Peacemaker*, January–February 1970 and March–April 1970.
4    'Message from Irene Zarb', *The Peacemaker*, January–February 1969, p. 2, and November–December 1969, p. 8.
5    M. Hamel-Green, 'Wanted for War', n.p.
6    Museums Victoria, 'An underground affair', https://museumsvictoria.com.au/article/an-underground-affair/ (accessed 24 November 2020).
7    *The Peacemaker*, September–October 1969, p. 1.
8    *The Peacemaker*, November–December 1969, p. 7.
9    'An Inquiry into Brian Ross' beliefs', *The Peacemaker*, October–November 1970.
10   *The Peacemaker*, August–Sept 1970, p. 1.
11   Brian Childs to Vivienne Abraham, 20 April 1969; Brian Childs, 'Statement of Present Beliefs', dated 5 June 1972; F.W. Jenkins & Co., Brief to Counsel, 7 June 1972; Deputy Crown Solicitor to Messrs F.W. Jenkins & Co., 15 December 1972, in Abraham papers, file: 'Brian Childs'.
12   'National Service Act breaches', *The Peacemaker*, April–May 1970, p. 7.
13   *The Peacemaker*, May–June 1970, p. 1.
14   'Charles Martin gaoled. He refused to comply', *The Peacemaker*, August–September 1970, p. 1.
15   *The Peacemaker*, May–August 1971 and September–December 1971.
16   These details are drawn from documents in Abraham Papers, file: 'Geoff Mullen'.

17 *Perth Independent*, 6 February, 1972, p. 5; *Weekend News*, 8 April 1972; Peter Cook [email to B. Oliver], 22 November 2020.
18 Senator Hartley Cant, Speech to the Senate 12 April 1972, *Hansard*, p. 1050, https://historichansard.net/senate/1972/19720412_senate_27_s51/#subdebate-71-0-s0 (accessed 23 November 2020).
19 D.T. Evans, Attorney General, answering a question from Opposition MLA, Mr Williams, Legislative Assembly of Western Australia, 27 April 1972, *Hansard*, pp. 1057–8. Also 'Cook starts at Guild today', *The West Australian*, 19 July 1972, p. 3.
20 Claude Stubbs MLC, Minister for Prisons, answering a question from Opposition MLC, J. Heitman, Legislative Council of Western Australia, 15 August 1972, *Hansard*, p. 2465.
21 'Unemployed graduates ... Cook was "the best"', *The West Australian*, 27 July 1972, p. 14.
22 Bill Thomas, survey response, 2020, and interview.
23 Mike Payne, survey response, 2020. Peter Kropotkin (1842-1921) was a Russian nobleman-turned-anarchist and a biologist who applied Darwin's theory of evolution to the Siberian ecosystem. He rejected the use of Darwin's 'survival of the fittest' theory to justify slavery, poverty and inequality. See https://www.rsb.org.uk/biologist-features/who-was-peter-kropothkin (accessed 29 August 2021).
24 *Canberra Times*, 7 December 1972, p. 9; *The West Australian*, 5 December 1972, p. 1; 6 December 1972, p. 3.
25 Australian War Memorial, 'Vietnam War, 1962–75', https://www.awm.gov.au/articles/event/vietnam (accessed 13 October 2020).

**CHAPTER 10** - 'It made me a left-wing activist for life'

1 Australia, Senate, *Debates*, 23 February 1971, p. 226, http://historichansard.net/senate/1971/19710223_senate_27_s47/ (accessed 22 January 2021); Department of Labour and National Service (WA) file 65/691 'Instructions re National Service statistics total strength 1965 to...'; Hamel-Green, 'The Resisters', p. 121; *Resist*, vol. 3, no. 1, 10 February 1971, pp. 1–2.
2 '11,500 Defy Draft', *Resist: official organ of the Draft Resisters' Union*, vol. 3, no. 1, 10 February 1971, p. 1.
3 D.H. Monroe, 'Civil Rights and Conscription' in R. Forward and B. Reece (eds), *Conscription in Australia*, St. Lucia, University of Queensland Press, 1968, pp. 20–21; G. Withers, *Conscription. Necessity and Justice*, Sydney, Angus and Robertson, 1972, pp. 108, 119, 152.
4 *Defence Amendment Act 1992 No. 91 of 1992* - ss. 7, (4) and (5). http://www.austlii.edu.au/au/legis/cth/num_act/dlaa1992248/s7.html (accessed 12 July 2013) and s. 9, 'Persons exempt from service', (h) (i). http://www.austlii.edu.au/au/legis/cth/num_act/dlaa1992248/s9.html (accessed 12 June 2013).
5 Michael Hyde, cited in G. Langley, *A Decade of Dissent: Vietnam and the conflict on the Australian home front*, St. Leonards, Allen & Unwin, 1992, p. 226; also Garrie Hutchinson, cited on p. 216.
6 Sandy, *Conscientious Objection*, n.p.
7 CO [Anon] [email to B. Oliver], 12 November 2020.
8 G.W. & E.I Truscott to Secretary, *The Peacemaker*, n.d., in Abraham Papers, file: 'Len Truscott'; R.S. Tuting to Professor Charles Birch, University of Sydney, 30 June 1969 and to Hon. Nigel Bowen, Attorney-General, 25 June 1969; Truscott to Bowen, 25 June 1969 in Abraham Papers, file 'Frank Tuting'.
9 Newspaper cutting from *Herald* (Melbourne), 16 June 1971, in Abraham Papers, file: 'Peter Graf' (emphasis in original).
10 'Letters', *The West Australian*, 12 May 1972.
11 Tony Pointon [interviewed by B. Oliver, Leederville WA], 31 October 2000.
12 McKeich, Paul, 'In My Life: "What are we fighting for... next stop is Vietnam"', n.p., personal memoir quoted with the author's permission; survey response (2021).
13 John Wilson, survey response, 2000. Except where otherwise stated, the following comments are

drawn from responses to my surveys in 2000 and 2020 and from emails or interviews with former dissidents.

14 Cahill, 'Crucible Days,' n.p.
15 Museums Victoria, 'An underground affair,' https://museumsvictoria.com.au/article/an-underground-affair/ (accessed 24 November 2020).
16 McKeich,'In My Life,' n.p.
17 McKeich, survey response, 2021.
18 See, for example, T. Greenwell, 'The myth of abusive protestors,' *Inside Story,* 24 April 2020, https://insidestory.org.au/the-enduring-myth-of-the-abusive-protesters/ (accessed 16 February 2021).
18 Sandy, *Conscientious Objection,* n.p.
19 Cahill, 'Crucible Days,' n.p.
20 P. Cook [emails to B. Oliver], 22 November 2020; 5 December 2020.
21 P. Cook and J. Perkins, 'Vietnam War Objector. Gary James Cook,' Obituaries, *The West Australian,* 31 July 2019.
22 Cahill, 'Crucible Days,' n.p.
23 Beale, 'Turning Point,' n.p.
24 See, for example, A. Vassiley, 'Occupy Perth' in C. Fox et al. (eds), *Radical Perth, Militant Fremantle,* 2nd Edition (Melbourne: Interventions Inc, 2019), pp. 47–58; also 'Global school strike for climate change movement resumes, with protests taking place across Australia,' ABC News, 25 September 2020 https://www.abc.net.au/news/2020-09-25/global-student-strike-for-climate-action/12702434 (accessed 19 November 2020).

# Image Credits

p. 2:     *The Peacemaker*, August 1950.
p. 16:    *The Peacemaker*, May 1951.
p. 25:    *The Peacemaker*, July 1952.
p. 31:    AWM P00474.036. Reproduced with the permission of the Australian War Memorial.
p. 34:    *The Peacemaker*, May 1954.
p. 36:    *The Peacemaker*, December 1955.
p. 37:    *The Peacemaker*, June 1955.
p. 50:    SLNSW_FL4574923. *Tribune* photograph, reproduced with the permission of the Search Foundation.
p. 52:    *The Peacemaker*, June 1965.
p. 62:    Reproduced with the permission of Michael Hamel-Green.
p. 67:    Photograph: Bobbie Oliver.
p. 71:    *Tribune*, 18 December 1968, reproduced with the permission of the Search Foundation
p. 74:    SLNSW_FL450982. *Tribune* photograph reproduced with the permission of the Search Foundation.
p. 77:    SLNSW_FL45229028. *Tribune* photograph reproduced with the permission of the Search Foundation.
p. 80:    SLNSW IE4530049. *Tribune* photograph reproduced with permission of the Search Foundation.
p. 84:    SLNSW_FL4527239. *Tribune* photograph reproduced with the permission of the Search Foundation.
p. 86:    SLNSW_FL4526536. *Tribune* photograph reproduced with the permission of the Search Foundation.
p. 96:    Photograph: Kay Bolwell. Reproduced with the permission of Kay Bolwell and Melbourne University Archives.
p. 99:    '9 Say NO', the Bill White Conscientious Objectors Defence Committee, Vivienne Abraham collection, held by the author.
p. 100:   Source: Vivienne Abraham Collection; photo: Bobbie Oliver.
p. 107:   AWM PO5394.003. Reproduced with the permission of the Australian War Memorial.
p. 114:   SLNSW_FL4540088. *Tribune* photograph reproduced with the permission of the Search Foundation.
p. 116:   SLNSW_FL450072. *Tribune* photograph reproduced with the permission of the Search Foundation.
p. 118:   SLNSW_FL4541059. *Tribune* photograph reproduced with the permission of the Search Foundation.
p. 120:   SLNSW_FL4541061. *Tribune* photograph reproduced with the permission of the Search Foundation.

p. 126:     Vivienne Abraham Collection, held by the author.
p. 128:     Photo courtesy of Michael Hamel-Green.
p. 131:     Source: Author photographed from booklet *We Resist Because: statements of conscientious non-compliers with military conscription*. Published by the Federal Pacifist Council of Australia and the Bill White Conscientious Objectors Defence Committee, 1970. Vivienne Abraham Collection.
p. 134:     *National U*, 24 March 1969.
p. 144:     Photo courtesy of Michael Hamel-Green.
p. 146:     SLNSW_FL4568126. *Tribune* photograph published with the permission of the Search Foundation.
p. 148:     SLNSW_FL4570691. *Tribune* photograph reproduced with the permission of the Search Foundation.
p. 150:     Photo: Leo Davis. Reproduced with his permission.
p. 152:     Photo: Leo Davis. Reproduced with his permission.
p. 158:     Courtesy of Michael Hamel-Green.
p. 160:     Photo: Graham Howe.
p. 167:     Cover *The Peacemaker*, Oct-Dec 1971. Photographer unknown.
p. 168:     Photos: Bobbie Oliver.
p. 172:     SLNSW_FL456570. *Tribune* photograph reproduced with the permission of the Search Foundation.
p. 174:     SLNSW_FL4565713. *Tribune* photograph reproduced with the permission of the Search Foundation.
p. 177:     *We Resist Because: statements of conscientious non-compliers with military conscription*. Published by the Federal Pacifist Council of Australia and the Bill White Conscientious Objectors Defence Committee, 1970, Abraham Papers 186: WAN-0038033
p. 186:     WAN-0038033. *The West Australian*, 18 July 1972, reproduced with the permission of West Australian Newspapers.
p. 200:     Photo courtesy of Rowan Cahill.
p. 201:     Photo courtesy of Michael Hamel-Green.

# Index

Abraham, Shirley: 98, 140.

Abraham, Vivienne: 3-4, 6, 22-3, 30, 35, 37, 70, 87-9, 92-4, 97-8, 105-6, 108, 117, 179, 182, 199.

Anglican Church (Church of England): 14-15, 19, 22, 26, 56-7.

Anti-Conscription Council of Victoria: 21-2.

*Anti-Militarist News:* 17, 19.

Anti-Vietnam War Moratorium Committee (AVWMC): 146.

Application for exemption: 18, 27, 39, 70, 73, 78, 89, 105, 108, 139, 195.

Australian Intelligence Security Organisation (ASIO): 54, 207.

Australian Labor Party (ALP): 154, 171, 175, 177, 188, 208.

Australian National University (ANU): 70, 154.

Australian Peace Pledge Union/Peace Pledge Union: 3, 15, 46, 69.

Australian Student Christian Movement (ASCM): 113, 117.

Bailey, Warren: 32.

Barker, Greg: 82.

Beale, Ken: 91, 103, 106-8, 203, 206, 209.

Beddow, Maxwell: 68-72, *71*, 91-2, 98, 103.

Beel, Geoffrey John: 31.

Bisset, David: 7, 113, 206.

Borodale, Neville: 32.

Bresland, Vincent: 154.

Bundesen, Keith: 21.

Burning draft card/s: *62*, 81, 83.

Bury, Leslie (Minister for Labour and National Service 1966-69): 79, 87, 93, 130.

Cahill, Rowan: 7, 59-60, *200*, 201, 204-5, 207-8.

Cairns, Dr. Jim (Member of Parliament, ALP): 35, 105, 141, 146, 177.

Campbell, Christopher: 87-9, 97.

Cannon, Bernard: 89, 202.

Cant, Hartley (Senator, ALP): 183-4.

Childs, Brian: 179.

Christadelphian/s: 18-22, 25, 27, 30, 32, 35, 40, 78.

Christian Israelite/s: 22, 40.

Chu, Benedict Bun Gee: 66.

Church of Christ: 21, 22.

Church of England (see Anglican Church).

Citizens' Military Forces (CMF): 11, 12, 20, 47.

Clements, Victor Paul: 31.

Coaldrake, Frank (Rev, Canon): 14, 53.

Collett, Noel: 78.

Collie, Raymond: 55.

Collocott, E.E.V. (Rev): 15.

Communist Party of Australia (CPA): 54, 64, 124, 145.

Compulsory military service/training (see also conscription): 1-2, 6,14, 17, 22, 46, 53, 169.

Conscientious non-complier (CNC): 49, 113, 125, 194-6.

Conscientious objector (CO)/objection: 4, 18, 23, 35, 40, *52,* 69, 71-3, 77, 78, 87, 92, 97-8, 104, 110, 129-30, 137, 139, 141-3, 157, 178-80, 193, 201-4, 207.

    Definition: 3.

Conscientious Objectors' Advisory Committee: 68.

Conscientious Objectors' Referral Scheme: 137-9, 157, 193, 194.

Conscription: 1-6, 12, 15, 17, 23, 33, 40, 45, 47, 49, 52-6, 60-1, 65-6, 68, 73, 79, 82, 91, 93, 113, 117, 122, 127, 130, 140-3, 154, 156-7, 159, 162-5, 183, 188 (abolished), 193-8, 205-7.

Constantine, John George: 30.

Cook, Gary James: 7, 154, 156-9, *160,* 164, 166, 169, 181, 183-9, *186-7,* 199, 200, 205, 209.

Court martial: 78-9, 98, 103, 106.

Court cases: 5, 14; 20-3, 26-7, 31, 32-6, 38-9, 55, 60-7, 69-72, 73-82, 87-9, 92, 97, 106, 110-11, 122-31, 133, 141-3, 164-5, 169-71, 176-81.

Courts: 13, 18, 19, 49, 58, 78, 92, 137-9.

    Melbourne City Court: 22, 65, 125, 201.

    Phillip Street Court of Petty Sessions (Sydney): 64, 66, *67,* 73, 76, 127.

    Sydney District Court: 64, 76, 92.

Covich, Danilo: 64.

Currie, Brian: 125.

Dalton, Anthony (Tony): *128,* 156, *158,* 159, 162-3.

Davies, Edward: 33.

Davies, Ian: 169, 183.

Davies, Joan: 7, 55.

Democratic Labour Party (DLP): 56-8, 83.

Democratic Rights Council of NSW: 15.

Department of Labour and National Service: 18, 61, 67, 76, 109, 124, 142, 155, 157, 164, 192, 203.

Draft resistance commune (Melbourne University, 1971); 162ff.

Draft Resistance Movement (DRM): 52, 166.

Draft Resisters' Union (DRU): *128,* 128, 155, 166.

Ernst, Martin: 65.

Federal Pacifist Council (FPC): 15, 23, 35, 36, 87, 92, 98.

Fines: 12, 14, 23, 35, 47, 49, 55, 69, 72, 82, 83, 89, 117, 122, 124, 125, 127, 130, 131, 133, 136, 139, 164, 170, 175, 176, 180.

Finkelstein, David: 171.

Foley, Jeffrey Ross: 65.

Ford, Brenda: 125.

Fox, Paul: *158,* 159, 162.

Fraser, Malcolm (Minister for the Army, 1966-68): 69-70, 92.

Gallup Poll (results): 57, 65, 78.

Gaol (see jail, prisons).

Geneva Agreements: 54.

Gerritsen, Rupert: 83, 143.

Golgerth, Joyce (founder of Save Our Sons): 53.

Gorton, John (Prime Minister, 1968-71): 122-3, 164.

Graf, Peter: 199.

Gray, Brian: 64.

Gray, Walter Henry: 32.

Greenwood, Ivor, Senator (Attorney General, 1971-72): 159, 165, 183-4, *186-7.*

Grondal, Donald: 30.

Gunning, Peter: 169.

Hamel-Green, Michael: 7, 60-1, *62,* 125, *128,* 138, 156, *158,* 159, *160-1,* 162-3, 175-6, 194-6, *201,* 201, 208.

Haylen, Wayne: 82.

Headland, Keith: 7, 203, 207.

Henderson, Wayne: 154, 166, *168*.

Henig, Ian Reece: 31.

Hill, Colin: 21.

Holsworthy Military Barracks/Military Correctional Establishment: 5, 20-1, 23, 24, *25*, 29, 35-7, 78, *96*, 99, 102, 105, 195.

Holt, Harold (Prime Minister 1966-67; Minister for Labour and National Service, 1949-58): 19, 49, 55, 72, *74-5*.

Hornby, Peter: *128*, 176, *177*.

Jail, gaol, prisons (See also individual prisons listed under Prisons): 6, 47, 48, 60, 73, 93, 99, 108, 122-5, 132-3, 136, 141, 142, 155, 157, 163, 166, 170, 171, *172*, 173, 175, 176, 177-81, 182, 189, 195, 199, 208.

Jehovah Witness/es: 18, 19, 20, 21, 22, 26, 27, 30, 31, 33, 35, 39, 40, 64, 175, 203, 206.

Jenkins, F.W. & Co.: 3, 98, 179.

Jensen, Graham: 133, 136, 169.

Jensen, Nadine: 82-3.

Johnson, President Lyndon (LBJ): *84-5, 86*.

Jones, Michael: 142.

Kapooka army training centre (VIC): 69-70, 78, 91-4, 106.

Karrakatta Barracks (WA): 104, 109.

King, Brian Dennis: 79.

King, Charles: 30.

Kitching, Robin Peter: 64-6, 68.

Lamont, John Christopher: 64.

Le Miere, Rene: 154, 171.

League for Freedom/League for Freedom and World Friendship: 17, 19.

Liberal Party of Australia (Liberal Party): 11, 61, 123, 184.

Lines, William: 154.

Marshall, Ian: 7, 203.

Martin, Andrew: 123.

Martin, Charles: 180-1, 183.

Martin, Robert W.: 189.

Mason, Brian Keith: 20, 23, 29.

Mass refusal strategy: 155.

Matteson, Michael Christopher: 7, 125, 129-31, 133, 154, 156, 162-3, 165-6, *167*, 169-71, 173, 183, 189, 208.

McKeich, Lorraine: 110.

McKeich, Paul: 7, 91, *107*, 108-10, 199, 203-4, 206.

McLean, Jean: *50-51*, 53.

McLelland, Ken: 189.

McMahon, William (Billy), MHR, (Prime Minister, 1971-72): 46, 154, 181, 184.

Melbourne University: 3, 4, 128-9, 159, 162 ff., 197.

Commune (1971): 157, 162ff.

Siege (1971): 157, 162ff.

Menzies, Robert (Sir), (Prime Minister 1949-66)/ Menzies government: 1, 6, 11, 15-6, 18, 20-21, 40, 45, 48-9.

Meredith, Stephen: 7, 208.

Military training: 1-3, 5, 11, 17, 22, 24, 33, 40, 46, 64, 92, 105, 110-11, 157.

Minister for Labour and National Service: 11, 19, 36, 36, 59, 65, 79, 87, 93, 139, 143, 154, 191-2.

Moratorium campaigns/marches: 72, 141, 144-54, *144, 146-7, 148-9, 150-1, 152-3*, 156, 159, 162.

Morrisby, Donald Stanley: 31.

Mowbray, David, Graham and Robert: 125, *128*, 130-3, *131*, 136-7, 201.

Mullen, Geoffrey: 125-30, *126, 128*, 181-3.

My Lai Massacre: 145.

*National Service Act 1951-59 (NSA)*: 5, 11, 15, 19, 24-5, 29, 47, 53, 76, 87-9, 93, 96, 113, 117, 122, 125-7, 132-3, 137, 140-2, 145, 154-5, 158, 164, 169-70, 178-81, 185, 192, 207.

*National Service Regulations:* 137, 157.

National Service Scheme: 5-6, 26, 34, 38, 40, 45-9, 63, 68, 112, 140, 155, 169, 193, 207.

National Service trainees/training: 11, 14, 32-3, 38, 47.

Newell, Frances: 7, *96*, 125, 176, *201*, 201-2.

Noack, Errol: 55.
Noack, Nigel Leonard: 31.
Non-combatant status: 13, 18, 26-7.
Non-complier (see Conscientious non-complier).
Norman, Raymond: 26-7.
O'Donnell, Denis: 91, 96, 98-9, 105, 122.
O'Toole, Robert Archer: 32.
Palling, Bruce: 141.
Payne, Mike: 7, 123-4, 170, 188-9, 202, 205-8.
*Peacemaker, The*: 1-5, 2, 14-15, 16, 18, 23-5, 25, 29-30, 33-4, 34, 36, 37, 38, 52, 53, 61-2, 68, 72, 83, 87, 94, 97-8, 113, 125, 136, 139-40, 167, 173, 177, 180, 183, 199.
Pearce, Ian: 140.
Pendlebury, Robert: 124.
Phillips, Graeme: 31.
Phillipson, Desmond: 91, 103, 105-6.
Pirate radio station (Melbourne University, 1971): 162.
Pointon, Tony: 7, 207-8.
Poole-Johnson, John: 91, 103-4, 106.
Porter, Piercy: 154.
Prestidge, Leslie: 33, 227.
Prisons (see also Holsworthy Military Correctional Establishment)
    Emu Plains (NSW): 182.
    Fairlea Women's Prison (Vic): 50.
    Fremantle Prison (WA): 157, 166, 173, 183, 185-8, 186-7.
    Goulburn Prison (NSW): 173, 208.
    Karnet Prison Farm (WA): 188.
    Long Bay Prison (NSW): 127, 130, 133, 136, 169, 173, 181-2, 208.
    Pentridge Prison (Vic): 175-6.
    Sale Prison (Vic): 176.
    Stuart Prison, Townsville (Q): 173.
Wooroloo Training Centre (WA): 183.
    Yatala Prison (SA): 180.

Protests (see also Melbourne University Commune, Melbourne University siege, Moratorium Campaign)
    Anzac Day, Sydney: 133.
    Battle of Forrest Place: 83.
    Department of Labour and National Service, Perth: 123, 142.
    Jensen protest at 1 RAR Welcome Home parade, Sydney: 82-3.
    Liberal Party Headquarters, Sydney: 122-3.
    Prime Minister's Lodge, Canberra: 114-5, 116, 122.
    Rockdale Town Hall, Sydney: 73, 74-5.
    St Andrew's Cathedral, Sydney: 133.
    Sit-ins: 114-5, 116, 117, 154, 206, 208.
    US Consulate, Melbourne: 123.
Puckapunyal training camp: 53, 98, 103-4, 107, 108-9.
Quakers (see Religious Society of Friends).
Questions (asked of objectors in court): 62-3, 67.
Rattigan, Peter: 171.
Referral (see Conscientious Objectors' Referral Scheme)
Reisenleiter, Gordon: 173-4.
Religious Society of Friends/Quakers; 18, 20, 26, 45-6, 108.
*Resist* (DRU Newspaper): 155-6, 192-3.
Returned Services League (RSL): 24, 33, 68.
Ripley, Julian: 143.
Rivett, Dr Kenneth: 6, 35, 93.
Robinson, Barry: 82.
Rodgers, Stipendiary Magistrate: 60, 66, 77-8, 88, 92.
Roman Catholic faith: 26, 56, 66.
Ross, Brian: 125, 176-8.
Ross, Donald James, 32.
Sandy, Geoffrey: 7, 140-41, 198, 204.
Save our Sons (SOS): 50-51, 53-5, 83.
Scates, Robert (Bob): 189.

Schapper, Derek: 154, 164.
Scott, John (AJA): 162-3, 259.
Seale, Clare: 78, 201.
Seventh Day Adventist/s: 18, 26-7, 31, 40.
Shipard, Carl Edwin: 38.
Sit-ins (see protests)
Snedden, Billie (Minister for Labour and National Service, 1969-71): 139, 154, 180.
Solitary confinement: 5, 98-9, 102, 105, 173, 183, 188.
Stead, Robert: 91-8, 103-4, 194.
Student Democratic Action (SDA): 117.
Sydney Conscientious Objectors Group: 117.
Sydney University: 59, 122, 133, *134-5,* 165-6, 170.
Thomas, Alexander (Sandy): 169.
Thomas, William (Bill): 7, 154, 164, 166, *168,* 169, 171, 185, 188, 205, 208.
Thurwall, John: 79.
Till, Donald: 32.
Time bomb (Dept of Labour and National Service, Perth): 142-3.
Townley, Athol (Minister for Defence, 1958-63): 38, 40.
Townsend, Simon: 5, 73, 91, 96, *96,* 98-9, *99,* 102, 106, 122, 125, *128.*
Townsend, Stephen: 125, 130.
Troy, Rodney: 31.
Truscott, Leonard: 199.
Turner, Ian: 139, *158,* 189.
Tuting, Frank: 199.
Underground: 6, 49, 143, 155-9, 162-3, 265, 165-6, *167,* 183, 185, 188, 195, 202, 208.
University of Melbourne (see Melbourne University).
University of Sydney (see Sydney University).
University of Western Australia (UWA):57, 83, 103, 109, 154, 156, 166, *168,* 169, 183, *186-7.*
Van de Wiel, Stanislas: 66-7.

Vick, Malcolm: 170.
Victoria Barracks, Sydney: 78, 130, 201.
Vietnam Action Committee: 54, 83.
Vietnam Coordinating Committee: 123.
Vietnam War: 3-5, 38, 49, 55-7, 65, 69, 79, *100-01,* 109, 113, 127, 140, 145, *168,* 175, 179, 195-6, 206, 208-11.
Vintilla, Peter: 154.
Volrath, Robin: 31.
Waddy, Ronald: 18-9.
Walker, Adrian: 7, 207.
Webb, Peter: 7, 202, 207.
West, Philip: 123.
White, William Phillip Orrick (Bill): 73-83, *74-5, 77, 81,* 88, 93, 96-7, 130, 198, 201.
Whitlam, Gough (Leader of the Opposition,1967-72; Prime Minister, 1972-75): 35, 41, 170.
Wilson, John: 7, 72, 147, 199, 207.
Women's International League for Peace and Freedom (WILPF): 15-7, 46.
World Council of Churches (Australian Council): 18, 20.
Wright, (Senator, Liberal Party): 191, 195.
Wrigley, Kenneth William: 32-3.
Youngman, Ian: 31.
Youth Campaign against Conscription (YCAC): 61, 82-3.
Zarb, John: *71,* 124, 175.

## BOBBIE OLIVER
# Published Books

**AUTHOR**

2019 *A Natural Battleground: the Fight to Establish a Rail Heritage Centre at Western Australia's Midland Railway Workshops*, Melbourne, Interventions.

2017 *Step Forward, Speak Out: a History of the Independent Schools Salaried Officers' Association and the Independent Education Union in Western Australia, 1960-2015*, Perth, Black Swan.

2016 *The Locomotive Enginemen: a History of the West Australian Locomotive Engine Drivers', Firemen's and Cleaners' Union*, Perth, Black Swan.

2007 *Jean Beadle: a Life of Labor Activism*, Nedlands, UWA Press.

2003 *Unity is Strength: a History of the Australian Labor Party and the Trades and Labor Council in Western Australia, 1899-1999*, Perth, API Network, Curtin University.

1998 Britton, N., Oliver, B. and Wettenhall, R., *A Decade of Pacific Disaster Aid: the Australian Overseas Disaster Response Organisation, the Australian Government and the Australian NGOs*, Townsville, Centre for Disaster Studies, James Cook University.

1997 *Peacemongers: Conscientious Objectors to Military Service in Australia, 1911 to 1945*, Fremantle, Fremantle Arts Centre Press.

1995 *War and Peace in Western Australia: the Impact of the Great War, 1914 to 1926*, Nedlands, UWA Press.

1992 *Work in Western Australia: an Annotated Guide*, Melbourne, National Centre for Australian Studies, Monash University; and Perth, The Centre for Western Australian History, UWA.

1992 *Towards A Living Place: Hospice and Palliative Care in Western Australia*, Perth, Cancer Foundation of WA.

**EDITOR**

2019 Fox, Charlie, Vassiley, Alexis, Oliver, Bobbie and Layman, Lenore (eds.), *Radical Perth, Militant Fremantle*, 2nd edn., Melbourne, Interventions.

2017 Fox, Charlie, Oliver, Bobbie and Layman, Lenore (eds.), *Radical Perth, Militant Fremantle*, Perth, Black Swan.

2016 Oliver, Bobbie (ed.), *1914: Mobilising for the Great War*, Canberra, Big Sky Publishing.

2014 Oliver, Bobbie and Summers, Sue (eds.), *Lest We Forget? Marginalised Aspects of Australia at War and Peace*, Perth, Black Swan.

2009 Oliver, Bobbie (Ed.), *Labour History in the New Century*, Perth, Black Swan.

2006 Bertola, Patrick and Oliver, Bobbie (eds.), *The Workshops: a History of the Midland Government Railway Workshops*, Nedlands, UWA Press.

ALSO BY INTERVENTIONS

## Australia's Pacific War: Challenging a National Myth
By Tom O'Lincoln

War is such a nightmare it's hard to believe any war can retain a positive aura for decades. Yet the vast conflict in the Pacific is a shibboleth for Australian politics to this day. Politicians in particular use its appeal to legitimise modern wars. Tom O'Lincoln's book questions every aspect of this syndrome. He argues that the Pacific War was an imperialist one on both sides, that the west cannot claim the moral high ground, and that wartime Australia was riven with class and other social conflicts. His aim is to challenge an Australian national myth.

"This thought-provoking book challenges us to re-consider what we assumed we knew about the Pacific war."
– Dr Peter Stanley, **National Museum of Australia**

ALSO BY INTERVENTIONS

**Radical Perth, Militant Fremantle**
Edited by Charlie Fox, Alexis Vassiley,
Bobbie Oliver, and Lenore Layman

*Radical Perth, Militant Fremantle* tells 34 fascinating stories of radical moments In the cities' past, from as long ago as the 1890s and as recent as Occupy: the revolutionary theatre of the Workers Art Guild; the riot of unemployed workers outside the Treasury building; rock concerts inside St Georges Cathedral; bodgies and widgies cutting up the dance floor at the Scarborough Beach Snake Pit; the Point Peron women's peace camp, and many more.

—— ALSO BY INTERVENTIONS ——

## Without Bosses: Radical Australian Trade Unionism in the 1970s
By Sam Oldham

*Without Bosses* gives a fascinating insight into radical currents in Australian trade unionism during the 1970s when rank-and-file trade unionists pushed the boundaries of their organisations, in some cases setting global precedents. This book revisits the better-known events, including the almost complete neutralisation of anti-strike laws through mass strike action in 1969 and the famous green bans of the Builders Labourers' Federation. it also details less well known but fascinating experiments with self-management and workers' control.

This book overflows with incredible and inspiring stories from a critically important period in Australian history. For anyone interested in labour history, left-wing ideas, and the power of unions, it is required reading.

www.ingramcontent.com/pod-product-compliance
Ingram Content Group UK Ltd.
Pitfield, Milton Keynes, MK11 3LW, UK
UKHW021324180426
11947UKWH00017B/1431